EDWARD ELGAR

Reproduction of Elgar's portrait painted in 1913 by Philip Burne-Jones,
which now hangs in Worcester Guildhall

EDWARD ELGAR

His Life and Music

by

DIANA M. McVEAGH

*Illustrated with 8 pages of photographs,
and music examples in the text*

LONDON
J. M. DENT & SONS LTD

PREFACE

To write the biography of a man, so recently dead, whom one never met is to make oneself unusually dependent on other people; the encouragement and help of Elgar's surviving relations and friends have made a responsibility also an exciting and absorbing quest.

My first debt is to Elgar's daughter, Mrs Elgar Blake, who has answered endless questions, lent me letters and photographs, allowed me to search the records at the birthplace, and given me a free hand in using this material. She has also very kindly read the book in proof.

Mr Harold Brooke, Mrs Joyce Crooke, Sir Percy Hull, Colonel and Mrs Leicester, the late Mr Littleton, Mrs Richard Powell, and Mr A. T. Shaw have lent me correspondence besides allowing me to question them. Father Kavanagh, Colonel Leicester, and the South Worcestershire Hospital Management Committee have given me access to unpublished manuscripts of Elgar's. Mrs Edgley has allowed me to quote from her late husband's letter, and Mr E. J. N. Hunter from his late father's. Mr R. J. Forbes has lent me two letters in his possession. The late Mr W. McNaught gave me his own collection of Elgariana. Sir Adrian Boult, Dr Moore Ede, Miss May Grafton, the Misses Beatrice and May Harrison, Dr Herbert Howells, Mr Jack Hulbert, Father Kavanagh, Mr Alan Kirby, the late Mr Mewburn Levien, Lady Muntz, Mr Albert Sammons, and Mr Frank Thistleton, either in person or by letter, have given me information. Though the opinions expressed in the book are entirely my own I thank all who have shared with me their memories of a man I was not privileged to know.

I am grateful to the publishers, particularly Messrs Novello & Co., who have lent me Elgar's music. Permission to include extracts from letters from Bernard Shaw to Sir Edward Elgar has been granted by the Society of Authors and the Public Trustee, and I also have to

v

PREFACE

thank the trustees of Elgar's estate for permission to publish extracts from his letters and other documents.

Finally, I want to thank Mr Eric Blom, who suggested that this book should be written; and Mr Frank Howes and Mr E. A. Hughes, who, like a pair of musical and literary godfathers, have guided, scolded, prompted, counselled, and cared for it throughout its growth.

DIANA M. McVEAGH

London and Porthcawl, *April 1955*

CONTENTS

ILLUSTRATIONS

Plates

Part One: The Life

—

CHAPTER I

1857–1873

EDWARD WILLIAM ELGAR was born on 2nd June 1857, at the village of Broadheath, three miles from Worcester.

His father, William Henry Elgar, the son of a builder, was one of a large musical family of Charlton, Dover. The name Elgar, in various spellings, was common on the south-eastern seaboard in the early nineteenth century, though by the twentieth it had become rare. Elgar believed it to be of Scandinavian origin and to mean 'fairy spear.' Not much is known of his forbears beyond two facts, themselves enough to show spirit in the family. His great-grandfather was hanged at Winchelsea for sheep-stealing. His great-uncle was a seafaring man; Elgar said he was a Dover pilot, and though this cannot be traced in the Trinity House records a pilot's clock hangs in the birth-place, and the British Museum has a letter from a William Elgar of Dover, dated 1813, concerning the filling of a vacancy in a preventive boat.

William Henry was apprenticed to the music firm of Coventry & Hollier in Dean Street, London. After the death of William IV, Queen Adelaide was living near Worcester, at Witley Court. Someone was needed to tune her pianofortes; the comptroller of her household applied to Coventry & Hollier, and in 1841 W. H. Elgar, a personable and well-mannered young man of nineteen, was chosen. Some eighty years later his son was to tend the instruments of King George V.

Besides tuning the queen dowager's pianos and those of her neighbours, W. H. Elgar opened a music shop in Worcester. In 1843, in a letter to his mother, he asked how his young brother Henry was getting on with his music, and by 1859 his business had increased enough for him to propose that Henry should join him. When he did so, the following year, the brothers settled in at 1 Edgar Street, conveniently near the cathedral, whose music they supplied. Henry had had experience as a tuner in London and Manchester, and now became organist of a Malvern church as well as assisting his brother.

W. H. Elgar, though a Protestant, became organist in 1848 of St George's Catholic Church, Worcester, a post he held for thirty-seven years. He took part in most local musical activities with violin or piano, and regularly played the violin in the orchestra formed for the Three Choirs Festival, into the programmes of which he introduced masses by Cherubini and Hummel. Elgar was proud of the fact that his father had been a pupil of Sutton at Dover, who in turn had been a pupil of Michael Kelly, the friend of Mozart. He was uninterested in book-keeping and his business never flourished, but he tuned his pianos with love, and rode to his work on a thoroughbred horse.

When he first came to Worcester he had stayed at a coffee-house kept by a Mr and Mrs Greening. Mr Greening had helping him a sister, Anne, a sweet-tempered, country-loving girl from Weston-under-Penyard in the Forest of Dean. She was the daughter of Joseph Greening and Esther Apperly of Westbury-on-Severn. Her baptism entry, recorded at Hope Mansel in February 1822, gives her father's occupation as 'labourer,' but possibly he bought himself a little land, for his widow is described in the census returns for 1851 as a farmer's wife. On 19th January 1848 William Henry Elger (*sic*), music master, son of Henry Elger, builder, was married to Anne Greening, daughter of Joseph Greening, gentleman. The residence of both is given as 6 High Street, Islington, Middlesex (which was at that time the Peacock Inn), and the bride and groom, both aged twenty-six, were married in the parish church. Why they should have chosen Islington for their wedding remains a mystery. They lived first at Worcester, presumably over the shop, where three children, Harry, Lucy, and Pollie, were born to them, and where Anne's widowed mother joined them. Then in 1856 they moved to a cottage at Broadheath. The village was small, merely a handful of cottages strung alongside the wide common from which it takes its name, looking towards the Malvern Hills. Here Joe, Edward, Frank, and Dot were born. Henry John (Harry) and Joe died in their childhood; Lucy Ann and Susannah Mary (Pollie) married,

ELGAR'S PARENTS

Left: William Henry Elgar. *Right:* Anne Elgar

His Parents and Home

and Pollie had six children; Dot became a nun and was Mother General of the Dominicans in England for her term of office; Frank carried on his father's business and became a well-known musical figure as an oboist and conductor at Worcester.

Edward was to be a composer. His childhood was simple and happy. He was baptized and brought up as a Catholic, his mother having become one through attending the services of the Catholic church where his father was organist. Music was part of his earliest life. His father earned his living from it and some of it was of first-class quality. At one concert in which W. H. Elgar played, the programme included a Handel concerto, extracts from Purcell's *Dido and Aeneas* and *King Arthur*, and the *Egmont* overture. His evenings were often spent in 'sundry fiddlings' for the sheer pleasure of it— 'We finish with a pipe and whisky.' Corelli was a favourite composer of his, and he often writes of playing Corelli quartets—'good stuff.' His personality—breezy, cheerful, and downright—comes out in his own account of a journey in 1843 to give a concert in Kidderminster:

We started for Kidder at ten o'clock on Tuesday about eighteen in number and a fine swell we cut I assure you. We started from the Punch Bowl Inn, a stage-coach for the occasion with four horses and two postilions. On the top of the coach were most of the instruments, double-basses, violoncellos, fiddles, and the devil knows what. I was stuck in the boot with that old monkey coat that I used to wear in Dover with my cap, and some with greatcoats, mackintoshes and a pretty lot we were. We sang all the way there and all the way back, and a good spree we had.

W. H. Elgar had a beautiful touch on the piano and played the organ well, and his music packed the church on Sunday evenings. At one annual collection for the choir and music £60 was taken in one day. A contemporary description of his procedure as organist is graphic: 'Old E. always handed round the snuff-box before commencing the mass, "damned" the blower, and began. Went out at sermon for drink at Hop Market.'

Anne Elgar was a Welsh Border countrywoman both of whose parents were Herefordshire folk. Though she bore seven children, five of whom grew to adult age, her talent lay more in the arts than in domesticity. A daughter described her as 'romantic by temperament and poetic by nature.' She wrote little poems, sewed fancy-work in coloured silks, and sketched churches and pretty bits of scenery while she waited in the pony trap for her husband on his business visits. Her love of learning lasted her whole life. As a woman of seventy-five she climbed the stairs to her grandchildren's nursery, and when she found them studying botany she joined their lessons. Her refinement of mind was apparent in her poised and gracious manner, even when serving behind the counter in her husband's shop. She read much and had a retentive memory which her son inherited. She would quote him her favourite passages—prose as well as poetry; translations from Greek and Latin as well as the English classics. She also encouraged in him a love of the English countryside, especially their own beautiful Worcestershire. Elgar spoke of her influence with great affection when he was made a freeman of Worcester.

When he was seven Edward went with his brothers and sisters to Miss Walsh's school in Britannia Square. Before this, in 1860, the Elgars had returned to Worcester for business convenience, and lived first at 1 Edgar Street and then, from 1866, at 10 High Street, the children only going back to Broadheath to stay at a farm for holidays. In the shop Edward was able to hear and handle other instruments besides the piano, and begged to be allowed to learn the violin. He was frequently able, too, to sit in the organ-loft during the services while his father played, and he himself began to practise the organ. He showed, however, no exceptional ability, and his parents naturally treated him like the rest of their children. It was, in fact, Joe who was nicknamed the Beethoven of his family, having, according to his sister Lucy, 'very remarkable aptitude for music from the time he could sit up in his chair.' But Joe died when he was seven, and Edward showed no such precocity.

It is true that one day, when he was about ten, he was found sitting on a river bank with a pencil and a bit of manuscript paper trying to write down 'what the reeds were singing.' (Was this what he caught in the trio of the First Symphony?) When he was twelve he heard Handel's 'O thou that tellest good tidings to Zion' sung in Worcester Cathedral, and afterwards taught himself to play it on the

Schooldays

violin. He was, as a boy, particularly struck by some modulations in Mozart's masses and in the minuetto of Beethoven's First Symphony, which he came across as a piano duet. But such signs, though interesting to the biographer of a great composer, do not reveal the composer in the small boy.

He was, perhaps, less keen on sport and more fond of reading than the average boy. But stories of his bareback riding—whether or not on the thoroughbred we do not know—dispel any idea that he was a weakling, and he had a country boy's observant eyes and quiet stride. He was as ready as any other lad for a practical joke. One Easter the Worcester Inland Revenue Office posted a notice which read 'Closed —back on Wednesday.' Late at night on Easter Sunday, Edward and a school friend, Hubert Leicester, slipped out and altered it so that next day a large crowd of holiday-makers read 'Closed—gone to the devil—back on Wednesday.' The same two boys, aged fourteen and fifteen, advertised in a local paper for 'a wife of cheerful temperament,' and when it appeared in print as 'a wife of cheerful temperature' Edward cut out the advertisement and sent it to the London *Figaro*, which paid him five shillings for it.

His first acquaintance with Shakespeare came through Ned Spiers, handy-man in his father's shop, who had been a member of a theatrical company. His declamations possibly had more gusto than style, but they led Edward to read the plays for himself. His mother was once fetched quickly by a disapproving neighbour to listen to Edward 'swearing at the top of his voice,' but Edward was merely quoting Shakespeare and went unscolded. He would have heard a few operas on the visits of the Haig-Dyer Opera Company to the district, probably *Faust*, *Norma*, *La Traviata*, and *L'Elisir d'amore*.

When he was eleven he was sent to Littleton House School, near Worcester. It was an establishment of some thirty boys taught by Francis Reeve, who happened to say these words in Elgar's hearing: 'The Apostles were poor men at the time of their calling; perhaps, before the descent of the Holy Ghost, not much cleverer than some of you here.' Elgar later admitted he never did his homework and always learnt it on the way to school, but as Reeve understood him he always came out top. His school friend Hubert Leicester thought

1857–1873

him 'a most miserable-looking lad—legs like drumsticks—nothing of a boy about him. One great characteristic, always doing *something*. When he stopped away from school, which he did about a third of the time, it was not merely to play truant.'

When he was fifteen he left school, after being head boy for the last nine months. He wanted to study music and had been learning German in the hope of going to Leipzig, but his father could not afford it, and he had to earn his own living. A friend of his father's offered to train him for law, and so, in June 1872, he was apprenticed to Mr Allen, solicitor, of Sansome Place, Worcester. It is on record that Mr Allen described his pupil as 'a bright lad' and that Elgar worked hard. Law, however, was less attractive than music, and there was, moreover, some trouble caused by a fellow apprentice. He began to consider changing his profession. His father, who was a better musician than man of business, needed help with his accounts in the shop, and there was, perhaps, an opening at Worcester for an adaptable young musician. Edward had had violin lessons from Frederick Spray, a local violinist who led the orchestra associated with the Worcester Glee Club. His access to the scores in his father's shop had made him familiar with the '48,' Mozart's masses, Beethoven's piano sonatas, and piano duet arrangements of his symphonies. Chance had given him as his text-books Stainer's *Composition* and *Harmony*, Cherubini's *Counterpoint*, Catel's *Treatise on Harmony*, and Sabina Novello's translation of *Succinct Thorough Bass*, then attributed to Mozart. He had given himself by trial and error a working knowledge of the cello, viola, and several wind instruments, and had learnt enough from Rink's and Best's organ tutors to deputize for his father at mass. He had already composed a few pieces. In Worcester Cathedral he had heard Tallis, Byrd, and Purcell; at the concerts of the Festival Choral Society he had heard Corelli, Handel, and Haydn; in his father's music shop and warehouse he had browsed to his heart's content; and sitting in his father's organ-loft he had become familiar with composers as diverse as Palestrina and Beethoven.

With this equipment he left Mr Allen's office in 1873 and embarked on his destined career.

CHAPTER II

1873–1889

EDWARD began his career by becoming assistant organist to his father at St George's Church (where he had already occasionally played) and by helping him in the shop.

Gradually his name became familiar as a violinist on programmes of local music-making. His first recorded public appearance was as Master Elgar in a band which played Mendelssohn, Bishop, Rossini, and Hullah at the Union Workhouse in 1873. It is significant to see how quickly the son outstripped the father as a violinist. In the Worcester Philharmonic Society's *Messiah* of 1875 W. H. Elgar and E. W. Elgar are among the seconds, with H. Elgar in the violas. By the 1879 *Messiah* E. W. Elgar was principal, W. H. Elgar led the seconds, H. Elgar led the violas, and F. Elgar (Edward's brother) was first oboe. No matter what a Worcester instrumental combination in the seventies or eighties might call itself, its personnel included the Elgars. W. H. Elgar had great respect for his son's superior musical gifts. As soon as Edward could scrape a violin (when he was about twelve) his father introduced him to the Worcester Glee Club. This club, which was established in 1810, met regularly at the Crown Hotel, drawing its members from the choristers and amateurs of the town. Members sat at long tables lighted by tapers, drank their tankards of ale, and smoked their churchwarden pipes—Edward smoked from the age of ten or eleven. On instrumental evenings they played Corelli, Handel, and Haydn, though during Edward's connection with the society the taste changed to Bellini, Rossini, Auber, Balfe, and sometimes Mozart. W. H. Elgar had joined the club shortly after his arrival in the city, and his son served it as violinist, accompanist, composer, and arranger. On 23rd October 1876 was performed the overture to *The Flying Dutchman*, arranged by Ed. Elgar. In 1879 he became the club's conductor.

Two years before this the Worcester Instrumental Society had been formed, and 'an efficient leader and instructor'—Edward Elgar—

7

1873–1889

engaged. He took every engagement that was offered him and began to build up a teaching practice. He managed to snatch a living, but it was meagre, and he found it worth while to score Christy minstrel songs at 1s. 6d. apiece.

Once again he wanted to go to Leipzig to improve his technique and qualifications, and once again he regretfully had to give up the idea. He could not afford it. London was the next best thing. He saved carefully, and in August 1877 went to London for violin lessons from Adolphe Pollitzer, leader of the New Philharmonic Orchestra and an established teacher. At the first lesson Pollitzer set Elgar one study to prepare; by the next Elgar had prepared the whole bookful. This enthusiasm, together with his musicianship, drew encouragement, but Elgar, who was living on 'two bags of nuts a day,' could not afford a sustained course of lessons and went back to Worcester. He returned to Pollitzer occasionally during the next few years, and took every opportunity of going to the Crystal Palace concerts, conducted by August Manns. Years later he described his concert-going in these words:

I lived one hundred and twenty miles from London. I rose at six, walked a mile to the railway station—the train left at seven; arrived at Paddington about eleven; underground to Victoria; on to the Palace, arriving in time for the last three-quarters of an hour of the rehearsal. If fortune smiled, this piece of rehearsal included the work desired to be heard; but fortune rarely smiled and more often than not the principal item was over. Lunch—concert at three—at five a rush for the train to Victoria—then to Paddington on to Worcester, arriving at ten-thirty.

He was becoming well known locally. In 1878 the Three Choirs Festival took place in Worcester, and Elgar, for the first time, played second violin in the orchestra. (By 1881 he was promoted to the first violins, and in 1884 he played under Dvořák, who very nearly forestalled him in setting *Gerontius*.) This festival, which is held annually during September in the cathedral cities of Worcester, Hereford, and Gloucester in rotation, provided Elgar with both education and opportunity. Through it he became acquainted from childhood with great religious choral masterpieces, and he grew up in an atmosphere of discussion, rehearsal, and performance of music.

8

Early Compositions and Local Music-making

He was composing all the time. In his own words:

I once ruled a score for the same instruments and with the same number of bars as Mozart's G minor Symphony, and in that framework I wrote a symphony,[1] following as far as possible the same outlines for his themes and the same modulations. I did this on my own initiative as I was groping in the dark after light, but looking back after thirty years I don't know any discipline from which I learnt so much.[2]

All the music performed at St George's was copied by hand, and the part-books in manuscript contain many short pieces (litanies and hymn-tunes) by E. W. Elgar, as well as a few by W. H. Elgar. The motets *Salve Regina* and *Tantum ergo* dated 1876 may well have been those sung at a concert in 1880; in addition there is a *Regina Coeli* dated 1876 and record of a *Domine salvam fac* in 1880. It is reasonable to suppose that Elgar wrote a good deal of music at this time for the church: he was assistant organist and his friend Hubert Leicester was choir-trainer; between them they ran the music. Possibly much has been mislaid. Perhaps even the composer, who signed his name with such a flourish, placed no great value on his efforts. He left a more permanent mark in his church: when recently the organ was cleaned, 'E. W. Elgar' was found scratched on two pipes.

He and Hubert Leicester formed at this time a wind quintet in which he played the bassoon, Hubert the first flute, Frank Elgar the oboe, William Leicester the clarinet, and Frank Exton (who worked at Worcester but was not a local lad) the second flute. The Leicesters lived only a few doors up the High Street from the Elgars, and the boys were always in and out of each other's houses. Edward very probably got something of his knowledge of printing from the Leicesters' press. Sometimes the boys serenaded their friends at night, playing by the light of a carriage lamp. Some of the music this wind quintet played was arranged, such as 'Hail, smiling morn' by Spofforth, 'Sweet and low' by Barnby, 'Now is the month of maying' by Morley, and 'Awake, sweet love' by Dowland. But most of it Elgar wrote himself. There is a set of *Promenades*—No. 2 is called 'Madame Tussaud's' and No. 4 described as 'somniferous'

[1] R. J. Buckley prints the opening in his *Sir Edward Elgar* (Bodley Head).
[2] *Strand Magazine*, May 1904.

1873–1889

—and a set of seven pieces called *Shed*, possibly because the instrumentalists rehearsed in a shed. A revivalist mission appears to have inspired the composer, for *Shed* No. 5 is called 'The mission, O Lord,' and *Promenade* No. 6 'Hell and Tommy.' About the five *Intermezzi* Elgar (when he borrowed the manuscript later) wrote: 'I like the *Shed* on the whole, but the *Intermezzi* are "mine own children."' All these pieces are dated 1877–9, when Elgar was between twenty and twenty-two.

His other spur to composition was the county lunatic asylum. Music was even more highly valued for its therapeutic qualities in those days than in these, and it was an asset in joining the staff of a mental hospital if one could 'double in brass.' The orchestra, comprising staff and attendants, was stiffened by local musicians, and the Elgar family had played in it certainly as early as 1877. Edward was made bandmaster in 1879 and spent one day a week at Powick. His duties were to coach his performers individually, to conduct the occasional concerts, and to lead the band at the weekly dances for the patients. His band consisted of first and second violins (two desks each), violas, cellos, and bass, piccolo, flute, clarinet, euphonium, and two cornets, with piano. For the concerts Elgar arranged music—one began with a selection from *Norma* and ended with the Soldiers' Chorus from *Faust*—and occasionally slipped in a piece or two of his own. A concert in 1882 included his *Air de ballet* (*Pastorale*), which was also played that year at a soirée of the British Medical Association at the Worcester Shire Hall, and a march, *Pas redoublé*. For the weekly dances he wrote quadrilles, lancers, and polkas, dating from 1879 to 1884. For each set he was paid five shillings.

In 1878 came the encouragement of his first public performance. At a Christy minstrel concert at the Public Hall, Worcester, the First Worcester Artillery Volunteers played *Introductory Overture*,[1] a new work written for the occasion by Edward Elgar. The following year the Early Closing Association performed his *Minuetto grazioso*.

In August 1880 Elgar went for a holiday to Paris with Charlie

---

[1] Of which there is now no trace.

Edward Elgar (standing) in 1888 (the year before
his marriage), with his brother Frank

First Professional Appointments

Pipe, his sister Lucy's husband. Here they saw Molière's *Le Malade imaginaire* and heard Saint-Saëns play the organ of the Madeleine. Elgar's appetite for things French had been whetted by a translation of Voltaire he had found among a pile of old books in the loft above the stable where his father kept his horse. This Paris trip was enlivened by some gay flirtation. In his article in 1933 about a meeting with Delius, Elgar wrote:

The scent recalled a romance of 1880, and I nearly—very nearly—turned to Barbizon. In that far-off time little did I dream that one day I should sit at the side of the President of the Republic. After my visit to Grez I decided to go to Barbizon, but when I passed the cross-roads the longing had passed away. That belonged to the romance of 1880, now dead.[1]

His set of quadrilles dated October 1880 has a Parisian accent. One is called 'L'Hippodrome,' another 'Champs Élysées,' a third, which makes use of a French song, 'Café des Ambassadeurs.'

On his return his musical appointments became more numerous and responsible. In 1882 he was engaged to play first violin in Stockley's orchestra at Birmingham. Stockley, besides conducting his Popular Concerts, was chorus master for the Birmingham Triennial Festival, and had, therefore, potentialities in the eyes of a young composer. The same year Elgar was invited to become conductor of the Worcester Amateur Instrumental Society, a position he held for seven years; he wrote analytical programme notes for the concerts. It is doubtful whether he could ever have obtained much polish from either this or his asylum band, but years later orchestras loved him because he was practical and unfussy and felt himself one of them. He had learnt, not in a conducting class with a guinea-pig orchestra, but by experience.

In 1879 he had gone to lodge with his elder sister Pollie at Loretto Villa, Chestnut Walk, Worcester, and in 1882 he moved to 4 Field Terrace, Bath Road, where he lived with Lucy and Charlie Pipe. At the end of this year he at last managed to go to Leipzig, not for two or three years' study as he had originally wanted, but for a two weeks' busman's holiday, crammed with all the concerts and operas possible, including Anton Rubinstein conducting one of his own operas.

[1] *Daily Telegraph*, 1st July 1933.

1873–1889

He was particularly interested by a work of Schumann's, *Overture, Scherzo, and Finale*. The organist of Worcester Cathedral, William Done, a man of conservative tastes, referred to Schumann's works as 'preposterous,' and Elgar was no doubt curious to hear them for himself. Done's choice of music for worship was confined to the Elizabethans and Purcell, for whom Elgar had little natural liking. His taste was already formed. Hubert Leicester was one day blowing the organ for him. He played something new and strange. Hubert ran round and said: 'Ted, what is that?' 'That, Hubert, is by a man who is not understood. You will hear more of him some day.' The music was the overture to *Tannhäuser*.

At the end of the next year, 1883, a short piece of Elgar's, *Intermezzo: Sérénade mauresque*, was played at one of Stockley's concerts at Birmingham. A press notice said: 'As Mr Elgar is not deficient in scholarship, has plenty of fancy, and orchestrates with facility, we hope he will not "rest and be thankful" but go on in a path for which he possesses singular qualifications.' The following year Elgar wrote *Sevillana* for a Worcester Philharmonic Society concert, which was conducted by Dr Done. A programme note by the composer gives an idea of his intentions and of his literary style at the time:

This sketch is an attempt to portray, in the compass of a few bars, the humours of a Spanish fête. It consists of three principal themes, which may be briefly characterized thus: 1st, an imitation of a Spanish folk-song, played by the violins on the fourth string; 2nd, a softer strain in the major, which may (or may not) be taken to represent *un passage d'amour*, for which, as in England, such gatherings are supposed to lend opportunity; and 3rd, a brisk valse measure in D major. Something very like an *émeute* takes place during the progress of this, missiles are freely thrown, and at least one stiletto is drawn—but these are only modern Spaniards, and no tragic result follows: 'Cela était autrefois ainsi, mais nous avons changé tout cela.' Quiet is restored, the itinerant resumes his song—the valse continues, and somehow or other all ends happily. It is not assumed that this little piece embodies an accurate representation of all the above; suffice it to say that amidst some such scene, and as a souvenir thereof, was it written.

On his next visit to London Elgar showed *Sevillana* to Pollitzer,

Decision to Compose—Engagement and Marriage

who gave him an introduction to August Manns, and *Sevillana* was performed at the Crystal Palace on 9th July 1884.

In August of that year Elgar went alone to Scotland. Here he discarded his ideas of becoming a concert violinist. Two incidents had helped to make up his mind for him. Pollitzer had sent him to hear Wilhelmj play Beethoven's Concerto at St James's Hall. There and then he had realized that such tone quality would never be his. And he had asked Pollitzer: 'Shall I ever be first-class?' 'You will be very good,' said Pollitzer. 'Shall I ever be first-class?' Elgar insisted, and Pollitzer had to say 'No.' Elgar now made up his mind to become a composer. He would practise only enough to maintain his orchestral positions and teaching. He would resign his appointment at the county asylum. All possible time must be given to composition.

On his father's retirement in 1885 Elgar became full-time organist of St George's. His position in the town's musical life was thus established. He wrote much music. A *Romance* for violin was played at an evening concert at the deanery in 1885 (and published the same year by Schotts), and 'A Soldier's Song' was sung at a Public Hall soirée in 1886. On 1st March 1888 his Suite in D, incorporating the earlier *Intermezzo: Sérénade mauresque*, was performed at Stockley's Birmingham concert, and again at Worcester, and some string pieces, *Spring Song*, *Elegy*, and *Finale*, were played by the Worcester Musical Union.

In 1886 Elgar became professor at Worcester College for the Blind. When a pupil, William Wolstenholme, went to Oxford in 1887 to sit for his degree, Elgar went with him and for three days acted as his amanuensis. His kindness towards fellow musicians was apparent. Once already it had been traded upon. A certain church musician wrote an anthem with orchestral accompaniment for a special occasion. At the rehearsal it became evident that his ambition had outstripped his ability. Elgar was persuaded to rescore the work, and at the performance the composer took all the credit. This unfairness hurt. Elgar, at twenty-nine, had to struggle for every mark of recognition as a composer.

On 22nd September 1888 Elgar's engagement was announced to

1873–1889

Caroline Alice Roberts. Miss Roberts knew her own mind very well and had some courage, for her relations did not approve of her choice of a delicate-looking musician, and by marrying him she forfeited a substantial legacy in an aunt's will. She was the only daughter of the late Major-General Sir Henry Gee Roberts, K.C.B., of Hazeldine House, Redmarley d'Abitot. She was born in India on 9th October 1848 and was baptized at Kutch, where her father, then a lieutenant-colonel, was political agent. Her mother was Julia, daughter of the Rev. Robert Raikes, of Longhope, Gloucestershire, and she could trace descent from the Robert Raikes who founded Sunday-schools. She had two brothers, both of whom followed in their father's profession. Her father had died in 1860, and after the death in 1887 of her mother (who left her her furniture, her carriages and horses, and enough property to bring in a small income) she had spent some time abroad and then lived at Ripple Lodge, Malvern Link. She was a lady of some literary taste and had published two novels and a translation of Hoffman's *Ritter Gluck*. She sang in a chorus affiliated to an orchestra in which Elgar played, and had also for two years been taking accompaniment lessons from him. Her love of music was real, even though her exceptional diligence of late had a little surprised her friends. Now the reason was made clear.

Edward and Alice were married in London on 8th May 1889, at Brompton Oratory. He was then not quite thirty-two; she was forty. A pupil of his remembered him at the time as 'a spare, dark, shy young man, standing by a piano and looking at me with a gaze that was at once difficult and aloof—a look that I was to see many a time in after years—as if he was half here and half in some other place beyond our ken.' [1]

Their honeymoon was spent in the Isle of Wight. On their return Elgar, fired by his wife's belief in him, resigned all his Worcestershire appointments. With high hopes, Mr and Mrs Elgar went to live in London.

[1] Letter from A. B. L.-W. to the *Henley and South Oxfordshire Standard*, 30th March 1934.

CHAPTER III

1889–1898

In London the Elgars took rooms at 3 Marloes Road, Kensington. Edward submitted songs and violin pieces to publishers, and some were accepted. He missed no opportunity of hearing music—the Monday and Saturday 'Pops' at St James's Hall offered a good mixed diet—and he and Alice kept a scrap-book of all their programmes. But there was as yet no way of earning a living in London, and after some months they returned to Worcestershire and made a fresh start at Malvern, where, before their marriage, she had lived and he had built up a teaching connection.

He worked hard at small pieces, and *Salut d'amour* was accepted by Schotts. This was played at the Crystal Palace on 11th November, and his Suite in D was played there on 22nd November and on 24th February of the following year. Encouraged by these performances the Elgars again came to London, staying first at Norwood in a house lent them by Alice's cousin, and then moving in March 1890 to 51 Avonmore Road, West Kensington. Both Edward and Alice had season-tickets for the Crystal Palace concerts. He travelled once a week to Worcester to teach private pupils, and in November 1890 this notice appeared in the *Musical Times*: 'Mr Edward Elgar begs to announce that he receives pupils for Violin, Accompaniment, Orchestration etc.'

That year the Three Choirs Festival was to take place at Worcester. The festival committee asked their native composer for a short orchestral work. Elgar wrote to introduce himself to Joseph Bennett, then music critic of the *Daily Telegraph*: 'I hope you will not think I am writing from egotistical motives, but it is a crucial time in the career of a young musician, and I was afraid you might question the committee's action in asking me to contribute to their scheme.'[1]   The

---

[1] This letter and the others to Bennett quoted below were published in the *Daily Telegraph*, 4th September 1937.

work, an overture, was unhesitatingly accepted by the committee. Dr Done, the cathedral organist, wrote to tell Elgar that it had needed no recommendation from him.   Novellos published it and it was per-formed, under Elgar's baton, at the secular evening concert, 9th September 1890, in the Public Hall, Worcester.   Thus *Froissart*, Elgar's first characteristic big-scale work, was produced a few weeks after the birth of his daughter, Carice Irene.

Froissart did not immediately meet with such a warm welcome as did Carice.   The *Musical Times* trusted that Mr Elgar would acquire greater coherence of ideas and conciseness of utterance, and the *Manchester Guardian* wrote: 'The work is cleverly designed.   Mr Elgar knows how to give graceful expression to his ideas, and some of his themes are very spirited.   The chief fault of the work is its excessive elaboration, and a tendency to monotony would have been more marked had the performance been less effective.'   The second performance, on 5th February the following year, 1891, at one of Stockley's Birmingham concerts, achieved a more definite success. Elgar was called to the platform and warmly applauded.

Between the two performances he had been working at a violin concerto.   This he destroyed before it was finished.   How much, if any, was recast for the concerto of twenty years later is not known.

In June 1891 the Elgars went back to Malvern and took a house in Alexandra Road which they called 'Forli.'   They were not to try their luck again in London for twenty-one years.   Elgar was forced to take up the teaching and playing appointments he had resigned after his marriage.   He led the orchestras of the Hereford Phil-harmonic and Worcester and Malvern Choral Societies, gave lectures at the Alice Otley School, Worcester, formed a ladies' orchestral class of which his wife was accompanist, and gave violin recitals.   Two programmes show the sort of things he played.   In 1891, at the Malvern Assembly Rooms, he played Dvořák's *Slavonic Dances*, Godard's *Adagio* and *Canzonetta*, and a *Romance* by Heitsch.   In 1892 he played Brahms's G major Sonata at Malvern Wells.

In May 1892 he began a new work.   This was no *salon* piece such

Struggles in London—'The Black Knight'

as he had offered London, but a cantata. His policy was wise. Dr Hugh Blair, then deputy organist of Worcester Cathedral, saw the manuscript by chance and promised to perform the work. It was called *The Black Knight* and was a translation by Longfellow of Uhland's ballad, *Der schwarze Ritter*. It was partly written on a holiday in Germany on which the Elgars were taken that summer by a Miss Baker, a friend of Alice's, and later stepmother of 'Dorabella' of the *Enigma*. They went to Cologne, Bonn, Mainz, Bayreuth (where they heard *Parsifal* twice, *Tannhäuser*, *Die Meistersinger*, and *Tristan*), Nuremberg, Munich, and Heidelberg (whence *The Black Knight* was posted to Novellos). The first performance of *The Black Knight* was on 18th April 1893, at the Worcester Festival Choral Society's concert, before a large, enthusiastic audience. The *Musical Times* thought that it revealed qualities in the composer which were bound to bring him rapidly to the front. Later that month Elgar went to London, staying at Norwood. He took the score of *The Black Knight* to Dr August Manns, hoping, no doubt, for a performance at the Crystal Palace where Manns was conductor, but no performance resulted. In August the Elgars spent their holiday on the Continent, hearing in Munich *Das Rheingold* and *Siegfried* for the first time.

That autumn the Three Choirs Festival was held at Worcester, and Elgar, in the first violins, played Brahms's *Requiem*, Parry's *Job*, and Stanford's Magnificat and Nunc Dimittis in A. On his programme of this festival he wrote that he had had to play in the orchestra to earn money, as he could gain no recognition as a composer. But he had as yet composed very little—only *Froissart* and *The Black Knight* of substantial size. That London had given him no recognition during his stay there remained a sore point with Elgar, yet it is hard to see what he could have expected. Certainly he had had bad luck; more than once a run-through at rehearsal of a piece of his was cancelled at the last moment. Sullivan was once unwittingly the cause of this, taking for himself rehearsal space that he did not know had been reserved for Elgar. What Elgar gained from his months in London was the chance of listening to an enormous amount of music and of studying the market open to composers. All his music, except

1889–1898

that for his church, had up to that time been instrumental. On his return to the midlands he began the long series of works fit to be produced at English provincial festivals.

Most of this music Elgar composed in the evenings, for, though his wife was able to help with the household expenses, he could not afford not to teach during the day (one pupil he started on a notable career was Marie Hall), and there is little doubt that he was overworking. Through his teaching he became acquainted with all the local music-lovers, and some of his friends are familiar through their portraits in the *Enigma* Variations. Among his colleagues Elgar came to know well the organists of the three cathedral towns, Hugh Blair and later Ivor Atkins (appointed in 1897) of Worcester, George Sinclair (appointed in 1889) of Hereford, and Lee Williams and later Herbert Brewer (appointed in 1896) of Gloucester. Of London musicians he knew few at this time, and one wonders whether, when he played the violin in the Hanley performance of Berlioz's *Faust* in 1893, Parry and Sullivan, who were present, would have known him even by sight. Parry, at forty-five, was already an honorary Doctor of Music of both Oxford and Cambridge, and was the next year to become Director of the Royal College of Music. His cantata *Prometheus Unbound*, produced at the Gloucester Festival of 1880, is considered a turning-point in the history of English music, and by 1893 he had followed it up with other choral works, including *Blest Pair of Sirens* in 1887, and four symphonies. Sullivan, six years older than Parry, had in that year written the thirteenth of his operettas in collaboration with Gilbert, and had been for ten years conductor of the Leeds Triennial Festival. Stanford, only five years older than Elgar, had been since 1887 Professor of Music at Cambridge, and had been on the staff of the Royal College of Music since that institution's foundation in 1882. He had a good string of operas and symphonies to his name. Cowen, Stanford's exact contemporary, had produced his 'Scandinavian' Symphony in 1880, and had just finished four years' conductorship of the Philharmonic Society, succeeding Sullivan. Mackenzie, ten years Elgar's senior, had taken over the Philharmonic Society from Cowen and had been since 1888 Principal of the Royal Academy of Music. All these men had shown from boyhood great

Friends and Contemporaries—'King Olaf'

musical gifts, had had the opportunity of thorough training, had produced substantial works, and now held positions of authority in the musical world. Elgar, at thirty-six, playing in the Hanley orchestra, had shown little sign that he was to outstrip them all.

One man, who was to become one of Elgar's most intimate friends, was already convinced of his genius. He was August Johannes Jaeger. Jaeger was a native of Düsseldorf who had settled in London and become music reader to Novellos. Until his death in 1910, he dealt with the publication of most of Elgar's music and became his friend, adviser, and champion. 'I am for ever pushing, and have pushed ever since I played your fine *Black Knight*, Mr Elgar's claim to attention.' The letters between the two men were voluminous and as revealing of their characters as of the music over the printing of which they took such care. 'I believe you *will* be happy,' wrote Elgar to Jaeger on his marriage. 'One can very seldom say this to men who show you the modern young woman they are going into partnership with: Lord pity 'em.' Their growing friendship was invaluable to Elgar, for Jaeger was able to act as intermediary between the composer and the head of his publishing firm, A. H. Littleton, who, himself more a man of business than a musician, found Elgar not the easiest person to deal with.

In 1894 *The Black Knight* was performed at Hereford in November and Walsall in December. Wolverhampton gave it the following February. In the summer of 1895 the Elgars went to the Bavarian Highlands for their holiday (they returned there again during the next three years), and on their return Edward wrote *Scenes from the Bavarian Highlands*. This was performed in the choral version at Worcester on 21st April 1896, and was later orchestrated.

Between June and December 1895 Elgar wrote his second cantata, *King Olaf*. 'More rain, more gout, more thunder, more dyspepsia, more liver, more music, less money,' he grumbled to Jaeger. 'But *King Olaf* is a mighty work. Wot ye that? In haste, Yours ever, Him wot rote it.' In December he was asked to write an oratorio for the next Three Choirs Festival, and he spent the spring at work on this, *The Light of Life*. In the autumn of 1896 both these works were produced, *The Light of Life* at Worcester on 10th September and *King*

1889–1898

Olaf during the North Staffordshire Festival at Hanley on 30th October. The founder of the North Staffordshire Festivals, Swinnerton Heap, had watched Elgar's career keenly. He had advocated a performance at Wolverhampton of *The Black Knight* shortly after its production at Worcester (Heap at one time was conductor of the Wolverhampton Festivals), and he it was who asked Elgar to conduct the first performance of his *King Olaf* at Hanley in 1896. The impact of the cantata on its audience was immediate and strong. It was exactly the kind of music that the people of the Potteries understood and liked. It has never taken root in London, but in 1932, thirty-six years after its production, Elgar again went to Hanley to conduct his *King Olaf*. Both the works produced in 1896, neither of them in the repertory to-day, lifted Elgar from local to provincial fame.

Of the oratorio *The Times* said that it was undeniably the work of a composer not only well cultivated and well trained in his art but also gifted in no small degree. The *Daily Telegraph* said about the composer of *King Olaf*: 'He adopts methods which I cannot recognize as of ideal value. But behind all his work lies the power of living talent, the charm of an individuality in art, and the pathos of one who, in utter simplicity, pours forth that which he feels constrained to say, and leaves the issue to fate.'

Punch recognized a new personality. 'What next? Mr Elgar's new cantata having been successful at the North Staffordshire Musical Festival, *King Olaf* will probably be followed by *Queen O'Smile*.'

King Olaf went on a round of successes: the Crystal Palace and Bishop Auckland in April 1897, Worcester in May, Liverpool and Camberwell in November, and Birmingham and Wolverhampton in February 1898. *The Light of Life* was performed at Hereford in April 1897, and *Scenes from the Bavarian Highlands* at Cheltenham in November.

In the meantime Elgar had written two works to celebrate Queen Victoria's Diamond Jubilee. The *Imperial March* was first performed at Queen's Hall on 25th April 1897 and subsequently, by command of the queen, at the state concert on 15th July. It was the only

Festival Successes—The Worcestershire Philharmonic Society

English work in the programme. *The Banner of St George* was performed in London (with piano and string accompaniment) by St
Cuthbert's Hall Choral Society, Kensington, on 18th May. This
little work had been heard in London before, on 14th March 1895.
There is a tradition at St George's Church, Worcester, that Elgar
wrote this when he was organist there. But he gave up this appointment in 1889. It is possible, however, that the version performed in
1895 had been written earlier for the church, though the connection
between the two St Georges is more likely to be fortuitous.

In 1897 Elgar became conductor of a new society, the Worcestershire Philharmonic, founded mainly to give him scope.[1] He
insisted on giving his services free for the first season, and concerned
himself, as all conductors of small orchestras must, with practical as
well as musical points.

Wedy night.

DEAR MISS HYDE,

    I Please coach your local shepherds.
    II Please have organ tuned and in good order.
    III Please see Foregate St station-master about trains—extra coach.
    IV Please have the streets kept quiet during the concert.
    V Please don't forget my chair—my back is in two pieces this p.m.
    VI God save the King.
    VII Also yours truly,

ED. ELGAR.

The naming of the society proved difficult; Elgar favoured the
Society for Prevention of Cruelty to Oratorios. Despite the conventional title eventually chosen the society flourished, with one
hundred and ninety-eight members during its first season, and with
Bantock, Cowen, Mackenzie, Richter, and Stanford among its
honorary members by 1902. Elgar chose as the society's motto
'Wach' auf!' which headed their note-paper, and each of their
concerts was introduced by this chorus from Wagner's *Die Meistersinger*.

[1] The old Worcester Philharmonic, with which the Elgars had been
associated, had died a natural death about 1889.

1889–1898

Their first concert, at which they gave the first performance in England of Humperdinck's *Die Wallfahrt nach Kevlaar*, was on 7th May 1898. They prided themselves on being up to date. 'It wd be rather nice to do something of Tchaikovsky,' Lady Mary Lygon wrote to Winifred Norbury in 1898, 'and with that and Dvořák, Dr Parry and Mr Elgar on our programme we shall be very advanced.' The programmes during the next five years reveal the idiosyncrasies of the conductor, who also wrote the programme notes. The proportion of music by French composers, modern as they were then, is high: Chabrier, Delibes, Gounod, Massenet, and Berlioz are all conspicuous. Contemporary English composers are well represented: 'If they are not disposed to let young England whoop! I shall not take it on,' Jaeger was told. Mackenzie's *The Dream of Jubel*, Stanford's *Last Post*, Cowen's 'Idyllic' Symphony, Parry's *The Lotus-Eaters*, as well as smaller things by Sullivan, Lee Williams, Walford Davies, Percy Pitt, Macpherson, Bantock, and, occasionally, Elgar himself, were conducted by Elgar during these years. He was determined that performances should be more than adequate—'We *must* do things properly whatever the cost' (an attitude he always retained towards his own music)—though when difficulties arose he was quick to tease: 'We want a big drum and cymbals for Friday—also a *gong*— can you borrow these—if not it is the secretary's duty to steal such things and *not* the conductor's.' He had no hesitation in threatening to resign when the standard dropped in 1902:

The chorus of the Philharmonic Society is singing so badly, and is so extremely ill prepared this season, that I do not see how it is possible to give a fair performance of the choral portion of the programme; under the circumstances I cannot conduct the concert announced for 11th December, and, as a consequence, it is unnecessary for me to come to any more practices.

In fact, he held this appointment until 1904, when he was able to 'congratulate the society on obtaining the services of [Granville Bantock] so splendid a musician and so lovable a man.'

Though Elgar had little time for recreation during the Malvern years, golf, cycling, beagling, kite-flying, and poker-work all took his interest. A poker-work design of the fire motif from *The Ring* hung in his study near a portrait of Wagner. Reading was, as always, his chief delight outside music, and the man who had found his first library in a stable loft now inaugurated a book club whose members interchanged their own books. Elgar worked either in his study, which looked out over the plain, or, in warm weather, in a tent on the lawn of their semi-detached house, whence he could look up to the hills. It was by looking at the hills that the idea for his next cantata came.

To have his music performed at the Three Choirs Festivals was encouraging; to have a work commissioned for the Leeds Festival was a mark of recognition. In December 1897 Embleton of the Leeds Choral Union wrote to Elgar asking the nature of the two works he was engaged on. Later that month Elgar wrote to Littleton of Novellos that nothing save 'the merest accident' would prevent his being asked to contribute a cantata to the Leeds Festival. 'I have hinted at other things, but it seems they want a cantata.' The idea for the libretto was his mother's. She described in a letter to her daughter Pollie a visit paid her by Edward and Alice when she was staying at Colwall.

I said oh! Ed. look at the lovely old hill, can't we write some *tale* about it. I quite long to have something worked up about it, it's full of interest. . . . 'Do it yourself, Mother' he held my hand with a firm grip. 'Do,' he said. 'No I can't, my day is gone by if I ever could,' and so we parted. And in less than a month he told me *Caractacus* was all cut and dried and he had begun to work at it.

It is a story of ancient British war against the Romans, fought on Mrs Elgar's 'lovely old hill.' Elgar wrote most of it at 'Birchwood,' a tiny cottage in the woods the Elgars had recently taken. 'May I thank you for not saying one word about the work, either for or against,' he wrote to Jaeger, 'and please *don't* yet or I shall surely die being on edge.' It was finished in early July and Queen Victoria was graciously pleased to accept the dedication. *Caractacus* was produced on 5th October 1898 at the Leeds Festival, with Medora Henson as Eigen, Edward Lloyd as Orbin, and Andrew Black as Caractacus. Elgar himself conducted. W. H. Reed played under him for the first time and described his appearance: 'A very distinguished-looking English country gentleman, tall, with a large and somewhat aggressive moustache, a prominent but shapely nose, and rather deep-set but piercing eyes.'

The *Manchester Guardian* hoped, concerning *Caractacus*, that some day Mr Elgar would advance beyond the dramatic cantata, which here as usual provided a hybrid and unsatisfactory form, and try his hand at genuine musical drama. 'Such is the vigour and resource of his music that one regrets to hear it thrown away upon manufactured verse.' 'All that he has to say,' said *The Times*, 'is his own. It suffers, if at all, from an excess of detail, not from any absence of interest or individuality.'

Elgar was forty-one. He had as yet written nothing that is to-day considered great. But his position in English musical life was secure.

CHAPTER IV

1898–1904

HIS next work *was* great. It was written during October and November 1898. Elgar was sitting at the piano one evening and played something, new to his wife. She liked it and asked what it was. 'Nothing,' he replied, 'but something might be made of it,' and went on to improvise, playing it in the different ways his friends might have done, had *they* thought of it. 'Surely you are doing something that has never been done before?' asked Alice. And so was born the idea of the *Enigma* Variations.

To Jaeger Elgar wrote:

As to myself, the following are FAX about me. Just completed a set of symphonic variations (theme original) for orchestra—thirteen in number (but I call the finale the fourteenth, because of the ill luck attaching to the number). I have in the variations sketched portraits of my friends—a new idea, I think—that is, in each variation I have looked at the theme through the personality (as it were) of another Johnny. I don't know if 'tis too intimate an idea for print, it's distinctly amusing.[1]

A year later he added: 'Really, Jaeger, it *is* a damned fine piece of work.'

Each variation is headed by initials or a pseudonym which have made identifiable the friends whose idiosyncrasies have been so affectionately caricatured. At the first performance these only heightened the mystery of the title and caused the music critic of *The Times* to write, a little crustily: 'It is evidently impossible for the uninitiated to discuss the meaning of the work,' though he had to admit that it was 'exceedingly clever, often charming, and always original, and excellently worked out.' Now that all the friends and incidents are familiar,[2] only the puzzle of the title remains. Elgar

[1] *Musical Times*, October 1900.
[2] Elgar's own account is published by Novellos in *My Friends Pictured Within*, and Mrs Richard Powell, herself 'Dorabella,' has described them with authority and charm in *Edward Elgar* (Methuen).

1898–1904

himself wrote in a programme note: 'The enigma I will not explain
—its "dark saying" must be left unguessed, and I warn you that the
apparent connection between the variations and the theme is often of
the slightest texture; further, through and over the whole set another
and larger theme "goes," but is not played.'

Even the composer's explanation is not crystal-clear, but it seems
that the enigma involves two problems—the 'dark saying' and the
larger theme that 'goes' but is not played. It has been suggested that
the enigma may not be a tune at all but an idea; but here those who
knew Elgar are adamant: there *was* a tune. Efforts have been made
to establish 'Auld Lang Syne,' 'God Save the Queen,' 'Pop goes
the weasel,' and such well-known tunes as a counter-theme. Mrs
Richard Powell ('Dorabella') believes 'Auld Lang Syne' to be the
tune Elgar had in mind, and her husband argued in favour of this in
Music & Letters of July 1934, turning it into the minor to fit the
original theme. But by leaving it in the major, in the relative key of
B♭, it seems a more credible counterpoint. Some people are convinced that the composer himself is enigma enough. But Elgar, who
when the work came out seemed almost to want his secret to be guessed
and teased his friends into racking their brains, in later years replied to
questions about it with answers as enigmatical as the enigma. The
people who knew the secret are dead, and it seems idle to speculate.

Is it possible, however, that one part of the enigma, the 'larger
theme' that goes 'through and over the whole set . . . but is not
played,' has been solved? The idea at the core of the *Enigma* is
friendship. Sir Thomas Browne in his *Religio Medici* wrote (and the
capital and italics are his): 'There are wonders in true affection: it is a
body of *Enigmas*, mysteries, and riddles; wherein two so become one,
as they both become two. I love my friend before my self, and yet
methinks I do not love him enough: some few months hence my
multiplied affection will make me believe I have not loved him at all.'
Elgar possessed this book; if he found in it the idea and title of the
Enigma will never be known.[1] Whatever prompted him to write
them, the Variations live on independent of the stimulus.

[1] I am indebted for this idea to my friend Mrs Cecil Dickenson, who
noted it in 1939.

'Enigma'

The work was produced on 19th June 1899 at St James's Hall, London. Hans Richter conducted. The score had been sent to him in Vienna by his London agent, Vert,[1] and he accepted the work, knowing little of the composer. Elgar told Jaeger that 'it wd be just too lovely for anything if R. did an English piece by a man who hasn't appeared yet.' This does not necessarily invalidate the story that it was through Parry's exertions that Richter came to perform *Enigma*: that Parry rushed off to Richter one wet evening with the newly written score under his arm.[2] It may have been to Vert that Parry went, finding Richter away, or even to Richter himself, without knowing that the work had already been accepted. But Elgar's Variations were accepted in their own right and won him a champion in Hans Richter who was to do as much in bringing his name before the public as he had done for Wagner.

The music made a decisive impression. It was Elgar's first big work to be produced in London, and the mystery attached to it attracted popular attention. Quite apart from this, the fantasy, brilliance, and delicacy of the music proclaimed that England had a composer, an orchestral composer, of strong originality.

In March that year the Elgars had moved to 'Craeg Lea,' Malvern Wells. Their new house was larger and more pleasant than 'Forli,' nearer to the Beacon hill, and with a great sweep of a view over the Severn plain from its windows. They still kept 'Birchwood,' where Elgar was able to go for periods of uninterrupted composition.

The year 1899 saw the production of *Sea Pictures*, a set of five songs for contralto and orchestra, at the Norwich Festival on 5th October. Clara Butt was the soloist. 'Both singer and composer were recalled over and over again,' said *The Times*, 'and the songs have undoubtedly been launched on a prosperous career.' Two days later they were performed in London at St James's Hall. Performances of *King Olaf* at Sheffield, *Caractacus* at Leeds, and an all-Elgar concert at

---

[1] 'I offered the work to Dr Richter (thro' Mr Vert who sent the score to Vienna).' Letter from Elgar to Littleton, March 1899. This is confirmed by 'Dorabella' and R. J. Buckley.

[2] Quoted by Dunhill in *Sir Edward Elgar* (Blackie) and by Plunket Greene in *Charles Villiers Stanford* (Arnold).

New Brighton, where Bantock was fostering English music, were further encouragement. Royal favour was evident. On 24th May Elgar conducted, by the invitation of Sir Walter Parratt (then Master of the Queen's Musick), at a concert which took place at Windsor in honour of the queen's eightieth birthday. At this was performed a collection, by some dozen living composers, of madrigals in praise of the queen, modelled on *The Triumphes of Oriana*, including Elgar's 'To her beneath whose steadfast star.' Many of his songs were included in a concert in the private chapel at Windsor on 18th October. *Sea Pictures* was given a command performance at Balmoral on 20th October. The year 1899 was a good one for the Elgars.

The success of his music and his more frequent appearances at important festivals brought Elgar into wider musical circles and made him new friends. Among these were A. E. Rodewald and F. L. Schuster. Rodewald was a Liverpool business man who had wealth and taste enough to make his musical influence felt in his city. He was a friend of Richter's, and at his home Elgar met many musicians, among them Ernest Newman. Elgar more than once stayed with Rodewald at Bettws-y-coed; part of *The Apostles* was to be written there. Rodewald's premature death in 1903 was a severe loss to Elgar. Frank Schuster's friendship was to remain his for much longer, until his death in 1927, and was to bring Elgar musical and social advantages as well as the affection and admiration of a discriminating friend. Schuster was always anxious to further Elgar's interests, and his position in London's musical life was no less strong because it was amateur. At his house in Westminster and his country home on the river near Maidenhead Elgar had the chance of mixing with distinguished people. When the Elgars went to America on tour, Schuster was made Carice's guardian.

On his wedding day Elgar had been given by Father Knight, the priest who married him, a copy of Cardinal Newman's poem, *The Dream of Gerontius*. When the Birmingham Festival committee asked him to write a major work for their 1900 festival his thoughts turned first to St Augustine. He wrote to Joseph Bennett in January 1899: 'I proposed St Augustine as a subject for Birmingham, but

'Gerontius'—Composition

"they" request that I will not take it up as it is too controversial: this is as I feared. I am now considering a purely scriptural thing, but have not fully decided.' In Mrs Elgar's diary there is a note about the 1899 Three Choirs meeting: 'Elgar walked with Father Bellasis' (Father Bellasis was at Brompton Oratory with Cardinal Newman), and the 'scriptural thing' was postponed; *The Dream of Gerontius*, which had simmered in his mind these eleven years, was begun. He knew perfectly well he was ready to write a great work. He wrote to Littleton of Novellos: 'Now I have to consider the subject, which must be sacred: can you suggest anything? And will your firm want the work? I want to make this my chief work and to devote myself to it with something like a free mind.' It was written at 'Birchwood.' He gave up all except major engagements and worked steadily and with fierce concentration. On 5th February 1900 he wrote to Jaeger: 'I am setting Newman's *Dream of Gerontius*—awfully solemn and mystic.' And finally, on 7th June: 'God bless you, Nimrod. Here's the end.'

Jaeger, reading the work in manuscript before performance, was remarkably prescient. 'You must not, cannot expect this work of yours to be appreciated by the ordinary amateur (or critic) after one hearing.' 'The more I study the work the more I marvel.' '*Gerontius* is miles ahead of anything you have ever done.' And over and over again references to *Parsifal*. 'Your *Gerontius* is the finest, because the most beautiful and ennobling work, since Wagner's sacred drama. Indeed, it is in a way another *Parsifal*.' Elgar's own happiness burst out with 'The trees are singing my music—or have I sung theirs?' over a quotation from 'Praise to the Holiest.'

It was produced at the Birmingham Festival of 1900 and given the place of honour on the Wednesday morning, 3rd October. Richter conducted and the soloists were Edward Lloyd (Gerontius), Plunket Greene (the priest), and Marie Brema (the angel). There is no doubt that the work did not receive the public success it deserved, and that this was largely due to a poor performance. It is difficult now, some fifty years afterwards, to distribute blame fairly. The facts must speak for themselves.

Swinnerton Heap, who was to have trained the chorus, contracted pneumonia and died on 11th June.   Stockley (in whose orchestra the young Elgar had played) was called out of retirement and did his best with a work antagonistic to his nonconformist outlook, and with a choir daunted by novel and difficult parts.   W. T. Edgley,[1] who sang in the performance, seemed to think that the choir had only six or seven weeks to learn *Gerontius* in addition to other new works.   This is borne out by a letter written on 9th June by Jaeger to 'Dorabella,' and quoted by her in her book, in which he says that 'the chorus parts will not be in the hands of the B'ham singers for another three weeks or more.'   Judging by the letters between Jaeger and Elgar this was an optimistic estimate.   Choruses do not normally rehearse during the holiday months of July and August, and it may well have been less than two months before the festival when rehearsals began in earnest.   There is some ground for thinking that Elgar was himself partly to blame for this: he always found proof-correcting laborious. Certainly the fact that the choir were supplied only with single-voice parts would increase the difficulty of learning a work in which soloists and chorus are so intertwined.   'One section of the choir had no idea what the others were doing (or not doing), and being a new work, we had not grasped the idea of the grand work as a whole,' wrote Edgley in 1950.   As a result of this, some members of the choir did not treat the work with due seriousness.   There was some light-hearted buffoonery among the basses which Stockley was apparently unable to control, though of this Edgley was unaware, and said that he and those around him knew the work well.

Elgar himself did not attend any but the final rehearsal.   Composers are not always an asset at rehearsals of their own works, but many of the choristers felt that in this case Elgar would have been helpful.   Edgley says: 'Quite early on in the rehearsals for *The Apostles* we had the great man, Elgar, to show and explain what he wanted.'   During the final rehearsal of *Gerontius* on the Saturday before the Wednesday performance, 'Elgar was alongside Richter, prompting him and trying to explain what he wanted . . . things got

---

[1] In 1950 Edgley wrote an account of the performance to 'Dorabella,' to whom, and to Mrs Edgley, I am indebted for permission to quote.

'Gerontius'—Production

very chaotic and everyone worked up to a high pitch and unfortunately E. E. more than anyone, naturally. He seemed desperate, with
whom I cannot remember, but it was not all "the choir" as most
people think.' Of Elgar's own words to the choir on that occasion
there are two first-hand accounts, both published in the *Birmingham
Post*. The first is a contemporary report by that paper's music critic.
'The rendering of this part did not satisfy the composer, and he
addressed the executants from the front of the orchestra. We venture
to think this was a mistake, and showed want of tact.' The second is
a letter printed on 8th March 1934 from a second soprano of the choir:
'Elgar's words at the rehearsal: "It is no better than a drawing-room
ballad," were not received in the large-minded spirit that their truth
demanded from a body of loyal singers.' It is clear that Elgar,
distraught by the flounderings of the choir, only made matters worse.

Edgley and many choristers wished that he had conducted his own
work, though, according to Herbert Thompson,[1] Richter followed
Elgar's tempi closely. Bax recorded [2] that a year later Elgar told him
bluntly: 'The fact is, neither the choir nor Richter knew the score.'
(It is significant that Elgar did conduct the first performance of *The
Apostles*.) Richter must, in his anxiety, have called the choir for extra
rehearsal: although Edgley says that there was only one combined
choral and orchestral rehearsal, and that the final one on the Saturday.
G. L. Graves, in the *Spectator*, 13th October 1900, wrote that the
amount to be learned was larger in quantity as well as more difficult in
quality than on previous occasions, 'while, to crown it all, it was
found impossible to give the choir a rest on the day preceding the
festival. As a matter of fact, they had six hours' rehearsal on the
Monday, and were thoroughly stale when they began their labours.'
'Second Soprano' recorded that 'on the morning of the performance,
Dr Richter came and stood on the steps leading to our dressing-rooms
and with unforgettable voice and gesture besought us to do our very
best "for the work of this English genius."' But it was too late.
The choir were overtired, apprehensive, and resentful. They dropped
in pitch, made ragged entries, and sang with little understanding.

[1] *Yorkshire Post*, 2nd March 1934.
[2] Arnold Bax, *Farewell, my Youth* (Longmans).

1898–1904

Gerontius was not the only work in that festival to be poorly performed. According to the *Sunday Times*, 'In Sir Hubert Parry's *De Profundis* we were rudely awakened to the fact that something was wrong,' and though the production of *Hiawatha* was praised the performance of the St Matthew Passion was considered 'worthy of a fourth-rate provincial choral society.' Clearly the Birmingham chorus was in need of a spring-clean. R. H. Wilson, the Hallé chorus master at Manchester, was appointed for *The Apostles*. Edgley remembers him as 'a dour and serious-minded man and very strict in his choice of voices for the choir.'

The true measure of *Gerontius* was taken by some people despite its unconvincing performance. Thompson, of the *Yorkshire Post*, declared: 'It is the most powerful and profound utterance of one of the most individual composers.' Graves summed up in the *Spectator*: 'Mr Elgar's work, in spite of the imperfections of the performance, created a deep impression by its beauty, its earnestness, and its distinction.' *The Times* was more cautious: 'A remarkable, and in some ways a beautiful, work.' Elgar's fellow musicians perceived its worth at a London orchestral rehearsal. According to the *Observer* dated the Sunday before the Birmingham performance: 'It made so very great an impression on the audience of musicians present' (among whom were Parry, Stanford, and Manns) 'that one of the most eminent of these roundly asserted *Gerontius* to be the finest work yet written by a British musician.'

It was left to the Germans to confirm that England had a great composer. Jaeger wrote to Mrs Elgar:

I sent the other day a score of E.'s variations to Prof. Buths of Düsseldorf, one of the ultra-moderns of Germany, great propagandist for Richard Strauss, and I enclose his remarks. . . . The firm, at my suggestion, have invited him to B'ham to hear some English music. He is conductor of the Lower Rhenish Musical Festivals. Do you guess something? But mum's the word.[1]

Buths came to Birmingham. There is a story (the authenticity of which nobody can now confirm or contradict, though it is traditional

---

[1] 18th September 1900.

German Performances of Enigma and Gerontius

at Novellos) that Buths was invited to hear *Hiawatha*, Coleridge-
Taylor being higher in favour than Elgar with the directors of
Novellos. What Jaeger, after showing tact in the handling of his
employers, said to Buths is not recorded, but it was *Gerontius* that the
conductor took back with him to Germany, himself translated, and
performed at Düsseldorf on 19th December 1901, with Ludwig
Wüllner, Antonie Beel, Willy Metzmacher, and the Städtische
Musikverein. He had conducted the *Enigma* Variations there on
7th February, and the success of both works was such that *Gerontius*
was repeated the next year, 1902, on 19th May during the Lower
Rhine Festival, when the soloists were Ludwig Wüllner, Johannes
Messchaert, and Muriel Foster. Richard Strauss, at a luncheon in
Elgar's honour, gave as his toast: 'I drink to the welfare and success
of the first English progressivist musician, Meister Elgar.' Elgar
described the first, December, performance in a letter to Novellos
which throws a good deal of light on himself and his ideas about the
Birmingham production.

As to the performance, it completely bore out my own idea of the work.
The chorus was very fine and had only commenced work on 11th November. This disproves the idea fostered at Birmingham that my work is *too
difficult*. The personnel of the chorus here is largely amateur, and in no way,
except in intelligence and the fact that they have a capable conductor, can
they (or it) be considered superior to any good English choral society. Of
the soloists, the contralto failed and I will say no more about her. [This
was not Muriel Foster, who was to become one of the most moving inter-
preters of the angel's part; Elgar came to have great admiration for her voice
and her attractive personality]; the bass was *fine* and the tenor, Dr Ludwig
Wüllner, was *splendid*, not in voice but intelligence *genius*—he carried everyone away and made Gerontius a real personage—we never had a singer in
England with so much brain—even here he is exceptional. Professor Buths
was unsurpassable as conductor and took *infinite* pains to make everything
'go'—all thanks are due to him. You will hear from Mr Jaeger about the
fuss made over me—I understand to an unusual extent, so I will not refer to
this very pleasant part of our visit.

I hope the exceedingly kind and liberal way in which you have
brought the work out may result in something more than an artistic
success.

1898–1904

So *Gerontius* became accepted as a masterpiece in Germany, though it had to wait two years before the second full performance in England. During the First World War the committee of the Philharmonic Society was discussing the lamentably small audience at their recent Elgar concert. 'But where *are* all the Elgar admirers?' asked somebody, and Beecham flashed: 'They are all of them interned.' There was more than a grain of evidence for it. Elgar, his disappointment aggravated by worry over a temporary illness of his wife's and a financial loss, let Jaeger know his bitterness the week after the Birmingham production. 'I have worked hard for forty years, and at the last Providence denies me a decent hearing of my work; so I submit . . . I have allowed my heart to open once—it is now shut against every religious feeling and every soft, gentle impulse for ever.' [1]

But he did receive, on 22nd November 1900, his first honorary academic qualification. At the instance of Stanford, then Professor of Music, and on the strength of the *Enigma* Variations, Elgar was made a Doctor of Music at Cambridge. He professed that his new title gave him no great pleasure—more than one letter of the time begins 'Kindly refrain from addressing me as *Doctor*,' or 'Why the divule you call me doctor I don't know!'—for he took pride in the fact that he had needed no university education; but he accepted the recognition for his wife's sake. His robes were given to him as a present (when it became obvious that he saw no reason to buy them for himself) by his fellow musicians headed by Parry, Richter, Bantock, and Henry Wood.

The year 1901 saw (besides the German performances of *Enigma* and *Gerontius*) the production of the *Cockaigne* overture on 20th June and the *Pomp and Circumstance* marches Nos. 1 and 2. In April Elgar described *Cockaigne* to Joseph Bennett, who was writing a programme note about it. 'It calls up to my mind all the good humour, jollity, and something deeper in the way of English good fellowship (as it were) abiding still in our capital.' London liked it, and it was repeated successfully at Gloucester on 11th September.

[1] 9th October 1900.

Rotary Photo

DR ELGAR

'Cockaigne' and 'Pomp and Circumstance'

On 19th October the two marches were performed at Liverpool. The first march had already been played at a concert of the Gloucestershire Orchestral Society. According to Mr Walter Pitchford,[1] who played the timpani on that occasion, Elgar wrote the tune and sketched the march one Sunday afternoon, on the back of an envelope. 'He played it over to Herbert Brewer, with whom he was staying, saying he defied anyone to say in what key the first ten bars were. When he came to the trio he said: "Listen to this. This 'll make them sit up." It did, and when it was played at the Royal Amateur Orchestra Society's concert King Edward is said to have told Elgar: 'You have composed a tune which will go round the world.' Elgar intended to write four more marches, one for a soldier's funeral, but this was never written. He did, however, write a funeral march that year which could very well be used instead, in the music to *Grania and Diarmid*, a play by George Moore and W. B. Yeats.

Also in 1901 Elgar wrote a *Concert Allegro* for piano at the request of Fanny Davies. She wanted a piece to play in a programme of English piano music. Elgar needed some tactful persuasion—after she had got her way Miss Davies wrote: 'I hope you will get to like the piano better!' [2]—but the work was written and performed at St James's Hall on 2nd December. After another performance at Manchester in 1906, at which Richter's opinion was 'I like it—it is rather like a marriage between Bach and Liszt!' [3] the manuscript was lost, and Elgar made no attempt to rewrite the work, although the rough copy which he kept indicates plans for turning it into a piano concerto. Neither this nor the one he began in his last years was published.

In February of 1902 Elgar was invited to write an ode for the king's coming coronation. His position as unofficial composer laureate, apparent at Queen Victoria's jubilee, thus became recognized. It was his intention to use in the ode the trio from the first *Pomp and*

[1] Letter from Walter Pitchford, Lamport Rectory, to the *Morning Post*, 28th February 1934.

[2] *The Times*, 12th October 1942.

[3] Letter from Edward Rice, a pupil of Fanny Davies, quoted in the *Daily Telegraph*, 8th December 1934.

1898–1904

Circumstance march for the words 'Land of Hope and Glory.' Jaeger did his best to dissuade him.

> I say, you *will have* to write another tune for the 'ode' in place of the 'March in D' tune (Trio). I have been trying to fit words to it, that drop to E and the bigger drop afterwards are quite impossible in singing any words to it, they sound damn' vulgar. Just try it. The effect is fatal. No, you must write a *new* tune to the *words* and not fit the words to this tune.[1]

But Elgar went his own way and turned a good instrumental tune into a bad patriotic song. The *Coronation Ode* was first given at the Sheffield Festival in October (though Clara Butt had sung 'Land of Hope and Glory' in London in June), as the coronation had to be postponed owing to the king's appendicitis. At its first London performance, at a concert organized by Henry Wood in thanksgiving for the king's recovery, it had a tremendous reception. Elgar was five times called to the platform. At a later performance, when someone congratulated him on 'Land of Hope and Glory,' he said with a a twinkle: 'Well, I've had that tune in my pocket-book for twenty years without using it!' [2]

Enigma, *Gerontius*, and 'Land of Hope and Glory' between them must surely have fulfilled the wish in a letter of 1898 to Joseph Bennett: 'I hope some day to do a great work—a sort of national thing that my fellow Englishmen might take to themselves and love.'

Gerontius, his greatest work, had so far brought him little financial gain. Conductors and choirs alike were wary of a work which had floored the Birmingham chorus, and though there were undoubtedly people who realized the quality of the music, it needed considerable resources and courage to perform it. All honour, then, to Worcester, Elgar's own city, for its gallant effort in May 1901, seven months after the Birmingham production. The Worcestershire Philharmonic Society gave a selection of the easier parts at the Public Hall. Elgar was still the society's conductor, but after his own work he played in the second violins while the leader of the orchestra conducted

[1] 6th December 1901.
[2] Letter from A. B. L. W. to the *Henley and South Oxfordshire Standard*, 30th December 1934.

Further Performances of 'Gerontius'

a piece of his own. Elgar had apparently feared that the work would fare no better than at Birmingham, for after the performance he circulated a letter to the members of the society: 'I was, a month or two ago, very much hurt at what I felt (erroneously, it seems) to be a want of interest in the practices. I know now that this was a mistake on my part, and can only say I hope the performers took half as much pleasure in its presentation as I did.' According to the *Musical Times* the large audience was 'profoundly impressed.' Even so to Elgar it must have been a pathetic performance, and he can in no way have been encouraged by the playing at the Three Choirs meeting at Gloucester that year of the Prelude and Angel's Farewell, of which *The Times* said: 'It is to be hoped that the two movements, which make a very effective selection, will be often heard in this way, even if we cannot hope for frequent revivals of the whole oratorio produced last year at Birmingham.'

At the following festival, at Worcester in 1902, it was given in its entirety, but in a de-Romanized version calculated to appease the Protestant clergy and audience, which left out the invocation to the Virgin and by such means tried to camouflage the letter of Catholicism even if not the spirit. 'In spite of these regrettable alterations,' said *The Times*, 'the performance, under the composer's direction, reached a very remarkable degree of excellence.' Jaeger had suggested [1] the removal of 'Joseph' and 'Mary' 'to a more distant background' before the work's production, foreseeing that its denomination would hinder performances at English festivals—'likely to frighten some d——d fools of Protestants.' The first performance fully to establish the work as a masterpiece was at Sheffield on 2nd October. *The Times* said: 'Dr Elgar's *Dream of Gerontius*, the emphatic success of which was delayed until the present year, is now to be ranked among the certain attractions for a festival audience. . . . The composer conducted with great skill and secured a performance which from every point of view must rank as the finest yet given in England.' A performance at Hanley in March 1903, again conducted by Elgar, reaffirmed the success of the work.

[1] 14th June 1900.

1898–1904

Although in 1903 it was performed in Chicago on 23rd March and New York on 26th March, the first London performance was not until 6th June. This was arranged by Elgar's own Church and took place in the unconsecrated Westminster Cathedral. The building, despite the exceptionally high price of the tickets, was packed, but it was unfortunate that the acoustics were poor as the building was as yet unfinished, so that even though Elgar conducted, the choir was the one which had recently been praised for its performance at Hanley, and the soloists were Wüllner (who had so excited Elgar at Düsseldorf), Muriel Foster, and Ffrangcon-Davies, the reception given to the work was cautious. The press seats were badly placed, and the critics did not wish to judge a work which they could not properly hear. The second London performance was on 15th February 1904, by the London Choral Society, which was formed for this purpose.

Meanwhile Elgar was writing a new work, *The Apostles*. It was not new in conception: that had taken place when the schoolboy Elgar heard Francis Reeve say: 'The Apostles were poor men at the time of their calling; perhaps, before the descent of the Holy Ghost, not much cleverer than some of you here.' An invitation to write a work for the Birmingham Festival of 1903 brought about its birth. The text Elgar himself compiled from the Bible and the Apocrypha. He started collecting material at the end of 1901 (after a summer holiday spent at Bayreuth to hear *The Ring* and *Parsifal*), although the music was not begun until July 1902. Ill health and depression dogged the writing of it. He wrote to Littleton on 15th February 1903:

I arrived home on Saturday not at all well—cold affecting liver of course: it stops *all* work and I must be contented to be idle musically the rest of my life I suppose and going away is not possible. Alas! However, I have been quite disillusioned as to the musical world for some years and so I say farewell to it without the slightest regrets.

Another letter in June 1903 is more serious if less dramatic.

I have been seeing my London doctor and my eyes are again in trouble— he forbids more work. Now I propose to the B'ham people that they

'The Apostles'

produce Pts I and II of *The Apostles*—this portion is complete in itself and may well stand alone. . . . The concluding portion of the work (Pt III to round it off), much of which was written first—you can have any time later.

To Jaeger, alarmed about his health, Elgar wrote: '*I'm not ill!* and it is of no use to postpone the work as I shall *never* get English vocal-ists—a complete cast that is—to do my work.'[1] He had already been obliged to reshape the bass parts to fit the available singers. It is evident from these references and from those in other letters that Elgar originally planned what now stands as *The Kingdom* as part of *The Apostles*, and was only deterred from completing the work by ill health, eye-strain, and the impossibility of finding 'singers *with brains.*' In July he wrote to Schuster from Bettws-y-coed, where he was staying with Rodewald, that he was fitter and getting on fast with the orchestration.

Jaeger made a detailed analysis of the work, about which Elgar, much touched, wrote: 'It is *superb* as a piece of informing dissection and you hit off every idea and feeling of mine.' Jaeger told Winifred Norbury that he had needed 'eight weeks' hard study, spending every spare morning, 4–7, and evening, 10–2 (or 3), on the difficult task.' The first performance of *The Apostles*, at Birmingham on 14th October 1903, had none of the hazards that had marred that of *Gerontius*. The choir had learnt its lesson. Elgar himself conducted and the singers were Albani, Muriel Foster, John Coates, Ffrangcon-Davies, Kennerly Rumford, and Andrew Black. The following May it was performed at Cologne at the Lower Rhine Festival, and Elgar, who went to hear it, wrote to tell Littleton that as a result of the festivities he was in bed with a chill, but that it was 'a splendid per-formance' and 'rapturously received.'

In November, after the production of *The Apostles*, the Elgars went to Italy. She spoke Italian; he could understand a little. While they were there they visited Verdi's home. Elgar had hoped to write a symphony, but this he found 'impossible,' and he wrote instead an overture, *In the South (Alassio)*. This piece is dedicated to Frank Schuster. After Schuster's death in 1927 Elgar wrote to his sister,

---

[1] 1st July 1903.

1898–1904

Adela, that he wanted something 'radiant, bright, and uplifting for dear Frank's memorial stone,' but could not find it. 'I have said in music, as well as I was permitted, what I felt long ago—in F.'s own overture *In the South* and again in the final section of the Second Symphony—both in the key he loved most I believe (E♭), warm and joyous with a grave radiating serenity.' [1] From Bordighera on 8th December 1903 he wrote to Schuster:

Alice and I have been out with a *donkey* all day up in the woods and mountains—donkey's name is Grisin—a lovely beast. We eat out of doors in the sun, so little does it take to make us happy!

I like the French now but can't get on with the Italian tonguage (good word). Bought some figs to-day—did not know the name, so asked for 'frutti per habilimenti d'Adam et Eva!' I got 'em.

Oh! that donkey, she is a love. . . . We are both riotously well and shall never come home.

But they did come home, and earlier than they had meant to. The weather became 'unbearable,' there was a 'bitter east wind,' and Elgar had 'crippling rheumatism and colds.'

The year 1904 saw three events which gave recognition and honour to Elgar. The first was an all-Elgar festival at Covent Garden. The idea came from Alice Elgar. 'Why have a Birmingham Festival, a Leeds Festival, and a Three Choirs Festival?' she asked one day at a party, with sublime partisanship. 'Why not simply an Elgar Festival?' One of her hearers agreed with her and the idea was passed on, with the result that Elgar received a letter from H. V. Higgins of the Grand Opera Syndicate. 'The idea has been suggested to me that it might be a good thing to organize an Elgar Festival. . . . Does such a scheme smile upon you?' There was some similar scheme afoot with Manchester, for Elgar wrote to Littleton to say that he chose Manchester for 'artistic preference' and Covent Garden for 'novelty.' The two schemes were amalgamated, and Elgar expressed himself satisfied, 'provided Richter will conduct.' Richter *did* conduct and brought the Hallé Orchestra, and the festival took place on 14th, 15th, and 16th March. The king and queen

[1] 20th August 1928.

Recognition

were present, and an assembly of the leading men of the day. Mrs Elgar had written to Schuster from Italy: 'Do you not think the King will come to the Festival? ... How should he be asked? You will say: "There, again, sheer audacity," but the Festival altogether is so wonderful (thanks to you) to think of that nothing seems impossible.'[1] Before the festival Elgar dined at Marlborough House to meet the king. *Gerontius* was performed the first night, *The Apostles* the second, and on the third the *Enigma* Variations, *Cockaigne*, the *Pomp and Circumstance* marches, *Sea Pictures*, and the new overture, *In the South*. To no other composer has England done such honour.

On 13th April Elgar was made a member of the Athenaeum Club under Rule II, by which 'a certain number of persons of distinguished eminence in science, literature or the arts, or for their public services' are elected each year.

On 5th July he was knighted. So was fulfilled his own prophecy made as a small, new schoolboy.

'What is your name?' asked the headmaster.

'Edward Elgar,' said the boy.

'Say "sir,"' said the headmaster.

And so the boy replied: 'Sir Edward Elgar.'

[1] 7th January 1904.

CHAPTER V

1904–1911

AT the end of June 1904 Sir Edward and Lady Elgar removed from Malvern, where they had lived for thirteen years, and went to 'Plas Gwyn,' Hereford. 'We arrived yesterday,' Elgar wrote to the Norbury sisters, 'and the men are settling in, Alice is in command, and in the expectation of vast tips, which they will not receive . . . they are piling on "My Lady" fourteen to each breath.' 'Plas Gwyn' stood above the Wye River, in a large garden, and had an orchard. Carice kept a white rabbit, Pietro d'Alba, to which Elgar dedicated a part-song. 'Pietro d'Alba' paraphrased the words of two folk-songs, 'The River' and 'The Torch,' which landed Elgar in difficulties over copyright. Elgar's big study looked out on to a veranda up which climbing plants grew. Here, in a Three Choirs Festival town, he was more in the swim of things than at Malvern.

After the knighthood further honours came quickly. On 6th October the University of Leeds made Elgar an LL.D.; on 26th November the University of Birmingham offered him the chair of music, the Peyton Professorship; he was made a member of the Maatschappij tot Bevoordering der Toonkunst of Amsterdam after a performance of *The Apostles* at Rotterdam on 2nd December; in the same month he was made an honorary member of the Royal Academy of Music; and in the following February Oxford University conferred on him a doctorate of music.[1] Becoming an Hon. R.A.M. brought him comments from friends who remembered his second name, William, which he had dropped in the Malvern days; E.W.E. had become R.A.M.

The Peyton Professorship Elgar was loath to accept: he disliked talking about music and his outlook was not academic. Birmingham pressed their invitation, pointing out that the £10,000 for the endowment of the chair had been given, 'the only condition being

[1] For further honours and degrees see Appendix C.

Sir Edward Elgar with Lady Elgar and their daughter,
Carice, at Plas Gwyn in 1910

Sir Edward Elgar with the Three Choirs Festival conductors, Sir Ivor
Atkins, Dr Percy Hull, and Mr Herbert Sumsion, after a rehearsal
of *Gerontius* at the Hereford Festival of 1933

Move to Hereford—The Peyton Professorship

that it should in the first instance be offered to and accepted by Sir
Edward Elgar, Mus.Doc., LL.D.' Elgar was far from being well
off. He found himself compelled to accept the position which had
been specially created for him, but on the condition that he should
shortly be succeeded by Granville Bantock. He gave eight lectures
(each preceded by intense gloom in the Elgar household and followed
by controversy in the press), the first on 16th March 1905. Three of
these were technical, on orchestration, Brahms's Third Symphony,
and Mozart's Fortieth. The other five dealt with the state of music in
England at that time, under the titles 'A Future for English Music,'
'English Composers,' 'English Critics,' 'English Executants,' and
'Retrospect.' Elgar's attacks on the lack of intelligence in English
oratorio singers and choruses, on the poor quality of much hastily
written musical journalism, and on the low standard of English
orchestral players compared with continental, were well deserved;
he had himself suffered from all three. English contemporary composers, however, were offended by his remarks about their work.
Much of what he said was merited and has already been confirmed
by the judgment of posterity. But Elgar, who was in his own
person the answer to his question 'What of the future for English
music?' was a composer and not an historian, and looked at the
scene from too narrow an angle of vision. He found that English
music was 'commonplace as a whole,' and said:

Some of us who in that year [1880] were young and taking an active part
n music—a really active part such as playing in orchestras—felt that something at last was going to be done in the way of composition by the English
school. . . . It is saddening to those who hoped so much from these early
days to find that after all that had been written, and all the endeavours to
excite enthusiasm for English music—'big' music—to find that we had
inherited an art which has no hold on the affections of our own people, and
is held in no respect abroad.

He spoke of the want of inspiration in English music, and went on:

Many respectable and effective works have been written during the twenty
years 1880-1900. To me they represent more or less—I will not particu-
larize—such a phase of art as in another way was represented by Lord
Leighton. There you had a winning personality, a highly educated man,

a complete artist, technically complete, but the result was cold and left the world unmoved. The musical works produced in the period named leave me in exactly the same way: I am amazed at the dexterity displayed in the finish of the works, but there is absolutely nothing new. The student of orchestration, the student of orchestral writing, will find nothing but what may be better learned from French or German composers.

This was all true, but it was not the whole truth. In taking his period of twenty years Elgar did not consider what had gone before it. He took little account of the aims of his contemporaries and still less of the higher quality of their music compared with that of their predecessors. Many of them were sincerely working to raise the level of taste and scholarship out of the vacuity of the mid-Victorian period. Their own compositions are now revealed to have fallen short of their ideals, but Elgar was never to surpass the poetic delicacy of Stanford or the unselfconscious nobility of Parry at their best, and they could never have written anything as meretricious as Elgar at his worst. Though what Elgar said was honest and bravely outspoken, his lack of perspective made him also say things that were both unkind and unsound. As a result, many musicians felt constrained to avoid his company.

That first winter at 'Plas Gwyn' little music was written. Elgar was attacked by one of his periodic fits of depression. 'I am still very low,' he wrote to Schuster in September, 'and see nothing in the future but a black stone wall against which I am longing to dash my head. And that's all: a pitiful end for a promising "youth"!' His Christmas greeting was no less bleak:

One line at this time (I *hate* it) because Alice says it's 'nice.' Oh! Lord. Well! I wish you everything nice and good—all, in short, everything I want and haven't got. I think that's about it.

Everything here is flat, stale, and distinctly unprofitable.

However, early in 1905 he was working on the *Introduction and Allegro* and a new *Pomp and Circumstance* march. The march he said was 'a devil' and the string piece was 'most brilliant with a real tune in it however.' (Jaeger had suggested something 'brilliant' for strings only, 'such as Bach could write ... even a *modern* fugue.') They

Visit to America—Freedom of Worcester

were first performed at Queen's Hall on 8th March. Richter, when he played the *Introduction and Allegro* at Manchester for the first time, sensed that the audience had not appreciated its true worth, and without any explanation played it all over again.

On 9th June Sir Edward and Lady Elgar sailed to America. This was a private visit for Elgar to receive an honorary degree of music from Yale University on 28th June, and the American press was full of regret that Elgar had not been asked to conduct. There was an elaborate reception at New Haven in his honour, and a friendship sprang up between him and his host, Professor Sandford. The *Introduction and Allegro* was dedicated to him.

The Elgars returned to Hereford in July. In September, at the Three Choirs Festival, Elgar received an honour which meant much to him: he was given the honorary freedom of the city of Worcester. The suggestion had come from the cathedral organist, Ivor Atkins, and it was Elgar's boyhood friend, Hubert Leicester, who, as mayor, made him a freeman. As he walked in procession through the High Street wearing his Yale robes, Elgar paused for a moment and saluted his father, who, too old to leave his house, watched his son from an upper window. Later in the year the city of Hereford asked Elgar to become its mayor. This he refused, mainly, no doubt, because he had not the time, but partly because, as a Catholic, he could not attend the cathedral services.

After the Worcester Festival, at which the *Introduction and Allegro* was played, Elgar went for a cruise with the Mediterranean fleet as the guest of Admiral Lord Charles Beresford. Schuster was one of the party, and so was Lady Maud Warrender, a music-lover who became a great friend of the Elgars when they lived in London. They had a rough trip, but Elgar enjoyed it. The fleet returned on 12th October, and Lord Charles wrote to tell Elgar that his band-master was several inches taller 'since your kind notice of him.' Lady Beresford asked Elgar to write something for her in remembrance of the Greek islands. He did, one of the very few piano pieces he ever wrote, called *In Smyrna*.

In October Elgar conducted *The Apostles* and the *Introduction and Allegro* at the Norwich Festival, and in November he conducted the first provincial tour made by the London Symphony Orchestra, during which *Sea Pictures* and the *Introduction and Allegro* were given nightly. This and the succeeding tours fostered the very pleasant association between Elgar and this orchestra, which was often to play his music at the Three Choirs Festivals. In April the proposal that Elgar be asked to conduct their symphony concert on 1st November had been carried unanimously by the orchestra's committee, and in September Elgar had presented a set of parts of the *Introduction and Allegro* to the orchestra's library, which had been founded with a gift of the *Enigma* Variations by one of the directors. But travelling always tired Elgar and gave him headaches, and he got 'frightfully sick of the tour.'

He was always subject to frequent minor ailments, colds, liver upsets, headaches, and occasionally quinsy. His letters at this time refer constantly to his poor health, as he was easily depressed and a peevish patient. 'We have still the cook who can't cook and can't get another and I have been very ill,' he wrote to Littleton in 1904. All through 1905 the fluctuations in his health were duly recorded: at best he was 'a poor thing.' Despite his military appearance his physique was by no means robust. Several times he went to Llandrindod for the cure. He wrote from there to Colvin in December 1906: 'We met like ghouls in the pump-room at 7.30 a.m. in the dark: mysterious and strange; hooded and cloaked we quaffed smoking brine and sulphur and walked thro' dim-lit woods, sometimes in snow.' Sir Sidney Colvin had recently become a friend of Elgar's. He was at that time Keeper of Prints and Drawings at the British Museum. Though he and his wife Frances were concert-goers, his main link with Elgar was literature, especially their common admiration for R. L. Stevenson.

During November and December 1905 Elgar was writing *The Kingdom*, which he intended as the second part of the trilogy of oratorios begun with *The Apostles*. When in June 1903 he had been forced to alter the plan of the work because of eye-strain he remembered his youthful tripartite idea, and on 28th October of that year he had written to Littleton: 'My ideas now revert to my colossal scheme of years ago—but I may not live to do it.' The irony of it! He lived

Scheme for the Trilogy—'The Kingdom'

long enough, but the work was never done. His scheme, as he put it in that letter, was this:

I *The Apostles* (which you have).
II A continuation as talked over with you.
III The Church of God (or Civitas Dei)!

Last Judgment and the next world as in Revelation: each work to be complete in itself—the one bearing to the other roughly:

I The schooling.
II The earthly result.
III The result of it all in the next world.

I have the IIIrd part libretto done in one shape, but of course when I begin work I shall go into pt II first! However, I want a rest now.

In December 1905 he was 'red-hot' in his work, but early next year he slipped and hurt himself on a holiday in New Radnor and wrote to Littleton that he was too overdone to finish the oratorio and had offered the first half only. Luckily he recovered enough to finish it during July and August. It was produced at Birmingham on 3rd October 1906. Elgar conducted and the soloists were Agnes Nicholls, Muriel Foster, John Coates, and William Higley. The third part was never to be composed. He wrote about it to Littleton from Rome in December 1907 (his mind already full of a symphony), that he had 'definitely and finally' given up the idea. . . . 'I am sadly disappointed with the commercial results of the last oratorios, and for the sake of my people must not waste more time in attempting to write high "felt" music.'

In April 1906 he paid his second visit to America, to conduct at the Cincinnati Festival in May. He gave the first American performance of *The Apostles* and also conducted *Gerontius*. Journalists described Elgar as 'the typical Englishman, silent, reserved, unsocial —until after dinner.' Lady Elgar—'small, plump, with laughing blue eyes and the prettiest manners imaginable' [1]—they found more approachable. Elgar's return was a sad one: his father had died on 30th April. Anne Elgar had died four years earlier.

During his third American visit in March the next year he

[1] *Cincinnati Post*, May 1906.

conducted *The Apostles* and *The Kingdom* in New York and concerts of his own music at Chicago, Cincinnati, and Pittsburgh. On this tour he had to leave Lady Elgar in England, for Carice had shortly before developed rheumatic fever. After his first trip in 1905 he had written to Littleton: 'My *feelings* are dead against coming here again but my pocket gapes.' Although royalties were coming in fairly well at this period his letters show that Elgar had not the money to do all that he wished. The move to 'Plas Gwyn' had been a heavy expense (he had even mentioned to Jaeger the possibility of taking violin pupils again), and it was only after some consideration that the Elgars again went to Italy, going to Capri, Naples, and Rome in January and early February 1907. Lady Elgar had written to Littleton in December: 'We feel we must give up our Italian journey . . . we cannot undertake it without financial anxiety.' But eight days later Elgar wrote to him: 'The doctor insists on rest' and 'Will you be so good as to send me some money!'

During 1907, tired and disinclined for extended work after the exertion of writing and producing *The Kingdom*, Elgar wrote only slight things and continued his lectures at Birmingham University. In May he attended the Morecambe Festival which Canon Gorton (who had helped Elgar collect material for *The Apostles*) had been instrumental in founding. It was for this competition festival that Elgar wrote many of his part-songs. Later that month he wrote the fourth *Pomp and Circumstance* march, which was first performed at Queen's Hall on 4th September. During the summer he was again having trouble with his eyes and was not allowed to read or write much. He disinterred his youthful pieces for a family play, and expanded and rescored them, making out of them two suites, *The Wand of Youth*. The first was produced at Queen's Hall on 14th December and the second at the Worcester Festival of 1908. Both were dedicated to men he had known in his young days—the first to Lee Williams, who had known Elgar's family and who had watched over Elgar's early festival appearances as a composer when he was organist at Gloucester; the second to Hubert Leicester, who had in all probability played the little pieces in their original state.

The Elgars spent the winter of 1907–8 in Rome. Elgar had

'The Wand of Youth'—A Symphony begun

French lessons at the Berlitz school and enjoyed taking his wife and daughter sightseeing.

I am trying to write music [he wrote despondently to Schuster at the end of the year], but the bitterness is that it pays not at all and I must write and arrange what my soul loathes to permit me to write what *you* like and I like. So I curse the power that gave me gifts and loathe them now and ever. I told you a year ago I could see no future: now I see it and I am a changed man and a *dour* creature. But not to you, dear Frank, not to you. Bless you.

Despite this Elgar was occupied with ideas for a symphony. He had great admiration for General Gordon and had long wanted to express this in music. As early as October 1898 he had mentioned a 'Gordon' Symphony to Jaeger, and in November of that year was 'possessed' by the idea. Jaeger wrote to him in November 1899: 'How *is* that "Gordon" Symphony getting on! You Sphinx!! *Why* dontcher answer??' Apparently the slow movement held him up, for Jaeger wrote in 1901: 'Wood tells me he hopes to do your symphony at the festival if it's ready. Now I don't suppose it will be ready unless you have had an inspiration for the slow movement yet.' Richter tried to encourage it: in 1904 he was 'hopeful,' but by 1905 he was following the advice of Psalm XXXVII: 'Wait patiently for it.' Elgar had already promised the work on two occasions in 1904, for the Covent Garden Festival and the Leeds Festival.

Now in Rome he turned to it again: the sketch in short score of the first movement is dated December 1907, though he wrote to Littleton that he saw little chance of the Symphony being finished. 'I can't tell how much I shall be able to work here: there are "voices most vociferous" and pianos most pianiferous in the street which is otherwise quiet.' He sent W. G. McNaught of Novellos a picture postcard of the Via Appia Antica over which he scribbled the first three bars of the symphony—the beginning of that great A♭ tune—and, underneath, the words: 'Here it was!' After his return to England in May 1908 he worked uninterrupted except by a visit to Ostend in August to conduct his own music, and the Three Choirs Festival in September. He had a little diversion in August—'Made soap yesterday between fits of scoring (nor scouring) the symphony. I have been vainly trying to persuade Carice to wash with it—strange how little encouragement I get!'—but in the same month he put the last note to the Symphony and told Schuster: 'You *will* like some of my latest phase, so do I.'

There is no indication that the work is in any way connected with Gordon: in fact, Ernest Newman, in his notice of the first performance, wrote: 'I may say that the composer assured me positively that this is not the "Gordon" Symphony.' If an earlier symphony was written, more than probably the composer destroyed it. Elgar wrote to Walford Davies: 'There is no programme beyond a wide experience of human life with a great charity (love) and a *massive* hope in the future.'[1] The Symphony bears the dedication: 'To Hans Richter, Mus.Doc. True artist and true friend.'

Richter, with the Hallé Orchestra, gave its first performance on 3rd December 1908, at Manchester. Although the work was to be repeated by him with the London Symphony Orchestra in London four days later, most of the London music critics were there. The enthusiasm was tremendous. Elgar was called to the platform after the slow movement as well as twice at the end. Bookings for the London performance were so heavy that an extra concert was arranged for the following Saturday, and the Symphony had its first two London performances in one week. Richter conducted the London Symphony Orchestra on both occasions, and he introduced the work to the players at its first rehearsal by saying: 'Gentlemen, let us now rehearse the greatest symphony of modern times, written by the greatest modern composer,' and he added: 'And not only in this country.'

The *Observer* remarked: 'At the first [London] performance the conclusion of each movement was marked by an outburst of enthusiasm and the appearance of the composer on the platform, probably a unique instance of sympathetic recognition and personal esteem.' This initial enthusiasm was sustained, and the work achieved the unprecedented distinction in this country of nearly one hundred performances in its first year. During 1909 and 1910 it was played in St Petersburg, Vienna, Munich, Leipzig, Berlin, Budapest, Frankfurt, Bonn, and Rome.

[1] 13th November 1908.

First Symphony—Death of Jaeger

After the production of the First Symphony 'music was off.' For several months Elgar devoted himself to chemistry—sometimes, as when a water-butt exploded, at some personal risk—in the hut in the garden at 'Plas Gwyn' which he called The Ark. He himself had fitted it up, tarred the roof, fixed shelves for his bottles, and made a telephone extension to the house.

In May 1909 Jaeger died. For some years he had been under sentence of death, spending his winters in Switzerland, though at the end he had come home. His unswerving devotion and the pains-taking care with which he criticized each new work had sustained Elgar through the early days before recognition came to him, and he was one of the first to perceive greatness in his music. 'Dear old Moss-head,' as Elgar called him, may have been taken to task for over-enthusiasm in the analyses which he wrote of Elgar's music, but in letters he never hesitated to speak his mind. Elgar made permanent his feeling for his friend in 'Nimrod,' which referred to one of the many occasions on which, as Elgar put it to 'Dorabella,' 'he preached me a regular sermon.' Many were the tributes paid in the press to 'the small German,' for several English composers besides Elgar owed him gratitude for his integrity and enthusiasm. On 24th January 1910 a concert was given in his memory at Queen's Hall. The programme was made up from the music of his favourite composers, some of whom (Elgar himself, Walford Davies, and Coleridge-Taylor) he had helped to make their name.

In February 1910 Elgar paid a surprise visit to the Worcester Glee Club, with which he had had so many associations in his young days. He took the chair, stood drinks, and listened to part-songs. A description of him by one of the party on that evening says:

Hair now very grey, but otherwise unchanged in appearances. Eyes open and shut rapidly and continuously, hands small, slender, and nervous. Right hand shakes nervously as it rests on table. Complexion rather dark, almost olive colour, strong, well-shaped moustache, nose almost hooked. Teeth large, strong, white and show when he smiles. Speaks rapidly, sharply, and distinctly. Not very loud but clear.

In April 1909 the Elgars went to Careggi to stay with Mrs Worth-ington at a villa she had rented there. Julia Worthington was an

1904–1911

American, a close friend of the Sandfords. She had met Elgar on one of his visits to the States, and she came to England for the next two summers. When he was back at 'Plas Gwyn,' Elgar began work on a violin concerto, but put this on one side to consider another symphony. A London Symphony Orchestra tour and the Leeds Festival interrupted work in the autumn, but during January and February of the next year he took out the sketches for the Concerto and played them over with Lady Speyer. Lady Speyer, the wife of Sir Edgar Speyer, the financier, who on occasion advised Elgar about his investments, had been before her marriage a professional violinist, Leonora von Stosch. She and Lord and Lady Stuart Wortley, who were midland friends of the Elgars, watched the Concerto grow, and during the early months of that year persuaded Elgar to continue with it when he became despondent and threatened to abandon the work. Claire Stuart Wortley, the daughter, interpreted the words on the sketch of the first movement, 'Where Love and Faith meet there will be Light,' as referring to this encouragement. Parts of the Concerto which Lady Stuart particularly liked were called the 'wind-flower' themes. In March Elgar began to work in earnest and took a flat in London, in New Cavendish Street, where W. H. Reed visited him frequently, playing Joachim to his Brahms, trying over passages as they were written and giving technical advice. Reed, who was a violinist in the London Symphony Orchestra and was made its leader in 1912, became increasingly intimate with Elgar from this time, and was, in Elgar's later years, one of his closest friends. He has described in revealing detail the part he played in the writing of the Concerto,[1] and described too Elgar's methods of composing as he saw them on his first visit to New Cavendish Street.

There was the composer, striding about, arranging scraps of manuscript in different parts of the room, pinning them to the backs of chairs and placing them on the mantelpiece with photograph frames to hold them in position. It was wonderful to note the speed at which he scribbled out another passage or made an alteration or scrapped a sketch altogether as being redundant.

---

[1] *Music & Letters*, January 1935.

Violin Concerto

From New Cavendish Street Elgar went to stay with Schuster at his Maidenhead house after a holiday with him in Cornwall. According to Reed, the Andante of the Concerto was written there, in a studio on the lawn by the Thames, though Claire Stuart Wortley recorded that Lady Speyer had played the movement on 6th February. Probably part of it was recast. In June Elgar went home and at 'Plas Gwyn' wrote the Finale. 'That last movement is good stuff,' he wrote to Schuster early in July. The complete Concerto was first played at a private party at Gloucester on the Sunday the Three Choirs Festival began. Reed played the violin part and Elgar the orchestral part on the piano.

The Violin Concerto bears a quotation in Spanish, 'Aquí está encerrada del alma de . . . . .' ('Herein is enshrined the soul of . . . . .'). The five dots are another enigma. Lady Elgar told 'Dorabella' that the soul was that of Julia Worthington.[1] Elgar's daughter cannot confirm this because she never knew, but Ernest Newman [2] has said that Elgar assured Basil Maine 'that the "soul" was feminine.' Mr Newman attached importance to the fact that there are five dots in the quotation instead of the printer's customary three. Certainly the name Julia has five letters, and so has Pippa, Mrs Worthington's nickname.

Elgar had seen a good deal of her during the previous couple of years and had become deeply attached to her, as indeed did most people who knew her, for she had a delightful personality. She was present at the private party at Gloucester in 1910 when the Concerto was first performed. Elgar had, in 1907, dedicated to her the part-song 'Deep in my soul.' Byron's words may have held some personal significance for them.

> Deep in my soul that tender secret dwells,
> Lonely and lost to light for evermore,
> Save when to thine my heart responsive swells,
> Then trembles into silence as before.

---

[1] Mrs Richard Powell, *Edward Elgar* (Methuen).
[2] *Sunday Times*, 21st May 1939.

There, in its centre, a sepulchral lamp,
Burns the slow flame, eternal—but unseen;
Which not the darkness of Despair can damp,
Though vain its ray as it had never been.

It is perhaps a little far-fetched to see a connection between the opening notes of this part-song:

Ex. 1ª
Andante espressivo

and those of the Violin Concerto:

Ex. 1b
Allegro

and yet the rhythm is identical, and, except that the song is major and the Concerto minor and that the notes of the song lie in the authentic compass of the scale and that those of the Concerto in the plagal, the pitch too is the same. Moreover, the similarity is not hidden in an inner part or in the middle of either work, but exposed in the very first bar of each. To express similar thoughts in similar musical shapes was characteristic of Elgar's subconscious mind. Here then, surely, is musical evidence to add to 'Dorabella's' testimony that the soul enshrined in this Concerto was Julia Worthington's.

The Concerto was produced at a Philharmonic Society concert on 10th November 1910. Kreisler, to whom the work is dedicated, played it and Elgar conducted. Before their first run-through in September Kreisler had written to Elgar, giving a hint of his working methods: 'You must not expect a finished performance, because I must always leave the technical study of the violin part of a new work to the end, in order to command it musically the better.' At the production Queen's Hall was packed, and violinist and composer were given an ovation.

The rest of that year Elgar worked with Ivor Atkins in the preparation of a new edition of the St Matthew Passion for use at the

The Order of Merit

Three Choirs Festivals, and at the beginning of 1911 he was at work on a second symphony. At the end of March he went again to America, this time not only to the United States but to Canada as well. This was on a tour by Coward and the Sheffield Choir to celebrate coronation year, in which Elgar had agreed to conduct *Gerontius* and *The Kingdom* on the American continent. The New World held little attraction for him. He found 'every nerve shattered by some angularity, vulgarity, and general horror.' To Colvin he wrote: 'I know I ought to be glad that perhaps I shall earn some money, but I would rather starve—if it were not for the others. Truly parts of the world are beastly!' While he was in America he accepted the London Symphony Orchestra's invitation to be their permanent conductor for the 1911–12 season. On his return he stayed for three months at 75 Gloucester Place, writing an offertory and a *Coronation March* for the forthcoming coronation of George V. According to Basil Maine, the march originated in some sketches made on an Italian holiday, mainly improvisations at the piano to accompany in fancy a procession of Italian lords and ladies.

Five days before the coronation the Order of Merit was conferred upon Elgar. 'Yes! It is really fine,' he wrote to Winifred Norbury, 'although few (country or county) people seem to know what it is: there's now nothing left for me to achieve.' But to Adela Schuster he admitted that he was 'very proud' of his 'newly apportioned fraction of the alphabet.' Parry, when he heard the news, said: 'He is the right person for it. You see, he has reached the hearts of the people.'

The month before this the Second Symphony was produced. Although most of the writing of this had been done in the first months of 1911, the sketches had been begun in 1909. The full manuscript score bears the names 'Venice—Tintagel' (what more romantic places could he have found to write a symphony?), and he was at Careggi and Venice in April and May 1909, and at Tintagel in April 1910. To Tintagel he went with Schuster on a motoring tour of Cornwall. 'I was so happy the whole time,' he wrote afterwards to Schuster's sister, Adela, 'that my letter might become an

C

essay "on the possibilities of earthly bliss."' The spirit of delight, perhaps? On 25th October 1910 he wrote to Lady Stuart Wortley:

I have also been making a little progress with Symphony No. 2 and am sitting at my table weaving strange and wonderful memories into very poor music I fear. What a wonderful year it has been! With all the sad things in the great public life—the King's death downwards—the radiance in a poor, little, private man's soul has been wonderful and new and the concerto has come!

Sanford Terry says [1] that in October it was in Elgar's mind 'to use in close context the present opening subjects of the scherzo and slow movement, and he explained that they represented the contrast between the interior of St Mark's at Venice and the sunlit and lively Piazza outside.' But when Terry reminded him of this in January 1911 Elgar said he had given up the idea. He also told Terry that the Symphony had no programme: it was simply the 'frank expression of music bubbling from the spring within him.' Canon W. H. T. Gairdner [2] states that Elgar told him it would be correct to say that the whole thing represents the 'passionate pilgrimage' of a soul.

On 29th January 1911 Elgar wrote again to Lady Stuart Wortley: 'I have recorded last year in the first movement to which I put the last note in the score a moment ago and I must tell you this: I have worked at fever heat and the thing is tremendous in energy.' The day before, Lady Elgar wrote in her diary: 'E. finished his 1st movement. He was hardly over a fortnight scoring and writing this from his sketches.'

The Symphony was finished on 28th February. It bears a dedica-tion to the memory of King Edward VII, and a quotation from Shelley: 'Rarely, rarely, comest thou, Spirit of Delight!' Whether Elgar meant the slow movement to be a funeral march to Edward VII cannot be deduced. From the dates above it would appear that the original sketches were made before the king's death in May 1910, but that the writing and orchestration were done afterwards, in 1911. In October 1910 he spoke of the slow movement as representing St Mark's Cathedral. Yet Lady Elgar's note in her diary, 6th February

[1] In some notes bound with sketches of the Symphony in possession of the Athenaeum Club.
[2] *W. H. T. G. to his Friends* (S.P.C.K.)

Second Symphony

1911, reads: 'Finished his 2nd (slow) movement. Very great and impressive. A. hears lament for King Edward and dear Rody [Rodewald] in it, and all human feeling. E. wrote it all from his sketch in one week.' A. stands for Alice, and whether she read into it a lament both for Elgar's king and for his friend, or whether he disclosed to her that that was his intention, it is hard to say.

Elgar conducted the first performance on 24th May during the London Musical Festival. Although the work was favourably received, it was not immediately acclaimed as the First Symphony and Violin Concerto had been, and Elgar himself was disappointed.

Towards the end of the year the Elgars began to consider moving to London. Sir Edward's engagements meant a good deal of travelling, and London was a better centre than Hereford. He was loath to leave the Wye country, and they worried lest the house in Hampstead they coveted should prove too expensive to run, but the decision was made, and at the end of the year the Elgar family left Hereford for London.

CHAPTER VI

1912–1920

THE Elgars spent Christmas with Admiral Beresford and his wife and moved into their London home early in the new year. Severn House, 42 Netherhall Gardens, Hampstead, had belonged to a painter and had a fine panelled studio which Elgar made his music room. Off it was a smaller room which he used as a study, shelved with his books. Elgar became house-proud and delighted in his new home, 'so warm and comfortable.' It was an elegant house, and before the move he and Lady Elgar had spent several months in lavishing care on the decorations. 'I wish you could see Severn House! We have been up to-day and it gets lovelier (and more expensive) every time.'

Once they were established in London their circle of friends expanded. Close friends such as Frank Schuster, Hugh Blair, Landon Ronald, and Billy Reed were, of course, frequent visitors, but besides these many others enjoyed Lady Elgar's hospitality and called to see them on Sundays, when they were 'at home.' Landon Ronald had been an admirer of Elgar's music since Parry had sent him to hear *Enigma*. 'Yesterday,' he told Ronald, 'I heard Richter perform the *Enigma* Variations by a Mr Elgar, which is the finest work I have listened to for years. Look out for this man's music; he has something new to say and knows how to say it.' [1] Through the years Ronald became a great friend of Elgar's and a particularly fine conductor of his orchestral music, though Shaw once wrote of him to Elgar: 'He wants to make more of every passage than you do. A composer always strikes an adorer as being callous. Same thing on the stage. Producers always want to overdo titbits.' [2] Philip Burne-Jones, Edward Burne-Jones's son, who had himself painted Elgar's portrait; Percy Anderson, who designed the sets for *The Crown of India*; and Lady Maud Warrender, a friend of the Schusters',

[1] Landon Ronald, *Myself and Others* (Sampson Low).
[2] 7th January 1932.

58

Severn House—'The Music Makers'

who sang and did much to encourage music in London—all came often to Severn House.

The first work to be written there was the masque *The Crown of India*, commissioned for the occasion of the visit of King George V to India. It was produced on 11th March at the London Coliseum and Elgar conducted throughout the run. It was, as a sumptuous spectacle, very successful. Elgar, in writing about it to Frances Colvin, showed his rueful streak:

When I write a big serious work e.g. *Gerontius* we have had to starve and go without fires for twelve months as a reward: this small effort allows me to buy scientific works I have yearned for and I spend my time between the Coliseum and the old bookshops: I have found poor Haydon's *Auto-biography*—the which I have wanted for years and *all* Jesse's memoirs—the nicest twaddle possible and metallurgical works and oh! all sorts of things. . . . I found a lovely old volume *Tracts against Popery*—I appeased Alice by saying I bought it to prevent other people seeing it—but it wd make a cat laugh. . . . My labour will soon be over and then for the country lanes and the wind sighing in the reeds by Severn side again and God bless the music-halls![1]

In February Elgar conducted a London Symphony Orchestra provincial tour, then began work on a setting of O'Shaughnessy's poem, *The Music Makers*. Like most of his works this had been in his mind for many years, certainly as early as 1904, for Jaeger wrote then inquiring about 'The Dreamers,' and Elgar referred to the poem in 1907 in a letter to Littleton. Work on this was interrupted in April by ear trouble for which he had treatment, and from which he luckily completely recovered. *The Music Makers* was produced on 1st October at the Birmingham Festival.

At the end of January 1913 the Elgars went again to Italy, staying at Naples and on Capri. Elgar had long had an idea of writing a work about Falstaff.[2] In Italy ideas grew and after his return to London on 23rd February he began work. He immersed himself in the character

[1] 14th August 1912.
[2] R. J. Buckley in *Sir Edward Elgar* (Bodley Head), published in 1904, mentions in the list of works a concert overture *Falstaff* as being in manuscript.

1912–1920

of Falstaff and read everything about him he could lay hands on. He drew particularly on Dowden, Morgann, and Deighton, all of whom he quotes in the analytical essay he wrote for the *Musical Times* in 1913. His estimate of Falstaff is revealed in a discussion with Bernard Shaw eight years later. Shaw wrote:

I am also convinced that Falstaff, like Don Quixote and Pickwick, suddenly grew out of a mere piece of street-boyishness. It is plain to me that Shakespeare intended Poins to be the witty philosopher of *Henry IV*— the Benedick-Jaques-Mercutio—and that Falstaff was introduced as a minor stage coward solely as part of the machinery of the robbery on Gads-hill. This explains the hopeless inconsistency of Falstaff's cowardice on Gadshill with his valour afterwards.[1]

Elgar held his own:

I can't follow you regarding Falstaff being, in a word, an afterthought (that is to say the extraordinary development) because I don't see how you can possibly get over his first scene with the prince. His *reality* and impor-tance seem to me to be shown from the first. Poins always was a puzzle: he is neither fish, flesh, fowl, or good red herring.[2]

During March and April Elgar was unwell. He suffered a good deal from small nervous ailments. In March he went to Llan-drindod Wells to drink the waters, and in April he took a house for the sea air at Penmaenmawr and worked there on the full score of *Falstaff*. In May he was back at Severn House, but not feeling fit and in one of his moods of pettish despondency. 'I am still ill and fit for nothing, and what is worse I have no *wish* to be of any use any more.' *Falstaff* was produced on 1st October at the Leeds Festival, Elgar conducting. The work was received respectfully but not with en-thusiasm, and at the first London performance on 3rd November the hall was not full. Elgar thought it his greatest orchestral work.

In the summer before the production of *Falstaff* Elgar was seriously considering some sort of operatic work. Sidney Colvin, always solicitous about his friend's inspiration, had approached Thomas Hardy with the idea of his co-operating with Elgar. Hardy was keen and willing for further discussion. Something founded on *The*

[1] 29th September 1921.   [2] 1st October 1921.

'Falstaff'—Projected Operas

Trumpet Major, The Return of the Native, or a part of *The Dynasts* was suggested. Elgar replied that for the present his affairs were in a 'chaotic' state regarding work: 'Chaliapin has been here and talking over many schemes for a great part for himself, Lear! for instance. . . . But there is also a scheme for an allegorical affair on a huge scale— these two things may hold me musically for some time, but I shall keep in mind the Hardy ideas.' [1] A few months earlier Colvin had written suggesting that Elgar should 'put into music the imaginations and the movement of Sir Guyon and the lover of Acrasia,' and had gone on to rough out a plan for a libretto—'the musical dream of a non-musician.' [2] But Elgar, though he must have taken down his copy of *The Faërie Queene,* for there are pencil references to suggested cantos on the letter, replied: 'As to Spenser—well! Yours is a great idea but difficult to illustrate; the music has already been written (Wagner, Strauss etc.) to other words.' [3] Nothing came of any of this and he wrote only small pieces the rest of that year, 1913, and the beginning of the next.

He was now fifty-seven, and at the height of his worldly success, secure in his reputation, esteemed in his country's capital city. He was in considerable demand both to conduct his own music and to lend distinction to social gatherings. His position was singular. The academic musical world was dominated by the same trio of personalities as when *Enigma* was produced. Parry was still Director of the Royal College of Music, though no longer professor at Oxford; Mackenzie was still Principal of the Royal Academy of Music; Stanford was still professor at Cambridge, and ever increasing his list of talented pupils at the Royal College of Music. To Elgar, who had been unknown when they were already holding these positions, the mastery of the first decade of the century unquestionably belonged, yet he ruled no institution, guided no disciples, shed no discernible influence. The man whose music had been received as *avant-garde* was already being seen as having found his sources in the past, and as having brought his country into the main continental

[1] 22nd July 1913.   [2] 17th March 1913.
[3] 26th March 1913.

61

stream of music as much by accepting continental traditions as by speaking within them with a distinctly English intonation. He was the origin of no modern school, and the younger composers left his position as yet unrivalled. Delius, his nearest contemporary, had buried himself at Grez, and his music was at that time received with little understanding in England. Vaughan Williams had written his *Sea Symphony* and his *Tallis Fantasia*, but his *London Symphony* was not to be produced until the next year. Holst's *Planets* suite was still unwritten; so were Bax's tone-poems *The Garden of Fand* and *Tintagel*. Elgar, isolated and aloof, stood like a giant between the two groups. No one in 1913 could have foreseen that nearly all his significant music had already been written.

Twice in the summer of 1914 he had occasion to visit Worcester. On the first he called on his old Uncle Henry and afterwards spent a day or two with his sister Pollie at Stoke. On the second, on an evening prowl round the city, he dropped in unexpectedly on his sister Lucy. They were on the best of terms and Elgar lovingly fingered the knick-knacks she had brought from their parents' home. 'Elgar remembered everything,' wrote his companion on the occasion, 'every book, picture, and ornament. Just before we left he said: "Where is that dead pheasant?" Sure enough there was an old painting of the bird over the parlour door.'

In June 1914 Elgar conducted *The Apostles* in Canterbury Cathedral with the Leeds Philharmonic Choir. Henry Embleton, who had made the arrangements, used this opportunity to discuss with Elgar the unwritten oratorio which he wanted Leeds to produce. Embleton cast his line skilfully and Elgar nibbled at the bait; the libretto was partly written and the music was sketched in his mind. In July, after a 'dreary and dull summer' during which he had been 'not at all well—dull and stupid,' he and his family went on holiday to isolated little Gairloch in Ross. It is quite probable that he meant to start work on the oratorio on his return.

They were still at Gairloch when war broke out on 4th August. They had to wait there several days until there was a car available to take them to the railway, thirty miles away. Back at Severn House Elgar wrote to Frances Colvin: 'Here we are busy and doing what we can to help. Carice Red Crossing from morning till night—Alice generally sympathetic—and I am constable Staff-Inspector to the whole district, no less. . . . We reduce our staff, finding them good places—no panic, please, only stern law and order and goodwill all round.' [1]

Elgar was in the Special Constabulary and the Volunteer Service— 'I am sure others could do the work better, but none with a better will,' he told Schuster. He sent his trombone to the Y.M.C.A. Musicians' Fund and after the Armistice became patron of the Music Corner in British-occupied Cologne.

There came a spate of war music. A song, 'Follow the Colours,' was first performed on 10th October at the Albert Hall; *Carillon* at Queen's Hall on 7th December; a symphonic prelude, *Polonia*, at Queen's Hall on 6th July 1915; *Une Voix dans le désert* on 29th January 1916 at the Shaftesbury Theatre; *Le Drapeau belge* at Queen's Hall on 14th April 1917; *For the Fallen* and *To Women* from *The Spirit of England* at Leeds on 3rd May 1916 (the complete work was first performed in London on 24th November 1917); and *The Fringes of the Fleet* at the London Coliseum on 11th June 1917.

Carillon, a recitation to music of Émile Cammaerts's poem, made a tremendous impression by its blazing patriotism, which matched brilliantly the need of the hour. Tita Brand (Mme Cammaerts), Réjane, Henry Ainley, and Constance Collier each performed the work, which on occasion lashed its audience, in that first winter of the war, to fervent demonstration. Early in 1915 Elgar toured *Carillon* with the London Symphony Orchestra—'dismal journetings in the north' he called it. Sidney Colvin drew his attention to Binyon's *For the Fallen* and Elgar saw Binyon to discuss using it. But there were difficulties in the way—Cyril Rootham had already planned a setting of the work. He withdrew when he heard of Elgar's intention, but by this time Elgar had perversely lost interest. Colvin wrote him a sharp letter [2] pointing out the injustice to Binyon, to raise his hopes and then crush them for a whim. The letter took effect, and the

[1] 25th August 1914. [2] See page 99.

three poems were set and published under the collective title, *The Spirit of England.*

In September 1915 the Elgars spent some time in the Lake District, 'trying to find a little rest and peace,' as Elgar wrote to Walford Davies. H. W. D.'s connection with him lasted from before 1900 till Elgar's death, though possibly it was not as close as the younger man, whose feeling for Elgar was just this side of hero-worship, might have wished. He wrote impulsively in 1900: 'I feel prompted to chuck away the despicable (if useful) reserves of humans when writing to you. If you are agreeable, please talk henceforth as if we had known each other for a hundred years,' but nineteen years later he found it 'rather criminal that the years slip by' without their 'comparing notes with the men who are at one with us on all deep issues, whose work we love; and I do not know whether you ever feel the same, but I simply hunger in musical loneliness for a real exchange of thoughts and hopes with you.' Davies was the only creative musician with whom Elgar had anything more than a professional acquaintance. In his letters Elgar was a little cautious in expressing critical opinions of Davies as a composer—he was always too overworked to have done more than glance at any newly arrived score—though of the 'Rocking Hymn' he wrote that he 'took this and always your music, among the highest and best things we have.' To the man he extended a helping hand. He had worked in 1900 to get his music produced at a Three Choirs Festival, using his own Worcestershire Philharmonic Society as 'a stepping-stone to the other thing,' and Davies knew his 'indebtedness' to Elgar when he was asked the next year to write a work for Worcester. When Elgar was professor at Birmingham he invited him to give two lectures there, and in 1913 offered to propose him for the Athenaeum. 'I am scarcely the proper person to do it but I should like to see it done.'

In 1915 Elgar wrote music for Algernon Blackwood's play for children, *The Starlight Express*, which was produced at the Kingsway Theatre: 'It has been a real joy to have something so pure and simple to do.' Early in 1916 there was another London Symphony Orchestra tour, and Clara Butt organized in May a week of nightly concerts for the Red Cross, at each of which *Gerontius*, *To Women*,

Photograph: Reginald Haines, F.R.P.S.

SIR EDWARD ELGAR AT SEVERN HOUSE

Friendship with Walford Davies—'Brinkwells'

and *For the Fallen* were performed. In January of the next year Elgar
wrote the music for a ballet, *The Sanguine Fan*, which was produced
at the Palace Theatre on 20th March.

In 1917 Lady Elgar found a cottage, 'Brinkwells,' near Fittleworth
in Sussex. Elgar was delighted by it. 'This place is divine,' comes
over and over again in his letters. Lady Elgar possibly found it less
divine, for, though picturesque, it was tiny, isolated, and devoid of
amenities. The villagers, who became accustomed to seeing him
striding through the woods on his long walks, knew him as 'Mr
Elgar,' and he often dropped in to choir practices and once played the
organ at a harvest festival service. The cottage was set high on a hill
in thick woods with a view down to the River Arun and across to the
South Downs. In the old country garden was a studio where Elgar
worked. But the river and the woods provided distractions. 'The
axe however claims me and I make huge fires in the wood, meanly
delighting in the fact that I can burn more than anyone I know—a
frame of mind I am ashamed of in the cold hours.' His wood-
chopping was welcome when the frequent sea-mists rolled up over
the cottage, and he became skilled enough in woodcraft to make hoops
for barrels. Sir Julian Corbett, the naval historian, and his wife
were their neighbours, and Elgar and Corbett had good walks together. Elgar was again bothered by eye trouble '(blepharitis, blessed
word!), which has made wreading and riting all as wrong as I have
spelt 'em.' Lady Elgar sent inquiries to the Colvins for a reliable
doctor in the district: 'You, having also a darling wife, will know
that Alice has been in nervous fits over my prettily swelled lid,
purple, look you, and what nicer colour is there in any rainbow?'
The Colvins stayed near them for a time. 'Oh! I wish you were
a mile this side of Petworth instead of the other,' Elgar wrote to them, 'I
should have descended upon you with a shower of trout this morning.'

Soon, however, he was at work again. During August 1917 he
had considered some 'Greek notion,' seemingly a second set of songs
from the Greek Anthology, but no translation satisfied him. W. R.
Paton's effort he 'detested almost wholly,' and asked Colvin:

Who, why, or what is the bony Paton? I cannot understand his

1912–1920

merciless transposition, quite arbitrary and mostly senseless. . . . I am angry, because Loeb, in his introdn, lays stress on the value of the 'classics' to people who read neither Gk nor Latin. . . . How amusing it wd be for me, with heaped-up ignorance, to review this anthology from the standpoint of the *very person* it is intended for.[1]

The idea was discarded, and by the summer of 1918 he was engaged in writing a violin and piano sonata, a quartet and a piano quintet. Billy Reed spent much time with him, exchanging axe for violin bow at Elgar's whim and playing with him in his woods and his music studio. Colvin wrote trying to interest him in an ode at the end of the war, but Elgar replied firmly: '*Peace* music is off.' Yet the month before the war ended Elgar took part in an activity that must have had the elements of celebration in it. Landon Ronald organized a concert of humorous music at Queen's Hall in aid of the Red Cross. Haydn's 'Toy' Symphony was performed with an all-star cast: Elgar played the cymbals, Moiseiwitsch the triangle, Frederick Cowen and Frederick Bridge the rattles; the nightingales were Irene Scharrer, Myra Hess, and Muriel Foster, and the cuckoos were Mme Albani (who came out of retirement for the occasion), Ada Crossley, and Carrie Tubb.

The winter of 1918–19 was spent at Severn House. Elgar was reluctant to leave the country, where he was in 'the seventh heaven of delight,' but 'A., poor dear, is not well and, of course, is bored to death here.' Despite his gloomy predictions that composition would be 'off' in London—'*telephones* etc. *all* day *and* night drive me mad!' —he worked all winter at a cello concerto. In June 1919 this was finished at 'Brinkwells'—'a real large work and I think *good* and alive.'

Reed, with Anthony Bernard, gave the first performance of the Sonata on 13th March 1919 at a meeting of the British Music Society, then, with Landon Ronald, the first public performance on 21st March 1919, at the Aeolian Hall, and he played the Quartet and Quintet with Sammons, Jeremy, Salmond, and Murdoch on 21st May. Bernard Shaw had heard the Quintet privately before and

---

[1] 17th August 1917.

Chamber Music—Death of Lady Elgar

wrote [1] to Elgar: 'The Quintet knocked me over at once: I said to myself, with the old critic's habit of making phrases for publication, that this was the finest thing of its kind since *Coriolan*. I don't know why I associated the two; but I did: there was the same quality—the same vein. Of course you went your own way presently.' But he 'solemnly protested' at the fugue: 'You cannot begin a movement in such a magical way as you have begun this Quintet and then suddenly relapse into the expected.' A good many years before, the Worshipful Company of Musicians had commissioned a quartet from Elgar, but so long elapsed before it was published that Elgar refused to accept the honorarium of fifty guineas. Cobbett [2] suggested Elgar should 'square matters' by writing a piano trio. Elgar agreed, saying he already had a sketch of a trio, but it never materialized, and eventually Cobbett persuaded him to accept the money. About the Quintet Cobbett says that it was Elgar's intention to write a piano part which should be one of five, not dominant, and also that he ranked the Quintet among his best works. During the summer Felix Salmond went down to 'Brinkwells,' and played the Cello Concerto with the composer. He produced it at Queen's Hall on 26th October. Elgar dedicated it to the Colvins: 'Your friendship is such a real and precious thing that I should like to leave some record of it.'

In the autumn Elgar went to Brussels and Amsterdam to conduct. After his return he and Lady Elgar decided they must sell Severn House. It was large and uneconomical to run. Elgar had written to Colvin that summer: 'I have ceased to take the smallest interest in affairs. I am—whatever turns up—done for commercially,' and, in reply to Colvin's inquiries: 'Do not, dear friend, think of finance: I am all right but I am depressed at having so many to think of—it's the future mainly for other people that hurts.'

Before the house could be sold Lady Elgar fell ill. During February she developed a tiresome cough and Reed noticed how 'she who had always been so full of vitality and energy was now

---

[1] 8th March 1919.
[2] Letter to *The Times* from W. W. Cobbett, 2nd March 1934.

often listless.' But no one thought it was serious. She was well enough to go in March to hear the three chamber works played by the London Chamber Concert Society. Suddenly the severity of her complaint was realized. She was in bed only a few days, and she died on 7th April 1920.

CHAPTER VII

1920–1934

His wife's death was a blow from which Elgar never fully recovered. Alice Elgar's gentle, unobtrusive manner had covered a character from which he had always drawn strength. It was more than the loss of a dearly loved wife—the greater part of his own will and resolution died with her.

Their friends rallied round them. Landon Ronald came to Severn House immediately he heard the news. Frank Schuster helped Carice to make all the arrangements. At the funeral Reed, with Sammons, Jeremy, and Patterson Parker, played the slow movement from the Quartet which she had loved. On 10th April 1920 she was buried at St Wulstan's Church, Little Malvern, where, in the early days of their marriage, they had worshipped.

After the funeral Elgar and his daughter, whom he found at this time of crisis 'a sterling good thing,' went to his sister at Stoke Prior, Worcestershire, and returned to Severn House at the beginning of May. There he found a letter from Walford Davies, and wrote to him:

MY VERY DEAR H. W. D.,

I am just back to a cold and empty home—alas—and find your sympathetic note. I can only say thank you for it.

All I have done was owing to her and I am at present a sad and broken man—just stunned. My daughter does everything and is wonderful about the hideous ghoulish business which civilization makes necessary. Death we know and expect and try to bear like men, but I cry out 'Leave me with my dead'—and creatures have to come in and count over her pretty valueless

1920–1934

little rings and the most private things to see what they are worth—it drives me to distraction, and I am no fit company for human beings.

Bless you and thank you.

Your old friend,

E. E.[1]

Engagements made previously had to be carried out. In May there was a performance of *The Apostles* to be conducted and a tour with the London Symphony Orchestra in South Wales. 'I am back from my attempt at conducting—which I did all right—but I am a sad, a weary, and a broken man.' After this he and Carice, to whom he turned completely after his wife's death, went to 'Brinkwells' and stayed there in seclusion for the summer. 'I felt I was no longer "in" the world, or rather that the old artistic "striving" world exists for me no more.' He had to go to the Three Choirs Festival in September, but lodged privately, seeing few people. 'I *made* myself go through the very glorious week at Worcester, but it was sad, sad beyond words. Nearly six months gone by, and the loss becomes greater every day.' Afterwards he returned to Severn House.

Eighteen years before, Elgar and Strauss had talked of Bach's organ works and had agreed that each would orchestrate one of the fantasies and fugues. Elgar's fulfilment of this pact was his only work this year: he orchestrated the Fugue in C minor. 'Now that my poor wife has gone I can't be original,' he told Eugene Goossens, 'and so I depend on people like John Sebastian for a source of inspiration.' [2] The summer of 1921 was spent mostly at 'Brinkwells.' Though he would not compose he would play, and Billy Reed frequently visited him, when together they would make music. He made no plans 'except that, as far as I can foresee, I am giving up everything in London and here. I have tried to take up the old life but it will not do and so there's an end. I feel like these woods all aglow—a spark wd start a flame—but no human spark comes.' [3] But his friends found him a little less withdrawn at the Hereford Festival that year. He joined in a large house party and afterwards wrote to congratulate Percy Hull, whose responsibility the festival had been, on his 'truly

[1] 1st May 1920.   [2] E. Goossens, *Overture and Beginners* (Methuen).

[3] Letter to Colvin, 27th July 1921.

The Widower

solid triumph.' Then, in a postscript, there is a flash of the old, impish Elgar:

There is an old song which we all used to love and love still:

> 'Bill Blossom was a nice young man   (1)
> What drove the Bury coach   (2)
> But bad companions was his bane   (3)
> As egged him on to poach.'   (4)

(1) That's me—I have been called this for years in private.
(2) Of course, my car has been called this for months.
(3) You, Billy Reed, etc. etc.
(4) This does not apply—yet? It is supposed to be a veiled allusion to the despicable practice of dropping into Sunday luncheons without invitations.[1]

On his daughter's engagement he made plans to leave Severn House. 'We are clearing up here,' he wrote to Sidney Colvin on 16th September 1921. 'A notice-board of sale is being put up—I am rescuing a few papers and a few books and go forth into the world alone as I did forty-three years ago—only I am disillusioned and old.' In October he took a flat, 37 St James's Place. One man with whom he resumed friendship at this time was Ernest Newman. Newman and Elgar had met at Rodewald's house in Liverpool when Newman was in business there, but some of his subsequent notices of Elgar's works did not please Lady Elgar, and he was not invited to Severn House. After her death the two men met fairly frequently. Elgar became increasingly attached to his many clubs and had just been elected a member of Brooks's. Microscopes still rivalled music paper, and though he would occasionally play Reed snatches from his third oratorio no more was written. No music at all came until 1923, when he wrote incidental music for a play by Laurence Binyon, *King Arthur*. Elgar himself conducted the first performance, on 12th March at the Old Vic Theatre.

His daughter was married to Samuel Blake in January 1922, and when she went to live in Guildford Elgar no longer had ties in London. He was hankering after the country, and most of all Worcestershire. He took a house called Napleton Grange, some

[1] 12th September 1921.

1920–1934

five miles from Worcester, and there his sister, who had been ill, spent the summer with him, recuperating. Still restless in his sorrow he went off on a trip to South America in November 1923. He sailed a thousand miles up the Amazon in the *Hildebrand*. There exists a tattered little diary with a few entries in his handwriting which tell their own story. Friday, 16th. 'Rough, not up.' Saturday, 17th. 'Rough, not up.' Sunday. 'Dressed.' 7th December. 'Crocodile.' On his return he went to London, staying at his flat, writing music for the Wembley Exhibition of April 1924. In May, Sir Walter Parratt died, and Elgar succeeded him as Master of the King's Musick. His duties were not arduous, for the sovereign's band had been dissolved by Edward VII; and he could not have found it strange to be expected to produce occasional music, for though the title had been Parratt's and not his, he had written music for every important royal and national occasion since Parratt's appointment in 1893.

He returned to Napleton Grange in October after a holiday in Scotland. Mary Clifford, a niece of Lady Elgar's personal maid, came as his housekeeper. Cars and dogs were at this time his main interests. He wrote to Percy Hull: 'I have decided on the newest Lea Francis, I think,' and again: 'We went to Coventry and wallowed in cars. I bought an Austin 7 a fortnight ago for my sister who loves it—the boys will drive it—I was *demonstrating* in the garden and backed into a row of loganberries. They fell never to rise again.' Margaret Harrison remembers how he used to love being driven in her car when they met at festivals, and would tease her to go faster. She and her sister, Beatrice, who played his Cello Concerto so memorably, gave him Merry Meg, the Aberdeen, who with Marco, the spaniel, and Mina, the cairn, shares so many of his photographs. Marco always had his place laid at table for meals. Mina, Elgar considered, had the disposition and appearance of a dowager duchess, and he delighted in taking her motoring dressed in goggles, a veil, and strands of Woolworth pearls. Though during his married life Elgar had never kept a dog, his liking for animals was deep. His dogs were his constant companions in his retirement and his concern for them figures in his correspondence. His envy of their uncomplicated

72

Retirement to Worcestershire

lives prompted him to send as his card at Christmas 1929 Walt
Whitman's lines which begin: 'I think I could turn and live with
animals, they are so placid and self-contain'd'; and his Christmas card
in 1932, written by himself, was in ironical praise of a puppy.

Between 1924 and 1930 he arranged for orchestra the overture from
Handel's D minor Chandos anthem, made arrangements of some of
his own music, and wrote incidental music for *Beau Brummell* and a
carol, 'Good-morrow,' which was sung at St George's Chapel,
Windsor, in 1929 as a thanksgiving for the king's recovery. *Beau
Brummell*, a play by Bertram Matthews, was produced in 1928 by
Gerald Lawrence at the Theatre Royal, Birmingham. Elgar
conducted on the first night. The idea for the carol, 'Good-morrow,'
came from Walford Davies, who wanted his choristers to sing and
record something of Elgar's. Elgar wrote back: 'I enclose some
words by old Gascoigne ... send me the words back and I am
quite prepared for you, dear friend, to say it will not do. Just a
simple tune, that's all.' In November 1925 the gold medal of the Royal
Philharmonic Society was presented to him by Sir Henry Wood, and
in 1928 a further honour came when Elgar was created K.C.V.O.

In the autumn of 1927 his lease of Napleton Grange was up. He
took a house, Battenhall Manor, for the winter. There the news
reached him of Frank Schuster's death, and he wrote to Schuster's
sister, Adela: 'By my own sorrow—which is more than I can bear to
think of at this moment (a telegram has just come), I may realize in
some measure what this overwhelming loss must be to you. I trust
you may be helped by the Holy Spirit you have loved and served so
well to bear this blow.' Schuster left Elgar in his will £7,000
subject to death duties, for saving his country 'from the reproach of
having produced no composer worthy to rank with the great masters.'

In the spring he moved to Tiddington House, near Stratford on
Avon. He took this house furnished from Lady Muntz, who
remembers his coming to view it: 'I met them on the doorstep, and
tho' I had not a clue as to who they were (for Sir E. had insisted his
name should not be mentioned), I won the old man's heart by inviting
the dog in too. After that, he was almost prepared to take the house
without seeing it.'

1920–1934

At Tiddington his old friend of *Enigma* days, 'Troyte,' spent much time with him, and his three nieces (including May Grafton, who had lived with the Elgars at Hereford and, for a short time, in London) took it in turns to spend week-ends with him. He loved the river at the foot of the garden, on which they would row in the boat he bought for them. In June another bereavement saddened him. His brother died. Frank, the oboist in their boyhood wind quintet, had been 'a great invalid to whom I have been devoting myself for the last four years in these parts.' Family worries came again that September, when his little niece, who had been living with him, became ill. 'I fear I tired you with a stupid recital of my own troubles,' he wrote to Adela Schuster, after a visit to her, and went on: 'I am a lonely man, although I do not say so to everyone, or, I might have said, to *any* one. If you feel you can write a little pencil note to me at any time I shall be sincerely grateful.'

While he was at Tiddington House he saw a good deal of Bernard Shaw. The two men came to know each other only late in life and their association, based on mutual interests, was one of chaffing good humour. In August 1929 Shaw wrote to Elgar before the Malvern Festival, telling him that Barry Jackson was 'bent on getting from you an overture for *The Apple Cart*; but on obtaining from Boult a rough estimate of the cost of an Elgar orchestra, and letting his imagination play on the composer's fee,' he gave up the idea. 'My own view was that six bars of yours would extinguish (or upset) the A.C. and turn the Shaw Festival into an Elgar one; but that would be a jolly good thing so. I demanded overture to *Caesar*, to *Methuselah* (five preludes), and a symphonic poem to *Heartbreak House*, which is by far the most musical work of the lot.'

For the Three Choirs Festival of 1929 Elgar took a house called 'Marl Bank' on Rainbow Hill at Worcester. His lease at Tiddington coming to an end, he bought 'Marl Bank' and moved into it in December. It was to be his last home. To Adela Schuster he wrote in September: 'Owing to the extraordinary state of music in this country I have to cut down all possible outlay, and am "retiring" to a very little house near Worcester as soon as the permanent move can be made—after that the rest is silence.' 'Marl Bank' was a

At Tiddington House and 'Marl Bank'

spacious house in a pleasant garden with a view all over Worcester and its countryside. At Worcester Elgar had many friends, some of whom, like Hubert Leicester, he had known since his childhood; some, like Winifred Norbury, from the *Enigma* days; and some, like Ivor Atkins, colleagues with whom he had worked. He joined in many of the town's activities and was a particularly keen member of the Archaeological Society.

In April 1930 he wrote *Severn Suite* as a test piece for the annual brass band contest at the Crystal Palace. It is dedicated to Bernard Shaw, who advised Elgar: 'If there is a new edition of the score I think it would be well to drop the old Italian indications and use the language of bandsmen. For instance—*Remember that a minuet is a dance and not a bloody hymn*; or *Steady up for artillery attack*; or *Now—like hell.*'[1] Elgar arranged *Severn Suite* for full orchestra for the Worcester Festival of 1932. In 1930 he wrote the fifth of the *Pomp and Circumstance* marches. The idea for the six-eight section suddenly came to him in the car going to Gloucester, and he scribbled it down on the only paper he had, the back of an ordnance survey map. He also began another suite, prompted by the birth of Princess Margaret, 'Dedicated by permission to Their Royal Highnesses the Duchess of York and the Princesses Elizabeth and Margaret Rose.' This was not finished until the next year, 1931, as he had a bad attack of lumbago which nagged him during the summer. For the festival he sent certain recommendations to Percy Hull:

I have made a note (notes—a whole chromatic scale I think) of the hates and dours—the dimes and tays—the tace and plimes—none of this sounds right but I refer to the rehearsals: it wd be kind if you wd get Foster (to whom greetings) as secretary to put in columns the opening times of public-houses and the times and places of the races:

thus:

CATHEDRAL	LICENSED PREMISES	RACES
Apostles, etc.	opening	

That *is* the way to live.[2]

---

[1] 28th September 1930.   [2] August 1930.

The *Nursery Suite* was first played at a private performance on 23rd May 1931, before the making of a recording by H.M.V. The Duke and Duchess of York were present and were so delighted by 'The Wagon Passes' that they asked for it to be repeated. The first public performance was at a Promenade Concert on 20th August.

In June Elgar was created a baronet. In November he was awarded the first Honorary Life Fellowship of the Worshipful Company of Musicians, and was filmed opening a new recording studio of the Gramophone Company at St John's Wood. In March 1932 a ballet by Ninette de Valois to *Nursery Suite* was produced at Sadler's Wells. During May Elgar arranged Chopin's *Funeral March* for full orchestra. In October he went to Belfast to conduct some of his own works.

Though during these years he composed little, he frequently accepted engagements to conduct, and became a familiar figure to generations for whom he had already made musical history. As a conductor he was variable: he could be superb, but his attitude was not professional. Eric Coates found him 'the most uncertain' of all the composers he played under. People who heard performances he conducted of his own music testify that they were most compelling. On the other hand, the stimulus had sometimes to come from outside; on one occasion, for instance, at a performance of *The Kingdom*, the chorus dropped in pitch right at the beginning; Elgar, apparently losing interest, simply beat time until the soprano sang to perfection 'The sun goeth down,' when his interest was rekindled and he conducted the rest of the work as one inspired. Sometimes, as he grew older, he obtained peculiarly intimate performances, conducting almost in self-communion, turning the pages as though reading to himself. He once told Littleton that other people's interpretations of his music were usually too 'assertive' for him; and he wrote to Jaeger about performances of his own works by other conductors that 'when they go as I like, elastically and mystically, people grumble. When they are conducted squarely and sound like a wooden box, these people are pleased to say it's better. It is a curious thing that the performances which I have hated and loathed

Daily Express

ELGAR CONDUCTING AT A RALLY IN HYDE PARK, 1931

Elgar as Conductor—Yehudi Menuhin

as being caricatures of my thoughts are the very ones held up as patterns!'[1]

Orchestral players were devoted to him. He never taught them their job and always considered himself one of them. Once a seven-year-old viola player, after one of his first professional engagements, asked Sir Edward Elgar, Bart, O.M., Master of the King's Musick, for his autograph. 'Certainly, my dear fellow,' was the reply, 'anything to oblige a colleague.'

Despite his many activities in 1931, his dissatisfaction with his own circumstances is revealed in his letter to Adela Schuster of 19th November: 'I can give no good account of myself, and the altered conditions in the musical world make the future most deplorably bad: I must give up my little car and many other small comforts, and walk for the rest of my life—after 31st December. However, most of the serious musicians are in the same plight.'

During the summer of 1932 he rehearsed his Violin Concerto with Yehudi Menuhin, then only fifteen, and together they recorded it. After a performance by Menuhin at the Albert Hall on 20th November, which he conducted, he wrote:[2] 'My dearest Yehudi and good friend: I am just being hurried away and steal one moment (I don't care if I miss the train!) to send you my warmest thanks for the complete artistry you showed us to-day. I shall write to your dear father (who saved my life twice in one day with the Ovaltine, bless him!) directly I get home.' And in the letter to Menuhin's father he writes of Yehudi's 'tender and affectionate candour to me (this I prize perhaps more than anything).' Early the next year he wrote to Menuhin: 'At my age old friends pass away and leave the world rather empty—this is inevitable and has to be faced. Your friendship in any case must be—is—a remarkable thing, and it has given me a new zest in life.' Out of their correspondence comes a picture of an elderly man not only moved by admiration for the playing of his young colleague, but touched and eagerly responding to his friendship. Elgar, in these last years, offered and asked for affection with warm

---

[1] 1st July 1903.
[2] The letters were published in the *Daily Telegraph*, 20th October 1934.

spontaneity. Often in his letters he speaks of his loneliness, surrounded though he was by those who cared for him, and sends a note to one or other of his friends begging for news of him.

In December 1932 three concerts were given by the B.B.C. to celebrate Elgar's seventy-fifth birthday. At one of these it was announced that the B.B.C. had commissioned a third symphony, and had made an arrangement with Elgar whereby he could compose with no financial worries. The first mention of the idea occurs in Shaw's letter to Elgar of 7th January 1932: 'Why don't you make the B.B.C. order a new symphony? It can afford it.' Landon Ronald acted as negotiator and the symphony was announced for the autumn of 1933.

At the same time he was writing a piano concerto, and during 1932 he began to play with the idea of writing an opera. This he had long wanted to do. Jaeger had written to him, wisely, in 1901: 'Don't cook up *Caractacus* for Covent Garden. It will never do. Write a real opera. *Wait* a year or two. . . . You can't alter a cantata into an opera, no one can.' [1] In 1913 there had been several operatic schemes afoot; these the war probably interrupted. From 'Brinkwells' he wrote to Walford Davies: 'Oh! about the opera—I never found a subject I cared about—I wanted something heroic and noble but I am only offered blood and lust in the way of libretti.' [2] Ricordis and Covent Garden had each approached him at one time on the subject, but both offers he had refused. In 1932 he asked Bernard Shaw for a libretto, to be told that his plays 'set themselves to a verbal music of their own which would make a queer sort of counterpoint with Elgar's music.' Then he hit on a play of Ben Jonson's, *The Devil is an Ass*. Even this he had considered years before and had pencilled notes into his own copy. In the late summer of 1932 he approached Barry Jackson for help in reducing the complex plot to a manageable libretto. Jackson, who lived at Malvern, near enough for frequent discussions, fell in with the idea enthusiastically, though at first he was doubtful over Elgar's choice of play. From the first-hand account he has written of their collaboration [3] it is clear that Elgar, for the first time since his wife's death, was seriously contemplating a major work.

[1] 12th December 1901.   [2] 8th October (?)1917–19.
[3] *Music & Letters*, January 1943.

Opera and Symphony—Visit to Delius

By March 1933 both *The Spanish Lady*, as the opera was to be called, and the Third Symphony were in full swing. Barry Jackson suspected that '*The Spanish Lady* again and again tempted him away from the symphony.' These works were no playthings of a composer's retirement such as had tantalized his admirers for the last thirteen years, but a promised resurgence of genuine creative activity.

Then in April 1933 he complained of pain which was diagnosed as sciatica. He was well enough to go away early in May—'I have been rambling (and racing) at Newmarket'—and to go to Paris at the end of the month to conduct his Concerto, played by Menuhin and the Orchestre Symphonique de Paris. He chose to fly (his first flight) and was brimful of enthusiasm for his new experience. The day before the concert he visited Delius at Grez-sur-Loing. They had met once or twice in London and Delius had been present at the production of *The Music Makers*, which he found 'too rowdy and commonplace' for his taste. Elgar took him some records of Sibelius and Wolf, and told Delius he would like to conduct his music. 'He was very genial and natural,' Delius told Eric Fenby, 'and altogether quite unlike what I had expected him to be.' The two composers discussed their methods of working and were at one in that neither of them used a keyboard; both admitted to being engaged on big works at that moment. They talked about literature (Elgar claimed *Bleak House* as Dickens's best novel, Delius championed *David Copperfield*), and then talked of Elgar's flying from England and the possibility of Delius's flying to England. Over a glass of champagne they remembered old friends. 'I left him,' wrote Elgar, 'in a house surrounded by roses, and I left with a feeling of cheerfulness. To me he seemed like the poet who, seeing the sun again after his pilgrimage, had found complete harmony between will and desire.'[1]

His friends found him quicker to tire at the Hereford Festival that year, and his sciatica troubled him. Early in October he was suddenly taken into South Bank nursing home and operated on for a malignant tumour. The operation could only alleviate, not cure. Though he lived for nearly five months his work was finished. On

[1] *Daily Telegraph*, 1st July 1933.

11th October he wrote to Hubert Leicester and his wife: 'This is a bad affair. However we have had some good times and I love you both.' On 20th November he had a collapse. To his daughter and his close friend, Billy Reed, he expressed his wish that no one should be allowed to 'tinker with' his unfinished music. They gave him their promise and he seemed content and rallied again. For some time he did not know that his illness was fatal and thought his pain was due only to sciatica, but gradually he himself realized the truth.

He had a good deal of intermittent pain—'There seems to be nothing that gives me anything but the shortest respite from this most agonizing pain, and what stamina I have is nearly used up by the incessant sleeplessness'—but in the intervals he found solace in thinking of his own countryside—'I lie here hour after hour thinking of our beloved Teme—surely the most beautiful river that ever was'— and in listening to his own music. During his illness Fred Gaisberg, Chief Recorder of the Gramophone Company, arranged that Harriet Cohen and the Stratton Quartet should record his chamber music, so that each time Gaisberg visited him there was a surprise to delight him. The Gramophone Company set up an instrument in his bedroom for him, and on one occasion he was amused to become his own salesman. He chose a soft needle for the record of *Cockaigne*, but had a message from his next-door neighbour asking him to play it louder. Again came a message, this time asking for the name of the piece, as the lady wished to buy it.[1]

Early in January Elgar was moved back to his own house. There was no more the nursing home could do for him. His joy at being among his own people and possessions was marred by the awful pain which he suffered. He became visibly weaker. His last contact with the world of music was made through the microphone. On 22nd January he was able to direct, from his bedroom, a recording of the Triumphal March and Woodland Interlude from *Caractacus*. The idea was Gaisberg's, who wanted Sir Edward to know that he was not forgotten. Engineers set up a microphone and loudspeaker in his bedroom. The London Symphony Orchestra, conducted by

[1] *Sunday Times,* 17th December 1933.

Illness, Death, and Burial

Lawrence Collingwood, in the London studio, listened to Elgar's voice criticizing their performance, and then recorded his works. Elgar heard the actual recording played back and said he was pleased with it.

As his end drew near he had periods of unconsciousness, but in between, and in the intervals of his pain, he recognized and sought comfort from those closest to him.

One day when the pain left him for a little he asked for a pencil and a piece of music paper, and as he lay there he wrote what was probably in his head as the end of his Third Symphony—or perhaps he meant it to represent the end of his life's work.

The following day the author [Reed] was again with him and he fumbled about in his pillow for a little without saying anything. Presently he found what he sought and handed these four bars of music [1] to the author, fighting back the tears which were choking him as he said: 'Billy, this is the end.' [2]

He died early in the morning of 23rd February. He was buried on 26th February, not in Westminster Abbey, for this offer had to be refused as he was a Catholic (nor, as once he had wanted, was he cremated and his ashes scattered in the River Teme), but, at his own wish, beside his wife. There was no mourning, no music, and only close relations and friends followed his coffin down the hilly graveyard at St Wulstan's Church, Little Malvern. At the time of his burial a low Mass of Requiem was celebrated at St George's, Worcester, the church where he and his father had been organists; the choir sang *Pie Jesu Domine*, his own setting composed for them. A few days later a memorial service was held in Worcester Cathedral for those hundreds of people in all walks of life who wished to pay him tribute.

On the opening day of the Three Choirs Festival in 1935 a window designed by Archibald Nicholson was dedicated to Elgar's memory in Worcester Cathedral, close to the spot where he had often stood listening at festivals. After Viscount Cobham, Lord Lieutenant of the county, had unveiled the window, Beethoven's *Equali* for trombones were played; the bishop then dedicated the window and the

[1] See example 5, page 129.　　[2] W. H. Reed, *Elgar* (Dent).

1920–1934

ceremony ended with the 'Nimrod' variation. The festival began with a performance of *The Dream of Gerontius*, which had provided the designer of the window with his subject.

In 1934 the cottage where Elgar was born was bought by the corporation of Worcester as a memorial to him. An appeal was made, under the guidance of Sir Landon Ronald, through the columns of the *Daily Telegraph*, for funds to make 'the cottage at Broadheath as dear to lovers of music as the national monuments at Stratford, Chalfont, and Grasmere are to lovers of poetry.' To this cottage Elgar's family and friends brought their personal mementoes of him; the garden was replanted to look as it did in his childhood, with shrubs and rose-trees given by people in Worcestershire who knew him; in these little rooms were gathered together the tangible signs of his heredity, his work, his fame, and his home. Here those who knew the man only through his music may see and touch the everyday things that were dear to him, that make him seem as real as any printed word may do.

CHAPTER VIII

ELGAR'S CHARACTER AND CAREER

EDWARD ELGAR was a man frequently misunderstood by his acquaintances—and loved by his friends.

His home life was happy. His and his wife's devotion to one another is borne out by countless stories. He made good friends. His letters to his intimates reveal warm-heartedness and loyalty. He was generous and quick to show appreciation. To Jaeger, who could not afford a bicycle and whose doctor had prescribed open air, he sent his own; and when Jaeger's health began to deteriorate Elgar fixed an appointment for him with his own specialist, took him to it, and paid for it. 'As to paying, yesterday was my wish and I am grateful to you for going with me, and there's an end of that matter.'[1] There is warmth and tact in his suggestion to Alfred Littleton that Jaeger, exiled in Switzerland, should analyse some of Elgar's early works so that he 'might feel he was not quite out of things.' Mackenzie, in his last illness, received every few weeks a boxful of flowers and vegetables from Elgar's garden. Then there is the story of Elgar's attending a local sale and finding he had outbid the wife of a great friend for a garden bench; that evening the bench was delivered to the lady. His first thought on buying a car was to lend it to the Colvins, who would otherwise have been confined to their house. His niece remembers him as a

> very charming personality, always full of sympathy and help where possible, to give pleasure and bring unexpected excitements where cheer was often needed in everyday life. A bottle of wine left on the doorstep when an old man was ill; a couple of pounds of salmon, when first in season, for a family who would probably never buy it; a lovely little puppy, bought when a favourite dog died, which happened as a surprise for my mother: these are the kindnesses I connect with Uncle E.

Any event of deep emotional significance brought out the best in him. Letters to his friends in their anxiety as well as their joy show a delicate, sensitive touch and occasionally a real feeling for words far removed from the bouncy jocularity which was partly affected, partly

[1] 22nd May 1901.

83

Elgar's Character and Career

the symptom of an inferiority complex. His own early struggles, though they left in him a bitterness, made him alive to the problems of others. After he and Walford Davies had recommended in 1921 that Percy Hull should be given an honorary degree, Elgar wrote to Hull:

You will forgive the following, I hope. Of course there are heavy expenses attaching to the degree: I feel sure however that these will not be allowed to fall on you in the end. If you should want any ready money (forgive the brutality of the phrase) let me advance anything you may want for the moment—these things sometimes occur at inappropriate times and this may be one. That's all. Don't be angry at my suggestion.[1]

He was generous in his support of his fellow composers. At the start of his career he gave practical help as amanuensis to the blind composer William Wolstenholme. His offer to Brewer to score his *Emmaus* for him (it had been delayed) saved Brewer's withdrawing it from a festival programme. 'I felt so much for Brewer's worries and thought if a week's work of mine could give him and his wife rest— I do know what it is to want it myself—I wd gladly give the week and more!'[2] We read of Elgar's encouraging the Three Choirs Festival committee to include the music of Coleridge-Taylor, Bliss, and Goossens in their programmes. It was he who recommended Holst's *Hymn of Jesus* to Percy Hull, with the result that its second performance was at Hereford in 1921. He was responsible for Bax's first Promenade Concert appearance. His frequent protests in later years that his works were too often performed at the Three Choirs Festivals ring true. For instance, he wrote to Hull in 1930: 'As to the concert, I think the people will have quite enough of me without the Vars and they might think the old work dragged in. . . . You may dislocate some person who shd have more consideration than me.' Letters to fellow artists, one at the end, the other at the beginning of his career, bear witness to his humility: 'I feel a very small person,' he wrote to Richter in 1910, 'when I am in your company, you who are so great, and have been intimate with the greatest'; and to Menuhin's father, near the end of his own life: 'I must be quite candid and ask you to consider if it will not be a risk for Yehudi's immense fame and position to be associated with me.'

[1] 26th October 1921.   [2] Letter to Jaeger, 4th July 1901.

Friendships and Enthusiasms

His most striking characteristic was exuberance. It bubbles out of his letters, jumps out of every page of reminiscence, and infects all the anecdotes about him. Whether it was music or cycling, Shakespeare or pond life, each subject claimed his complete absorption. Kite-flying at 'Forli' (for a time he had the Meteorological Office forecasts sent to him every day), chemistry at 'Plas Gwyn' (where he patented the Elgar Sulphuretted Hydrogen Apparatus), and billiards at Severn House, which he played, according to Reed, to rules of his own—to each he abandoned himself in turn. His delight in his own music was intense. 'Gosh! man, I've got a tune in my head,' he would write, or 'I shall be *thrilled* by *King Olaf* after thirty-six years. It *does* sound well.' Though by no means a first-class conductor, he could by his enthusiasm spur an orchestra to superb performances. This same enthusiasm could persuade his Three Choirs Festival house party to summon their morning tea with toyshop instruments in the absence of bells. He had an appetite for information on every subject and a memory for detail that impressed his friends: so much so that Colvin could in all seriousness write to ask him whether a condor had ever been kept in captivity.

He loved all the good things of life. In a speech at the Malvern Drama Festival he claimed to have been to twenty-nine theatres in one month, and one Courtneidge-Hulbert revue he saw twelve times. When Jack Hulbert asked him why he liked such light musical entertainment, Elgar replied: 'I like the little tinkling tunes.' He enjoyed the company of theatrical people, and numbered several actors, including Gerald Lawrence, Norman Forbes, and Allan Aynesworth, among his friends. He followed racing—had he not learnt the good points of a horse from the thoroughbred his father rode?—and enjoyed nothing more than to back his fancy on the Worcester racecourse. It was Dan Godfrey who led him astray.[1] He kept a separate banking account for his racing bets, and reckoned that he usually evened out by the end of a season, although 'Peterborough' of the *Daily Telegraph* wrote: 'When Sir Edward Elgar was alive it was said to be advisable to find out which horse he was

---

[1] Eric Coates, *Suite in Four Movements* (Heinemann).

Elgar's Character and Career

backing in any race and then back something else, for bookmakers, who were awestruck by Sir Edward's infallible skill in picking losers, could only attribute it to some mysterious power; hence the *Enigma* Variations.' He loved the sea. 'I wish I could share a good rough sea with you—this I love. My own great-uncle was one of that superhuman breed—a Dover pilot—and I have the sea very much in my veins,' he wrote to Menuhin, and he enjoyed his Mediterranean cruise, his trip up the Amazon, and his passages to America and Italy. When he was seventy-six he made his first flight and enjoyed it so much that he enthusiastically recommended flying to Delius. He became increasingly fond of his clubs and of the civilized pleasures they afforded him. One could say of him, in Johnson's phrase, that he was 'a very clubbable man.' He appreciated food, wine, and pretty dresses, and his manner had a touch of gallantry in it. In later life he became something of a dandy and insisted on a newly cleaned suit for every public appearance. He was proud of his military appearance and liked nothing more than to be mistaken for a major-general. In fact, he frequently protested ignorance of, and lack of interest in, music, and as he grew older adopted the rather tiresome pose that his hobbies were of greater importance.

Hobbies came and went, but his love of literature remained with him all his life. Implanted by his mother, who knew her English and Greek authors—'You know I was brought up on the old translations of the classics'—fostered by the haphazard collection of books dumped above his father's stable (he remembered particularly Baker's *Chronicles*, Drayton's *Poly-Olbion*, and Sidney's *Arcadia*), this love made him an avid and adventurous reader. He had a special admiration for R. L. Stevenson: 'The man is so healthily good to one's soul and body,' he wrote, and even on his journey back to London at the outbreak of the First World War he visited Edinburgh. 'There I *would* stay for a day or two to steep myself in R.L.S. I had been longing to do so for years.' His taste ranged from Aristophanes and Voltaire—'I cannot do without their works'—to O. Henry—'I am astounded and delighted by the collected things.' He was something of an authority on eighteenth-century prose and politics, and *The Times Literary Supplement* published on 4th September 1919

Taste in Literature

a column-and-a-half-long letter from him on 'Gray, Walpole, West, and Ashton—the Quadruple Alliance.' When he was in Rome in 1908 he wrote to Walford Davies: 'I could not reconstruct the ancient period or the Renaissance: I could only efface the present by peopling the place with folk living from 1650–1800, Evelyn, Horace Walpole, etc., etc. I felt a classic failure but learned much and want to learn more.' His lifelong reading of Shakespeare resulted in *Falstaff*, a character he knew well enough in 1898 to quote in a letter. His acquaintance with Shakespeare was not limited to the printed page: 'In G. Barber's production of *Winter's Tale* he made Autolycus hide his face when he mentioned he went about with troll-my-dames, suggesting that he was thinking of improper women —it means a sort of gambling bagatelle board.' His criticism is at times swiftly responsive. 'I have been reading Quiller-Couch's *Studies in Literature*—and am amused and sometimes annoyed: he mostly quotes the right things and "engaged" me by his "Donne": surely no other two lines in any language are so *packed* and concise as "Love, any devil else but you, Would for a given soul, give *something* too." This is wonderful.' It is extraordinary, in a man so widely read and so devoted to literature, that his own style should sometimes be so cumbersome and his choice of texts so undiscriminating.

His interest in books extended to their making as well as their contents. His advice to Colvin was thoroughly practical. '*Do* have a *good* INDEX . . . *Farrer and Liddon* have marvellously minute indexes and get quoted out of all relation to their worth in consequence.' He had a knowledge of printing. 'I am always interested in these sort of books, as Baskerville, who was a Worcester man, altho' he worked in Birmingham, sold his types to Paris and from them the first collected edn of Voltaire was printed.' He took meticulous care over the setting out of his own music—'I have to be careful of my ninepenny slurs' he once said—and wrote an introduction to a treatise on music notation by Elliot Button, published by Novellos. 'Printing, and all that belongs to it,' he said, 'has had a fascination for me since I was first permitted to pull a lever in Leicester's office in Worcester fifty years ago.' He once went through with his niece a programme of a Three Choirs Festival, corrected in red ink

Elgar's Character and Career

sixty-four printer's errors, and drew up his bill thus: 'At the agreed rate of $\frac{1}{2}d$. per dozen errors the old-established firm of Grafton & Elgar (Errata Hunters) claim the net sum of $2\frac{1}{2}d$. for sixty errors; the balance of four errors is presented to the Widows and Orphans Fund.' Though his letters—like most people's written in haste—were frequently careless, he would have made an excellent proof-reader.

He had a tremendous capacity for laughter. When he was in the mood his boisterous high spirits overrode all other considerations. Though he was facetious rather than witty he was an amusing *raconteur* and quick in repartee. He delighted in puns, anagrams, and spoonerisms. His daughter's name, Carice, he compounded from his wife's, Caroline Alice. The name of their second home, 'Craeg Lea,' was an anagram of the name of the family who lived there: E., A., and C. Elgar. He liked crosswords, cryptograms, enigmas. Words fascinated him (though more for the sheer sound of them than for their subtler shades of meaning), and he collected swear-words as a boy might collect stamps. Some of his teasing, ragging letters, full of misspellings and play on words, are extraordinarily schoolboyish and heavy-handed, even in a period when such things were popular. He must have been aware, even if only subconsciously, of the streak of crudity in his nature, for Jaeger's criticism of some passage as 'crude' rankled for an unexpected length of time, and Elgar, with a typical exhibition of that crudity, spelt the word 'crooood.'

Temperamentally he was highly strung; this showed physically in the quick, jerky movements of his hands and in a little mannerism he had of blinking rapidly. Like many highly strung people he tended to exaggerate and was subject to swiftly changing moods of dejection and effervescence. His response to life was always emotional, not intellectual. He was quick-witted rather than intelligent, and though his interests were wide his opinions were not always without bigotry. The self-education which his aspiring character had acquired gave him an alert, keen mind, not blunted—but on the other hand not broadened—by the academic training which never came his way. His musical achievement is perhaps all the greater for this.

Though in private he could poke fun at pomp and circumstance,

Facsimile of a page from a letter by Elgar, with his caricature
of himself in court dress

Elgar's Character and Career

he could in his public life provoke charges of pomposity. People could laugh gently at his royal progress about the Three Choirs towns and nickname him 'the pouter pigeon,' about his London telegraphic address, 'Siromoris,' a palindrome made up from two of his honours, and about the obvious pride with which he wore his decorations. Yet he had reached a notable position and he filled it with distinction. He delighted in every honour done to him, not only gloating like a schoolboy over his drawerful of medals and ribbons, but proud for his colleagues that their calling should be recognized. When Jaeger teased him about getting 'spoilt,' Elgar explained: 'I haven't any [conceit] except that I always resent familiarity from outsiders and I *do* stand up for the *dignity* of our art, not profession.'

His life had become far removed from theirs, but to his Worcester family and friends he remained always Ted Elgar. On all his visits to Worcester he called on his relations, and when he retired he had many of them to stay with him and helped them in what ways he could; they in return gave him the companionship he craved for. For Worcester, though he spent none of his creative life there, he cherished an almost passionate love. He delighted in examining old prints of the city, chatting about his childhood and wandering round his old haunts, when he would talk 'rapidly, eagerly, but in a curiously low voice as if to himself' of people and things gone by. He was a countryman at heart (his speech never quite lost its soft Worcestershire burr), and it was a wrench for him to leave his three rivers, Wye, Severn, and Teme, when it became necessary to live in London. 'Most of my "sketches," that is to say the original thoughts reduced to writing, have been made in the open air. I fished the Wye round about Mordiford and completed many pencil memoranda of compositions on the old bridge.' In his Malvern and Hereford days he was a keen walker and cyclist, and at 'Brinkwells' he took up wood-cutting and trout fishing. He came to love Sussex almost as much as Worcestershire. 'I have never seen anything so wonderful as the sun climbing over our view in golden mist. I see now where Turner found such sights as Norham Castle.' It is significant that those who remember his happiness, his affection, his gaiety, knew him as a

The Countryman and the Professional Musician

countryman: those who found him moody, crusty, discontented, knew him as a Londoner.

For despite his kind-heartedness and eagerness to be liked, his yeoman stock sometimes betrayed itself by a lack of social small change. He could be tactless. He could be rude. His sensitive, shy nature hid itself behind a gruff, abrupt façade, and if he were caught off his guard by an unexpected meeting or an unwanted introduction his manner could be downright unkind. But many of these casual meetings were made immediately after a performance of his own music, which possibly he himself had conducted, when his nerves were jangling. Often he could be persuaded to apologize, which he would do so charmingly that his rudeness would be forgiven. What Elgar wrote of Frank Schuster might very well have been said of himself: 'Only his most intimate friends could realize how easily that sensitive soul was lacerated.' It was his misfortune that he would take personally many a remark or incident that was not so meant. Some of his acquaintances suffered a rebuff followed by years of silence for a reason beyond their control. Such set-backs as he had in his career he never allowed his triumphs and honours completely to obliterate. He was suspicious of patronage and condescension. He lacked the easy arrogance of breeding that can dismiss small criticisms as of no account, and was pricked into a petty retort or bruised into taciturn silence. A true countryman, he disdained diplomacy, but was too sensitive an artist not to demand it from others.

When he felt, often without just cause, that his music was slighted, he was quick to take offence and slow to forgive. This may have been due in part to natural temperament. In part it may have been an occupational disease: in Wales we have a phrase, 'cythraul y canu' (literally 'the fiend of singing'), for jealousy among musicians—who would not be musicians if they were not highly strung. In part it may have been due to the self-consciousness of a man who, having climbed (not without the aid of a guide) from obscurity to fame, was expected to acquire a new code of social conventions. Whatever the reasons, there is no doubt that for years on end he was not on speaking terms with one or another of his fellow musicians.

Elgar's Character and Career

Of these estrangements the most widely known and the most regrettable was with Stanford. It lasted on and off for twenty-seven years, and English musicians felt distress at that dissension between two of their leaders. Neither of them had the most placid of tempers, and probably no one except themselves knew the full truth of the matter. The trouble started in 1897 when Elgar lent Stanford a score of *The Banner of St George* and asked for his opinion. 'It's all very well having fine raiment; but there must be a fine body to put it on,' was Stanford's reply, which was fair comment, but an ill-considered remark to make personally to a touchy friend. By 1900 the quarrel had been patched up, for Jaeger wrote to Elgar: 'The result of your Stanford *entente cordiale* is that he is going to do your Variations at the College. They have bought score and parts already.'[1] Stanford *did* perform the Variations and *Sea Pictures* at the R.C.M.,[2] and in 1901 Parry wrote to Elgar asking him to judge the annual composition examination in company with Stanford: 'I should like you to come and so would Stanford.'

According to Colles and Plunket Greene (who quotes a supporting letter from Herbert Thompson), it was on Stanford's recommendation that Elgar was given his Cambridge degree. And that this was more than the necessary formal consent by the Professor of Music is indicated in Thompson's letter by the words: 'C. V. S. is pressing us to give him a degree.' The fact that Stanford was not present at the ceremony has been taken as a deliberate slight to Elgar. This may have been Stanford's intention. But the degree was not given at the big June congregation but in November, when Stanford (who was a professor at the R.C.M. as well as at Cambridge) may have had professional commitments elsewhere. The fact that he sent a telegram regretting his absence (which was a necessary polite formality) shows that he was not at Cambridge that day.

One thing is certain. Stanford recognized the quality of the younger man's music. Though his pupils were accustomed to Stanford's snorting 'Stinks of incense!' about *Gerontius*, Vaughan Williams recalls how he and Lady Stanford walked out together

[1] 4th February 1900.

[2] *Sea Pictures* on 15th March 1900, *Enigma* on 13th December 1901.

Elgar and Stanford—The Estrangement

after its first performance and she said to him: 'Is not that a fine work!' The words were hers, but the opinion was palpably her husband's. Herbert Howells once played through the first part of *Gerontius* to Stanford, who at the end said with great emotion: 'I would have given my head to have written Part I of *Gerontius*.' So to read that Stanford championed Elgar's music at Leeds (when he was conductor of that festival) does not come as a surprise. Plunket Greene quotes a letter of 1902 in which Stanford regrets 'the apparently curt dismissal of Elgar's *Dream of Gerontius*,' and four letters of Stanford's urging that Leeds should not in resentment cut out of their 1904 programmes all Elgar's music because he had not produced for them his promised symphony.[1]

In 1903 Elgar was elected to the Athenaeum Club. Parry and Stanford were his sponsors. Parry wrote to Elgar: 'It was kind of you too to allow me to be one of your godfathers for the A. club. I didn't write to you about it because Stanford wanted me to enter your name as soon as possible and said it was unnecessary to write to you about it.'[2]

In June 1903 *Gerontius* was performed for the first time in London. On 20th April Elgar had written to Littleton:

Stanford has been here and *deeply* commiserates with me on the cathedral performance: thinks it is a *great pity* for *my* sake, etc., etc. all on account of the deadly bad acoustics of the building, etc., etc. *Is* there anything in all this? . . . I quite appreciate Stanford's kindness in pointing out that the performance *must* be disastrous—they say that about anything I do or compose. . . . The fact is if anything can be *said* not done to throw cold water on the thing it will be done.

This letter was written from 'Plas Gwyn': had Stanford journeyed to Hereford to see Elgar? Stanford's warning was shrewd: the acoustics did spoil the performance.[3] Elgar's reaction to sound advice, given well beforehand, was one of sardonic suspicion.

In 1905 in his inaugural lecture at Birmingham Elgar discussed, in disparaging terms, English music since 1880. He recalled at one point Strauss's remark that 'some Englishmen of later days are not

---

[1] *Charles Villiers Stanford* (Arnold).   [2] 2nd June 1903.
[3] See page 38.

Elgar's Character and Career

quite so great as Brahms,' and at another he said: 'Twenty, twenty-five years ago some of the rhapsodies of Liszt became very popular. I think every Englishman since has called some work a rhapsody. Could anything be more conceivably inept! To rhapsodize is one thing Englishmen cannot do.' Is it unreasonable that Stanford, many of whose works were produced between 1880 and 1905, who had studied in Germany and never quite, in his large-scale works at any rate, escaped Teutonic influence, and who had in the last few years written two rhapsodies—is it unreasonable that he saw in these remarks deliberate jibes at himself? According to Plunket Greene 'the real estrangement of Stanford dated from that time.'

In 1920 Elgar wrote a letter to *Music & Letters* commenting on Shaw's article on himself in the previous issue. In this letter he makes it quite clear (as their correspondence confirms) that between himself and Parry relations had always been cordial. 'All I am concerned with is the mention of Sir Hubert Parry's name with the implication that he in some way slighted me. This is quite a mistake.' Parry maintained strict neutrality between Elgar and Stanford, though it is said that, even though he never showed it, he never quite forgave Elgar for his attack on English music.

In 1920 Stanford attended Lady Elgar's funeral at Little Malvern. He was uninvited and unexpected. At the end of the service Reed found Stanford at his elbow saying: 'Tell Elgar I *had* to come. I daren't go to the graveside as the doctor has absolutely forbidden me to stand in the open air without a hat, but tell him how sorry I am that I just felt I *must* come.'[1] Elgar's reaction is revealed in his letter to Schuster of 18th April:

Of Stanford's presence at the funeral I was unaware until after the ceremony. I only regard it as a cruel piece of impertinence. For years (? 16) he has not spoken to me and has never let me know why, although we have several friends in common.

His presence last Saturday was a very clever 'trick' to make it appear that after all, he is really a decent fellow, etc., and that *I* am the culprit—that the fault (if any) of our difference (which only exists by his manufacture) is

---

[1] Plunket Greene, *Charles Villiers Stanford* (Arnold). W. H. Reed, *Elgar as I knew him* (Gollancz).

Elgar and Stanford—The Reconciliation

wholly *mine* and not his. As to his wanting to show respect and the like, I do not believe a word of it and never shall do: it was a mere political trick. . . . For the good things he has done in the past I still hold respect.

Two years before Stanford's death the two men were brought together and shook hands. The occasion was the unveiling of the Parry memorial at the Gloucester Festival of 1922, the place was Brewer's lawn, and the intermediary was Brewer himself. 'In a burst of generosity Stanford exclaimed: "Let's forget all about it." Elgar, still at a loss to know what exactly they were required to forget, consented.'[1]

The truth is, the incident or incidents that caused their quarrel were negligible beside the fact that the two men were temperamentally incompatible. They would not have got on had they been cooks instead of composers. Stanford, with his Irish blood, was always spoiling for a fight. Elgar, whose guard was never as good as he would have wished, was too easily pinked. And when he was, his wounds always took a long time to heal. In his sulks, his exaggerations, his enthusiasms, his moodiness, and his craving for praise he was often like a child.

I am still at heart the dreamy child who used to be found in the reeds by Severn side with a sheet of paper trying to fix the sounds and longing for something very great—source, texture and all else unknown. I am still looking for this—in strange company sometimes—but as a child and as a young man no single person was ever kind to me.[2]

And like a child he was often most lovable when his foibles were most apparent.

To his wife Elgar was husband, child, and protégé. Her belief in his genius was unshakable. She saw greatness in him before he had written one great work. She married him against the advice of her family, for she married, as these things were then reckoned, beneath her. She encouraged him to give up teaching and helped to support them both with her private income. She taught him much, for though he had instinctive good manners—his mother was a woman

[1] Plunket Greene, *Charles Villiers Stanford* (Arnold).
[2] Letter to Colvin, 13th December 1921.

Elgar's Character and Career

of great natural dignity, and had not his father been chosen to serve a queen?—when first they met he was still, though nearly thirty, gauche and shy. She had always his career at heart and it was she who persuaded him to leave Worcester for Malvern, Malvern for Hereford, and Hereford for London. She picked him as an outsider, put her money on him, groomed her shaggy country colt, used spur and curb to train him, and brought him to the show-ring of London.

In her certainty that the man of her choice was the greatest English composer she condemned without trial anyone who could criticize adversely one bar of his music, one action of his behaviour. There was room in her life for no one but him, and to serve him she devoted herself with fanatical zeal. She made herself his nurse, his watch-dog, his governess. She ministered to his every ailment and cared for him so thoroughly that Jaeger was once provoked into writing to 'Dora-bella': 'Can't you get Alice to reduce the size of her medicine chest?' In trying to shield him from irritations, worries, and distractions she undoubtedly kept away many people who would have wasted his time, but in so doing she must also have kept away people who could have cultivated his talents. Her sense of social obligation occasionally overrode his artistic judgment. When he was too poor to employ a librettist, well-meaning friends would send their offerings. If Elgar should storm that such stuff was impossible to set, it was Mrs Elgar who persuaded him that feelings must not be hurt. She was an efficient Martha: though not herself domesticated—she had always been accustomed to servants—she saw that Elgar's home was comfortable and well run. Frank Schuster called her 'an indefatigable hostess and *marvellous* manager.' Alice appeared a gentle, womanly creature. But she was deceptive. It was she who saw that works were finished, proofs corrected, letters answered. It was she who nightly ruled the music paper that was to be his stint next day. She might sound persuasive, humble, entreating: she was inexorable.

Though she was no musician she shared her husband's aspirations and ideals. The furthest her criticism or help would go was a gentle hint that one passage seemed to her less perfect than another. Her own creative gifts she turned to his account. She had, before her marriage, written two novels—one, in two volumes, *Marchcroft Manor*,

Alice Elgar—Religion

and one in blank verse, *Isabel Trevithoe*—and some poems, several of which her husband set to music. After her marriage she would never speak of her own work, only of his. His happiness was her only wish. She laughed at his outrageous jokes and teasing remarks even when she could not match them (she was more fastidious—and less sensitive —than he), and apologized for him to their guests when she considered him too exuberant. Her life was not always easy, and if sometimes she was too tired and care-worn to amuse him herself, she sent him out to play with those who could.

Her death, when he was sixty-three, ended Elgar's life as a creative musician. His musical development had been slow. By 1889 he had written nothing of any account whatsoever. His marriage had affected not only his life as a man but also his career as a musician, for his wife provided him with both the encouragement and the opportunity for composition. Immediately after their wedding he began the long string of works which showed his talent, but she had to wait ten years before her claim of genius in him was vindicated. Jaeger's praise in 1905 was well deserved: 'The triumph is *yours* no less than his.' Elgar's own tribute to her he wrote a little over a year after her death: 'There is no work left for me to do: my active creative period began under the most tender care and it ended with that care. All my friends, dear though they may be, seem rough, violent, and in most cases *coarse* in comparison—no more.' [1]

She had given him what he needed most—devotion and faith, unquestioning and absolute.

Elgar and his wife were Catholics. She was converted four years after her marriage. He was not born into a Catholic family, for his father, though organist of a Catholic church, was an Anglican until shortly before his death, and his mother was converted to Catholicism only after her marriage. In Elgar's home, as in that of his parents, the practices of his religion were not always observed. It is certain that he was neglectful in attending the services of the Catholic Church, and it is probable that there were times when he questioned its doctrines. But throughout his life he supported and remained a

[1] Letter to Colvin, 9th August 1921.

Elgar's Character and Career

member of the Roman Catholic Church; in his last illness he affirmed his allegiance to it; and on his deathbed he received extreme unction.

Paderewski was once asked at a party: 'Who is Elgar and where did he study? Was he at any conservatorium?' 'No,' said Paddy. 'But who was his teacher?' 'Le Bon Dieu,' answered our friend.[1]

Elgar was self-taught. The education, musical and general, of the future Master of the King's Musick cost £56 10s. The account is drawn up in Elgar's handwriting on the Lord Chamberlain's office note-paper as follows:

		£	s.	d.
Expenses, in full, for general and musical education.				
1866 School 4 years				
—7 Miss Walsh,		16	0	0
—8 11 Britannia Square,				
—9 at £1 per qr.				
1870 3 years.				
—1 Mr Reeve,		18	0	0
—2 Littleton House, Lower Wick,				
£1 10s. per qr.				
Books and music				
Grammar, geography, etc.		2	15	0
Pianoforte instruction bk, etc.				
Pianoforte lessons,				
2 qrs		1	0	0
Before 9 yrs old				
Violin lessons, Mr Spray, Worcester,		3	0	0
2 qrs 1874				
Violin lessons, Mr Pollitzer, 1877–8		15	15	0
		56	10	0

Musically the fact that he was self-taught was no tragedy. No one can accuse Elgar of lack of technical facility, and the personality of his

[1] Letter from Schuster to Elgar, 26th November 1902.

EDWARD ELGAR M.R.

Attitude to Press, Public, and Publishers

music is the stronger for his having come under no one influence during his adolescence. But it had a far-reaching effect on his life. He had behind him the backing of no institution, and every mark of recognition had to be fought for by himself alone. Not unnaturally he was prone to suspect deliberate hindrances. The fact is that his music gained the recognition it deserved. Once his *Enigma* was composed it was immediately performed and immediately acclaimed. Before that his work had been received, as press notices quoted in this book show, with fair comment, encouragement, and the repeated hope that his best was still to come. Elgar's lifelong grumble that he had received neither the fame nor the payment that he deserved may fairly be balanced by a tribute to his own tenacity, his wife's encouragement, the system of the English provincial festival, and the perception of the English audiences and critics, all of which had a share in turning a Worcester music teacher into a man who was not only recognized by his countrymen as interpreting their own way of life, but who forced other countries to realize that England had once more produced a composer. Yet the twist in his character gave him a perverse pleasure in refusing to admit the admiration of critics, colleagues, and public for his music, and the universal respect and affection for himself as a man. Though he claimed indifference to all opinions except his own, he became increasingly convinced that his music was neglected and unappreciated. In his later years he grumbled at the fickleness of the British public, and was fond of hinting that works lay completed in his desk drawer that he would not publish because nobody wanted them. As early as 1915 this attitude had drawn a sharp rebuke from such an admirer as Sidney Colvin. 'I think you take far too censorious and jaundiced a view of your countrymen. . . . You cannot in your heart fail to believe that there is a big minority passionately sensitive to it [art], to whom your work makes all the difference in their lives. . . . It is mere self-deception to blind yourself to the existence of this minority.'[1]

Still, there was some justification for his attitude. His career, his

[1] 13th April 1915.

99

Elgar's Character and Career

music's popularity, his financial position, all went through vicissitudes during his life.

Elgar was the victim of his own temperament and circumstances. English composers of his period were either the sons of gentlemen, from whom they had inherited a private income, or they held professional posts. Elgar was the son of a tradesman. Temperamentally he was unsuited to academic work: his brief professorship at Birmingham showed this. His tours in America were undertaken mainly for financial reasons. Although no other English composer has had such honour done to him, none of these honours carried remunerative award, and this caused Bernard Shaw to write to him in 1928: 'Why don't they make us duty-free instead of giving us O.M.s and the like long after we have conferred them on ourselves?' It was a bitter quirk of fate that Elgar's most poorly paid compositions became the most popular. *Salut d'amour*, the copyright of which he sold for two guineas (a sum not unreasonable in those days for a *salon* piece by an unknown composer), must have brought its publishers thousands. He exaggerated only enough to make a good story when he gave half a crown to a street violinist playing *Salut d'amour* with the remark: 'It's more than Elgar ever made out of it!' Novellos, who had published Parry, Stanford, and Mackenzie to their credit but not their gain, were not enthusiastic when yet another festival cantata composer appeared; between 1895 and 1897 Elgar's expenses were greater than his receipts. And when that composer brought to them an orchestral work (with the scores of Parry's and Stanford's symphonies getting dusty on their shelves) they were positively discouraging. *Enigma* brought Elgar little money.[1] He received a nominal fee for the score, and royalties only on arrangements other than orchestral. Though this meant more in those days, when music-lovers bought piano arrangements where they would now buy gramophone records, it did mean that orchestral performances of Elgar's most popular orchestral work brought the composer no benefit. His long fight for performing rights was the result of this personal experience. *Gerontius* was published by Novellos only after much

[1] 'The Variations have brought me in about eight pounds (!).' Letter to Jaeger, 10th August 1904.

Royalties and Rewards

persuasion by Johnstone of the Birmingham Festival committee, and it was not until its resounding success in Germany that Novellos felt safe in offering Elgar an exceptionally high percentage royalty for his next oratorio. But *The Apostles* is a difficult work demanding large and experienced forces, and the nature of the music is not as appealing as that of *Gerontius*. As the royalties on his works went up, perform-ances of them went down. That the financial disappointment weighed heavily on him is proved by his letter to Littleton in 1907, quoted on page 47. Had Novellos been more far-seeing the third oratorio might now have existed, and Elgar might not have replied to Harold Brooke's query about it, on an evening stroll at a Three Choirs Festival: 'The public doesn't want it, it won't pay Novellos, and it won't pay me.' The First Symphony would undoubtedly have been produced earlier (though whether that would have been an artistic gain is a moot point) had there been enough money in it to make the amount of work worth while. The idea was in his mind as early as 1897. Jaeger wished he were wealthy enough to commission it, and in 1900 Rodewald wrote: 'Think about my proposition regarding your symphony. Don't be proud but sensible.' But Elgar *was* proud and would not accept money from his friends, and there was in Edwardian England no way in which a composer could be given full-time employment as, say, Haydn was in eighteenth-century Austria.

The coming of the gramophone made a great difference commer-cially to Elgar. As early as 1914 gramophone and pianola royalties were substantially increasing his income, and they continued to do so until his death. But because of the war he lost heavily in foreign investments, and it was sheer bad luck that the run of the stage production of *The Fringes of the Fleet*, which was earning Elgar big money, was curtailed—though even so it was a long one—owing to Kipling's whim. Certainly Elgar had bad luck. And certainly he was not avaricious: he was concerned more for his dependants than for himself, and he was a generous man. But even so his constant references in letters and speech in his later years to his lack of money are not strictly borne out by the comfort and style in which he lived.

The rise and fall of his music's popularity were capricious. In his

Elgar's Character and Career

life of seventy-six years Elgar can only have been fully satisfied with his reception during five or six of them. His productive years of greatness were short: *Enigma* in 1899 and the Cello Concerto in 1919 mark their boundaries. Complete recognition in this country did not come until 1903, and reached its peak with the First Symphony in 1908. Between these years his popularity was immense. The reception given to the Second Symphony in 1911 was sober (though the press was full of approval) and caused Elgar to ask Reed: 'What is the matter with them, Billy? Why do they sit there like stuffed pigs?' The Violin Concerto, by its nature more attractive to the public than a symphony, and with Kreisler as the soloist, almost rivalled the First Symphony in immediate success. *Falstaff*, after a successful production at Leeds, was given its first London perform-ance to 'an array of empty benches.' At the end of the war there was little demand for Elgar's music. The audience at the Philharmonic Society's first post-war concert, at which *Falstaff* and the second *Pomp and Circumstance* march were played, was so small that the committee, despite its respect for Elgar, was forced to reduce performances of his works. The production of the Cello Concerto in 1919 did nothing to help, for Elgar's public no doubt expected a work of like propor-tions to the Violin Concerto, and this wistful quasi-chamber work made no decisive appeal.

During the twenties Elgar's music did suffer neglect. The reasons for this are diverse. He himself was in retirement and producing no new works. The post-war audiences were out of tune with King Edward's composer laureate. There was a new generation of composers who were producing their own *Enigmas*. Only in the cathedral cities of the west was Elgar's music faithfully performed year after year. The Three Choirs Festivals, where Elgar began and ended his musical life, not only remained devoted to him and cherished his traditions of performance, but relied on his works as the mainstay of their programmes. In London his orchestral music was less often heard. The *Daily Telegraph* recorded in 1926: 'So rarely has Elgar's First Symphony been performed in recent years in London that it may well come as a new experience to many of the younger folk.' In 1927 *The Times* said: 'We get so little nowadays of Sir Edward Elgar's

His Music and its Audience

music in the ordinary repertory of orchestral concerts that a programme devoted to it and conducted by himself is particularly welcome'; and of the same concert noted later in the week: 'The hall was half empty . . . and the gallery was scarcely fuller than the stalls.' During the last few years of his life Elgar's works suffered less neglect. (The word neglect is itself a relative term. Was it not simply that, after their astonishing vogue in the early years of the century, they were now taking their rightful place in the concert repertory?) 'Public interest in the Second Symphony of Sir Edward Elgar appears to be on the up grade,' wrote the *Daily Telegraph* in 1930, and the 1931 Promenade Concerts prospectus contained a greater proportion of Elgar's works than that of previous years. The three concerts arranged by the B.B.C. to honour his seventy-fifth birthday must surely have demonstrated the deep regard in which his music was held. 'How are we to convince him,' asked *The Times*, 'that we are not callous? The audience of Wednesday did its best. One can think of no living composer who is so certain as he to be listened to with rapt attention by a crowded Queen's Hall through a long evening.'

Perhaps in his heart he was convinced. He knew his own worth. Once, listening at home to a recording of his *Falstaff*, he said simply, after Shallow's orchard interlude: 'That is what I call music.' Callous he may have thought us, but he knew that his music would survive after he himself had gone. Caustic yet considerate, suspicious yet warm-hearted, reserved yet impulsive, intolerant yet sympathetic, rude yet gallant, boisterous yet sensitive: provocative though his character may be, the man is less important than his music.

Part Two: The Music

CHAPTER IX

SKETCH-BOOKS, JUVENILIA, AND TRIFLES

AMONG Elgar's earliest compositions were those written for the church choir of St George's in 1876, when he was nineteen. They are exactly the sort of thing that any English provincial organist in that year might have written, except that they are more fluent than the average untrained nineteen-year-old might be expected to produce. The part-writing is sedate, with an occasional chromatically altered note at cadences (the chromatic passage from a *Credo* of 1872–3, which Buckley quotes and Maine mentions, seems to be an exception); there are *fugato* passages, tidily worked out; there are suave solos for the sopranos, joined later by the altos a third below. They are extremely singable, and St George's must have counted itself fortunate in its organist.

There are some instrumental pieces in sketch-books dated round about 1879, when he was twenty-two, with no idea of performance (except in his own circle) or of publication. The interest of the sketch-books is mainly biographical. They show him arranging Christy minstrel songs, writing motets and hymns for his church (the hymn published as 'Hear Thy children' in *Westminster Hymnal*, No. 151, and quoted in the *Nursery Suite* was written in 1878), and training himself by exercises. Here are chords laid out in specimen arrangements for orchestra; here are the Greek modes studiously written out and labelled; here are pieces by Mozart, Beethoven, Corelli, Leybach, and Weber scored for different orchestral combinations.

A good many of the original compositions in these well-worn, brown-covered manuscript books were later published. Written here in 1879 was the *Romance* for violin and piano, Elgar's Opus 1, published in 1885. *Sérénade mauresque* was written four years before its first performance in 1883. The song 'Is she not passing fair?'— not published till 1908—was written in 1886. At least one of the

105

Sketch-books, Juvenilia, and Trifles

Vesper Voluntaries and the *Cantique* of 1913 were first played by the wind quintet. Occasionally an early idea seems subconsciously to have been used in a later work: the sequence of modulations at 'The door swung wide' in 'The Wraith of Odin' (*King Olaf*, 1896) was composed in 1879, as were the opening bars of *The Black Knight* (1893); Elgar himself, looking over the books years later, noted the fact in red ink and added: 'How strange!'

The *Wand of Youth* and *Severn* suites absorbed the best of the instrumental pieces in these sketch-books. In the *Severn Suite* for brass band, published in 1930, with selections from it later arranged by Ivor Atkins to make an organ sonata, all the music from cue nos. 50 to 52 and 54 to 57, and the tune of the Minuet, was written by 1879 for the wind quintet. Of the Overture to the second *Wand of Youth* suite, the opening up to cue no. 3 was written in February 1879 for small orchestra, with only an odd note's difference from the 1908 version. 'Moths and Butterflies' was outlined in short score, and only the passage between cue nos. 30 and 32 (and correspondingly 34 and 36) underwent substitution in the later version. 'The Wild Bears,' all except cue nos. 55 and 57 (and correspondingly 61 and 63)—in the sketch-book other material exists here—began life in 1879 as a quadrille for the patients of Powick asylum to dance to. The waltz tune which swings through the 'Sun Dance,' as characteristically Elgarian as one could want, was written in 1879. More than this of the *Wand of Youth* suites may have been written at this early date, but now cannot be traced. Elgar himself destroyed much manuscript. Also, these sketches only show the latest, not necessarily the correct date of composition, as the music was written for a play performed by the Elgar family as children, and by 1879 Edward was twenty-two. It is possible that the dates are those of copying, though the sketches have the look of originals.

It is plain that whatever was worth while in these early sketches Elgar himself salvaged. Nearly always when the eye lights on a characteristic tune or twist of harmony it is only to recognize it as part of a later work: it is no use digging for lost masterpieces. The opening of one of the *Intermezzi*—'mine own children'—for the wind quintet shall stand representative of the unpublished Elgar:

In Manuscript and in Print

Most of his early published pieces are for violin and piano, more than likely written for himself to play at local concerts. They are melodious and pretty but quite unmemorable. The *Sérénade lyrique* of the same year as *Enigma*, the two similar *salon* orchestral pieces published in the two years following *Falstaff*, and the two published in the two years before his death are all inoffensive and mildly charming, but not stylish or witty enough to place them above dozens of such trifles by other composers, or individual enough to class with Elgar's other pieces of comparative length, such as *Dream Children*. *Mina*, his last complete work, named after his dog, is a little echo of the 'Lullaby' in *From the Bavarian Highlands*. The earliest pieces of any consequence are those of the Suite in D, Op. 10, which reveal a very minor talent but several points that were to become characteristic. The most pleasant examples of the *salon* style are *Chanson de matin* and *Chanson de nuit* (1901) for small orchestra. The rich string tune of *Chanson de nuit*, with accompaniment of divided violas and thrummed harp, is unmistakably Elgarian; even in Op. 15 he liked the harp. In the sprightly *Chanson de matin*, at letter D, is a foreshadowing of the *appassionato* phrase that forms the climax of the Cello Concerto's slow movement.

CHAPTER X

SECULAR CANTATAS

ELGAR'S first cantata is *The Black Knight* (1893). The text is Long-fellow's translation of the ballad *Der schwarze Ritter* by Uhland. It tells of a jousting competition on the Feast of Pentecost when no cavalier could outdo in valour and strength the 'monarch's stalwart son' except an unknown sable knight, who dances 'a measure weird and dark' with the king's daughter, and, at the banquet which follows, gives her and her brother a fatal drink of golden wine. The fustian libretto is typical of its time. Cowen's *The Water-Lily*, also produced that year, has the same mixture of chivalry, romantic im-probability, and sorcery, and the two composers write the same sort of music for their cavaliers, though Elgar's setting for the tournament at Hofburg is a shade brighter than Cowen's at Caerleon.

Elgar described his work as a 'symphony for chorus and orchestra' and set it in four scenes, each continuous and without easily detach-able airs. The importance of the orchestra is such that the chorus takes second place: in each scene it borrows the orchestra's tunes, and there are long stretches where it is subservient to the orchestra or doubles it, which produces odd vocal writing at times.[1] (A particu-larly horrid example comes from *The Banner of St George* where the words 'Alas! his bravest knights are slain' are set to this metre: ♩ ♪ ♩ ♩ | ♩ ♪ ♩ ♩ | ♪ ♪ ♪ ♩ | ♩ ♩. But then, the words themselves deserve little, and one can hardly blame Elgar for setting to almost a monotone 'waves a mighty shadow in.' The orchestral writing, on the other hand, is competent and occasionally characteristic.

Elgar, as was the custom in these festival cantatas, attaches particular themes to particular people and ideas—the Black Knight himself has an ominous Klingsorish arpeggio—but most of the music is descrip-tive and independent of leitmotives. The opening of the third scene is pretty and the setting of the banquet is in Elgar's grand manner.

[1] When the work was reprinted Jaeger suggested an alteration at a point where 'the singers cannot at present get the words in edgeways.' (10th December 1897.)

'The Black Knight'

He relies for dramatic power too much on harmonic sequences moving limply step by step: fear at the Black Knight's entry into the lists, mournful concern of the old king for his children, pathos at the drinking of the fateful draught—all are expressed by this method. He tries in the same way to give excitement artificially to dull music in the Gudrun, Sigrid, and Thyri scenes in *King Olaf* and in the final chorus of *The Light of Life*; and while Orbin and Eigen plead with Claudius at the end of *Caractacus* the orchestra takes a two-bar phrase sequentially step by step through six keys. Such rigidity very quickly makes a sequence stale.

The king's anguished outburst, 'Take me, too, the joyless father,' is set to a progression with melodic *appoggiaturas* of the type Elgar employs in the cantatas at emotional crises. (Ironbeard's dying song in *King Olaf* and Christ's question 'Dost thou believe on the Son of God?' in *The Light of Life* are other examples.) Almost invariably, as here, the *appoggiaturas* or struck suspensions resolve downwards, are in the melody, and are sequential; most often, as here, the interval between the dissonant note and the bass is a seventh, sometimes it is a fourth, sometimes a seventh and fourth alternately, as in the other two instances mentioned above and in example 24, page 161 from *Enigma*, which shows a more refined treatment of what is in the cantatas an immediately recognizable Elgarian idiom.

The Black Knight's dance owes what weirdness it has to the flattened supertonic in both melody and harmony resulting from the Neapolitan sixth, a chord Elgar (and his contemporaries) used extensively at this period, though nowhere more persistently than he did here; in the same work the youth 'fell from saddle-bow' to it, and in *The Light of Life* the blind man prays for light by means of it. Elgar's liking for the flattened supertonic triad prevailed into the oratorios: Magdalene's 'revelry' motive in *The Apostles* uses it.

Despite its weaknesses *The Black Knight* has genuine creative impulse behind it, a vitality and a freshness the more obvious because unhampered by self-criticism or self-consciousness. The opening scene, for all its square phrases, is gracious, the macabre touches to the knight himself are effective for their period, and the whole work is full of fingerprints as common to the mature as to the callow Elgar. It is

Secular Cantatas

a compact cantata, and the balance of the dramatic and the lyrical is just right. Its lack of distinction lies in the musical material out of which it is built.

The Banner of St George, produced in 1897 for the Diamond Jubilee, though at least partly written two years before, is a bad work. It is a short ballad in two scenes with an epilogue, and though the libretto by Shapcott Wensley offers dramatic scope, the language appeals only to the wrong emotions. A dragon threatens the town of Sylenë; the king's daughter offers herself as a sacrifice; St George appears, rescues the maiden, slays the dragon, and leads the community singing.

The best of the music is undistinguished; the worst is atrocious. The melodies are of the glib type that made Cowen's *The Rose Maiden* so popular with small choral societies. Much of the choral writing is of the worst facile part-song style. Elgar's reliance on repetition is here an undoubted weakness: in the first scene one figure in the 'hope' theme is repeated *ad nauseam*, twisting aimlessly in and out of keys. Triplets decorate the 'fair maid' and 'comely daughters' tunes; in the cantatas Elgar's ladies always lean towards compound time—compare Thyri in six-eight, Gudrun and Sigrid in nine-eight, and Eigen (as she waits for Orbin) in twelve-eight. There is some combining of themes near the end which shows Elgar's deftness: two previously heard motives are woven into the accompaniment to the broad tune of St George's chivalry. But such things cannot disguise the poverty of this music.

Elgar's most individual choral work before *Gerontius* is *King Olaf* (1896). It has the vigour and directness of *The Black Knight* with a more commanding technique and more freshly minted themes. It also has a good many of the same faults. The libretto is taken from Longfellow, padded out by H. A. Acworth. Longfellow's verses have an easy if rather mechanical rhythm, but the text is a hotch-potch of inconsistencies and irrelevancies. The legend of Olaf comes from the Norse sagas, and Elgar set it as if it were being told by a gathering of bards, whose leader introduces each episode in a recitative, and some of whom take solo parts of individual characters. The work is therefore a series of scenes.

'The Banner of St George'—'King Olaf'

The introduction has the atmosphere of 'Once upon a time,' and it is straightway evident that here is real imagination. 'The Challenge of Thor,' who defies Christianity, is well constructed, terse, with a hard strength produced in part by the *ostinato* bass and the rhythm ♩♩·· ♪♩♩♩, which, as Reginald Nettel [1] points out, Beethoven had used to symbolize the heroism of Egmont. Cowen's *The Water-Lily* again provides a parallel scene. In *Olaf* the chief bard summons Thor: 'Him who rives the heav'ns asunder'; Cowen's Merlin calls 'Spirits of the storm, awake!' Both Thor and the storm spirits sing of raising a tempest to terrify the world. Elgar's chorus is much more extended than Cowen's, but both composers use the same technical device of repeating a fragment of scale in the manner of an *ostinato*. By comparison the force of Elgar's music, for its period, is clear, particularly when Cowen's spirits hurl their bolts with a diminished seventh and Elgar's with a blunt energetic tune.

Olaf hears Thor's challenge and sails into Trondheim to accept it. Here the inconsistency appears. His motive is a double one—the conversion of heathen Norway to Christianity and the unchristian desire for vengeance for his father's death and his own banishment. 'King Olaf's Return' anticipates the writing of Gerontius's part, for it moves easily between recitative and *cantabile* and from one tempo to another; its tenor lines are suave but its feeling is intense. Olaf is met by Ironbeard and his men, worshippers of Thor, to whom he offers the peace of Christianity. Ironbeard defies Olaf. The music is urgent and swift. Olaf shatters the image of Thor, and Ironbeard is mortally wounded in the struggle. The true, tough warrior calls on Odin and, after an emotional affirmation of his faith, dies with 'axe in his hand, with sword upon thigh, and face to his slayer.' Surely such a death could only strengthen the belief of his followers? But no! In an ending to the scene, dramatically false, the men of Trondheim feel 'the power of Christ,' watch the 'golden censers' swing, and sing a 'solemn hymn.' That the music of their conversion predicts the chromaticism of the later Elgar, and that the atmosphere and lay-out for chorus and orchestra slightly foreshadows that of the priests and

[1] *Music in the Five Towns* (Oxford).

Secular Cantatas

assistants over the long pedal point in *Gerontius*, by no means mitigates its ill-timed appearance, while the sentimental hymn which follows is incongruous. Up to this point *King Olaf* has been an attractive work, with a full-blooded enjoyment of tune and rhythm that is exhilarating and in keeping with the rough vigour of the subject.

Olaf now entangles himself with three ladies in turn, and Elgar finds them as difficult to deal with as did his hero. Ironbeard's daughter, Gudrun, very properly resents being married by Olaf merely as atonement for murdering her father, and on her wedding night prepares to stab him. Olaf wakes, asks: 'What is that, what is that, that gleams so bright, so bright above thy head?' in a recitative as bald as the words, and not believing her reply that it is a bodkin for binding her hair, sends her packing. The music is unconvincing. Sigrid, 'the haughty queen of Svithiod,' who is introduced by charming dotted thirds and sixths which entirely belie her character, converses with Olaf in music whose stylized nature is absurdly at variance with the lack of diplomacy shown by both, refuses to resign her gods in exchange for Olaf's hand, and when Olaf strikes her, saying: 'Thou hast not beauty, thou hast not youth, Shall I buy thy hand at the cost of truth?' curses him in a recitative that unexpectedly grows into an outcry of genuine passionate revenge. Thyri, the third lady, sings of spring but thinks of her lost dowry which she has forfeited by fleeing from King Burislaf to Olaf, who has married her. She is not placated by Olaf's offering of angelicas, and only sings in duet with him after his promise to recover her lands. In her solo she falls into the shape of phrase that is characteristic of Elgar's lyrical passages of this period, familiar in the *Serenade*, the tenor 'spirit' aria in *The Light of Life*, Eigen's 'At eve to the greenwood' in *Caractacus*, and 'Music, sweetest child of heav'n' in the *Coronation Ode*. Though Elgar beats Cowen when it comes to evoking the spirits of the storm, his lovers are as conventional as Cowen's. Neither Olaf and his ladies nor Orbin and Eigen achieve the tenderness in Mackenzie's *The Rose of Sharon*. Both Thyri and the Beloved sing of the flowers and birds of spring, but while Mackenzie's glows with paint, Elgar's picture is like a photograph.

In between Olaf's scenes with the three women come two ballads.

'King Olaf'

'The Wraith of Odin,' in which a mysterious one-eyed stranger visits Olaf's feast, is an advance in gruesomeness from *The Black Knight*, and the chorus of gossips, who tell of Thyri's flight to Olaf's court, is a delightfully gay piece. In the last scene the defeat of Olaf by Svithiod's forces is picturesquely done, but the epilogue shows the same confusion of character as the conversion scene, and after Olaf's mother hears a prophecy that St John will continue Olaf's fight for Christ in Norway, the work ends in an atmosphere of synthetic religious emotion whose music was compounded in the same laboratory as *The Banner of St George*. Moralizing at the end of a cantata, whether relevant or not, was, of course, not peculiar to Elgar. Most composers of the period chose libretti which ended with an exhortation to praise God, Love and/or Peace, or Country. Barnett hymns 'the dear God who loveth us' and Cowen 'good St John'; Mackenzie declares 'Argo's fame will never die' or ends in praise of Scotia. Elgar had not the taste to avoid the convention in *Olaf*, *The Banner of St George*, and *Caractacus*, and on the principle of *corruptio optimi pessima* his emotional gusto turned into vulgarity what in other composers seemed like complacency.

If Elgar and his librettist could have made up their minds whether Olaf was to conduct a crusade or an act of piracy, could have dispensed with Gudrun and Thyri, and developed Sigrid, into whom, at least momentarily, the composer had insight, *King Olaf* might still deserve an occasional hearing. What is remarkable about it is that the leitmotives are more flexibly developed not only than in the previous works, but than in *Caractacus* and some even later works. For instance, the 'sailing' motive becomes, in the bass and transformed, the germ of two quite new passages. The use of leitmotive is dramatic, especially at the reminiscence of Ironbeard's dying song when his daughter stands over his murderer; when Sigrid's 'curse' motive rises out of the sea-music as Olaf drowns, followed by his motive in the minor for the first time; and in the shrewd quotation, as Olaf is pursued by Sigrid's husband, not of his 'grace and beauty' motive, but of his love-duet with Thyri.

Coming after *King Olaf*, *Caractacus* (1898) is a retrogression. It is a more complex work, but less imaginative. Elgar wrote his share of

Secular Cantatas

bad music, but not much of it was dull. A lot of this is. Particularly is the vocal writing commonplace; when independent of the orchestra it is stodgy, and the setting of the words, though less arbitrary than in *The Black Knight*, is ordinary. Elgar's verbal rhythm is much on a par with Cowen's, though what always distinguishes Elgar from Cowen is the interest of his accompaniments; Cowen far more often resorts to mere figuration. But even *King Olaf*, Elgar's best cantata from the verbal point of view, has nothing of the unobtrusive subtlety of Somervell's *The Forsaken Merman*, produced the year before.

The libretto of *Caractacus*, based on historical fact, was by H. A. Acworth and concerns a battle between the British king and the Roman forces. Caractacus is falsely encouraged—why is not made clear—by the ArchDruid to take the offensive, and Orbin, who is betrothed to Eigen, the daughter of Caractacus, is cursed and expelled by the Druids when he tries to tell the king the true meaning of the omens. The British are defeated, and Caractacus, Eigen, and Orbin go before Claudius in Rome. Their brave conduct gains his pardon, and all, in the manner of Victorian librettists—though it was Elgar's suggestion that they should 'dabble in patriotism' [1]—join in predicting the fall of the Roman Empire and the ascendancy of the British. The plot is more credible than that of *King Olaf*, but the versification is as much of a stumblingblock to honest appreciation of the music. It is arguable that the poor quality of these cantatas is more the librettist's fault than the composer's. But the composer picks his librettist, and Elgar had the whole range of English poetry, of which he was a selfprofessed student, to choose from. Parry and Stanford had shown the way. Fine libretti do not make fine cantatas—Barnett went to Coleridge and Keats, and what of his work lives now?—but it is hard to take seriously music written to the libretto diction of Elgar's early cantatas.

Elgar is most successful with the martial side of his story. The fighting themes associated with Caractacus and Orbin have a spirited swing, and the report of the battle and the sombre lament of Caractacus and his troops (one of Elgar's few excursions into an uncommon

[1] Letter to Jaeger, 21st June 1898.

'Caractacus'—The Cantatas and their Background

time-signature—that of seven-four) have, if only slightly, something of the quality of tragedy. The flimsiest part of the work is the sacred dance and the invocation by the Druids of their god, which is all pleasant enough music but has no connection with 'mystic circles,' 'brooding godheads,' or 'sacrificial knives'; the Druid maidens, like the youths and maidens in the next scene, narrowly escape a simper. In this next scene the pastoral setting is attractive, but it is dramatically weak for Orbin to recount to Eigen the reading of the omens. For Eigen's 'Thine in death, to thy latest breath' there are twining chromatic triplets with which at this period Elgar expresses sweetness and innocence; there was a hint of the manner in Olaf's and Thyri's scene ('Sweet and fair as thou'), the prelude to *The Light of Life* is full of it, and 'Only let the heart be pure' from the *Coronation Ode* is extraordinarily like this *Caractacus* passage.

Caractacus shows a more systematic use of leitmotives than previous works, dovetailed in the intricate and resourceful way that was later used in *The Apostles*. The second scene particularly, where the omens are read, is worked very largely from themes already heard. The method differs slightly from that used in *King Olaf* in that here the motives are fitted together and there they were transmuted: one model is made from meccano and the other from plasticine. In this *King Olaf* forecasts *Gerontius*, and *Caractacus* more *The Apostles*.

These four early cantatas differ only in degree, not in kind, from the sort of thing composers were turning out each year. They are written within the conventions of the low standard of musical and literary taste of the provincial England where Elgar was born and did his early work. They give no indication, however easy it is to be wise after the event, that with extraordinary suddenness he was to burst these conventions and that a *Caractacus* was to be followed by a *Gerontius*. Their position when compared with the cantatas of Parry and Stanford is piquant: none of them approaches in consistency of style, taste, and merit, say, *The Pied Piper of Hamelin* or *The Revenge*, yet Elgar's next choral work was to make all such comparisons negligible. His cantatas stand out from their background not by originality or even by promise, but by their zest, their sturdiness, and their highly mannered idiom. It is almost as easy to recognize Elgar

Secular Cantatas

in a page from them as in a page from the mature works. His personality is marked from the beginning, but then one would have had every excuse to judge it as the personality of talent, not genius: a gifted but limited personality, satisfied with near-commonplaces, and with little promise of real development.

It was 1912 before Elgar again turned to the secular cantata, and this was *The Music Makers*, for contralto, chorus, and orchestra—a pleasant work to sing but not quite so satisfying to listen to. O'Shaughnessy's ode appealed to Elgar because it matched his own creed, admitted in one of his Birmingham lectures, that by placing his lever in heaven the artist can move the world. Yet the work fails to convince. There is in it plenty of lovely music, very personal to Elgar. The prelude is almost an anthology of his characteristics, the first entry of the voices—probably the simplest bit of choral writing he ever composed—never fails to thrill, the mention of inspiration brings a passage as visionary as anything in *The Apostles*, and the climaxes sound firm and full. But for all that the work as a whole is pretentious and only in a superficial sense catches the spirit behind the poem. Each line of the poem, each new idea or mood, is aptly illustrated, but for a work on this scale that is not enough. The effect is restless, and there is not enough musical development to justify the frequent repetition of the words. There is much dull imitation between the vocal parts and an occasional falling back into the old trick of phrases repeated by sequence in step. Many of the themes are undistinguished: the orchestral tune, for instance, at the words 'Till our dream shall become their present,' which sits heavily on the second beat and heaves itself up with a triplet on the fourth, might have come from a pre-*Gerontius* cantata. The harmony is luscious and there is less counterpoint threaded through it as stiffening than in Elgar's other works of comparable length. The emotion of the whole work, though keenly felt, is trite. There is no reason why a dream should not die to a drawn-out diminished seventh, or 'Ye of the past' to a *fp* held unison, but the devices sound faded; one might have hoped for fresher invention from Elgar. He squeezes the last drop out of the contralto soloist by much *rubato*, and from the passage discarded from

'The Music Makers'

Gerontius[1] by richly dissonant suspensions, but there is just not quite enough genuine stuff in the work: it remains a good setting of the poem, not a re-creation.

Elgar uses in *The Music Makers* self-quotations from *Enigma*, *Gerontius*, *Sea Pictures*, the Violin Concerto, and both the Symphonies, as well as snatches from 'Rule, Britannia' and the 'Marseillaise,' to suggest what he called 'typical national fables' (which, however, rarely make their point in performance). The allusions of these quotations are sometimes clear to anyone who knows Elgar's works, as is the phrase from *Sea Pictures* at 'Wand'ring by lone sea-breakers,' but the listener needs biographical knowledge to understand that the 'Nimrod' variation is apt for 'But on one man's soul it [light] hath broken' because Jaeger once gave Elgar the encouragement he needed at a critical moment; and sometimes a knowledge of Elgar's own mind to realize that he quotes the *Enigma* theme in connection with desolation and the isolation of the artist because it symbolized for him his own loneliness at the time it was written.[2] There is nothing against a composer's quoting his own works—in this case the *Gerontius* reference at 'A singer who sings no more' is very affecting—but in *The Music Makers* the dozen or so quotations do nothing to integrate what is originally a not very strong design.

[1] See page 130
[2] Ernest Newman, 'The Music Makers,' *Musical Times*, September 1912. At the end of the full score of the Variations Elgar wrote: 'Bramo assai, poco spero, nulla chieggio (Tasso).'

CHAPTER XI

RELIGIOUS CHORAL WORKS

WHEN they met in 1933 Delius asked Elgar why he had wasted so much time writing long-winded oratorios. 'That is the penalty of my English environment,' was Elgar's reply.[1] Elgar was not primarily a choral composer. His first work of any size was instrumental, the first work to demonstrate without doubt his genius was instrumental, and once his position was securely established it was instrumental works he wrote by choice. But the English public at the end of the last century, faithful to their *Messiah* and *Elijah*, recognized their native composers by commissioning choral works for choral festivals. The majority of such works served their purpose and sank into oblivion, as in other countries many operas and symphonies do, and there is no evidence that the men who wrote them would have been more successful if the committees had asked them for orchestral, not choral works. So it is a paradox that *Gerontius*, the one religious choral work of unquestioned genius that chorally minded England has produced, should have been written by a man all of whose natural tendencies were towards the orchestra. Elgar's reference that he had 'hinted at other things'[2] rather than a cantata to the festival committee that commissioned *Caractacus* is significant.

The 'penalties' of his environment were four: *The Light of Life* (1896), *The Dream of Gerontius* (1900), *The Apostles* (1903), and *The Kingdom* (1906).

The Light of Life is the conventional oratorio of its period and birthplace, with a few redeeming flashes of true Elgar. The libretto is weak. It tells the story of the healing of the blind man, partly in the

[1] Eric Fenby, *Delius as I knew him* (Bell).
[2] See page 23.

'The Light of Life'

words of the Bible and partly in the words of the Rev. E. Capel-Cure, who arranged it.

> All joy is dead,
> All gladness fled,
> And life has missed its mark

is perhaps the worst example of bathos.

The work, which is short, is written in set numbers of recitative, aria, duet, and chorus. In two of them a soloist alternates with the chorus. The first, 'Seek Him that maketh the seven stars,' fore-shadows *The Apostles*, though here the blind man, outside the temple, sings of his distress in juxtaposition with the chorus of praise inside the temple; Judas's song is superimposed on the psalm, so making a keener contrast. Leitmotives characterize persons and ideas and are set out in the orchestral prelude, *Meditation*, which is sometimes played as a concert piece. The recitatives are stilted, much of the harmony is flaccid, and 'Doubt not thy Father's care' and 'Thou only hast the words of life' are the worst type of sentimental female song. Christ's final words, 'Father, I will that they be with Me,' are set to music of a banality all the more shocking because of the strange beauty of the passage immediately before.

For strange and prophetic beauty there is in the work. The passage in thirds for sopranos on page 27,[1] 'Thou hast borne the sinner's sentence,' has affinity of atmosphere with moments in the later oratorios and also with the passage between cue nos. 3 and 6 in *To Women* from *The Spirit of England*, where the thought in the words, of wounds, is the same. The accompaniment to the Lord's words to Moses (page 52) has a ghostly likeness to the accompaniment at one point of 'Dead rides Sir Morten of Fogelsang' in that little master-piece of eerie effect, 'The Wraith of Odin' in *King Olaf*. The orchestral interlude on page 74 is harmonically the rich, mellow, chromatic Elgar of the Cello Concerto.[2]

Elgar is recorded as having said in badinage of the fugue that 'I thought a fugue would be expected of me. The British public

---

[1] Vocal score published by Novellos.
[2] See pages 209–10.

Religious Choral Works

would hardly tolerate oratorio without fugue.'[1]   In fact this fugue, 'The wisdom of their wise men,' and its succeeding numbers are the best section of the work.   The taut counterpoint, the contrast of the following eight-part harmonies unfolding in contrary motion, unaccompanied, from G major to E major to express 'And the eyes of the blind shall see,' and then the floating, spiritual tenor solo and the vigorous chorus of Pharisees give the work a solid core.

The Apostles, produced three years after Gerontius, is the first of a group of three oratorios on the subject of the founding of the Christian Church.   The plan of these oratorios was several times altered and the third was never finished.   The Apostles and The Kingdom are related both textually and musically, and must be considered as a sequence as well as separately.   It was Elgar's wish that they should be performed on consecutive days.   The trilogy is admirable in its intent and impressive in its scope.   The music throughout has a high seriousness and gives evidence of the reverence and thoughtfulness with which the composer approached his self-appointed task.

The libretti were compiled by the composer himself from the words of the Bible.[2]   In this way he ensured dignity of language and safe-guarded himself from the doggerel of some of his earlier works.   His scissors-and-paste method of telling a New Testament story by taking sentences out of their context from the Old and New Testaments and the Apocrypha enabled him to expand the passages of reflection in the narrative, but the imagery he thus obtained occasionally perplexes more than it illumines.   Obscurities of detail in a libretto are of little account if the force of the music is strong; the more serious criticism here is one of structure.   Elgar took upon himself a double responsi-bility, for when librettist and composer are one, virtues and weaknesses alike are magnified.

The Apostles is divided into two parts, with choral prologue.   The first part begins with Christ's prayer in the mountain at night, the morning psalm, the break of dawn, and the choosing of the Apostles.

[1] R. J. Buckley, Sir Edward Elgar (Bodley Head).

[2] The Musical Times, July 1948, has an article by 'Dorabella' on the sources of the libretti.

Libretti of the Trilogy—Characterization of Judas

There follows a setting of the beatitudes, 'By the Wayside,' and an Act 'By the Sea of Galilee,' which shows the remorse and conversion of Mary Magdalene and the miracle of Christ's walking on the waters. Part II opens with an orchestral introduction and depicts Christ's betrayal by Judas, his arrest, the mourners at Golgotha, the scene at the sepulchre, and the Ascension. A large orchestra, chorus, and six soloists are employed. Though the work comprises choruses, recitatives, and solos, the divisions are less sharp than in *The Light of Life*. The episodes flow into each other without break except between the Acts, and the forces are often combined in *ensembles*.

The work is cast in a grand mould, and for such scenes as the splendid, blazing dawn, the storm on the lake, and the Ascension Elgar used a vivid orchestral palette. Vocally the *ensembles* are finer than the solos. The interplay of the many voices in their various rhythms at the end of the first Act produces a wonderful web of sound, complicated yet light-textured. The great 'Proclaim unto them' (cue no. 116) and 'Give us one heart' (cue nos. 229–31) roll like thunder. Particularly moving are the passages for women's chorus: the affecting part-writing of 'And the Lord turned' (cue nos. 164–6) and the ethereal chording of 'What are those wounds in Thy hands?' (cue no. 225).

Elgar understood Judas to be not a betrayer but a man whose zeal overreached itself, who wanted to force Christ's hand by placing Him in a position from which there was no escape except by the assertion of his earthly as well as his spiritual dominion. For this view—'I have taken the ancient view of Judas's character' [1]—Elgar gave as his authorities Theophylact, referred to in Whitby's *Commentary*, and Whateley's *The Characters of Our Lord's Apostles*. Authorities matter less than that this interpretation was musically the right one for Elgar, who had (in Magdalene, the demons, and Falstaff) less insight into wickedness than into virtue. By regarding Judas as mistaken rather than as a wilful wrongdoer Elgar commands sympathy for him without distaste. Judas is from the outset differentiated from the other

---

[1] B.M. Add. MSS. 47904–5. With the sketches are commentaries by Elgar presumably at one time planned for publication.

Religious Choral Works

Apostles by a more impetuous and decisive vocal line when ambition grips him, and the tension of the work mounts steadily to his great tragic monologue in Part II.   To set this monologue against a background of a psalm within the temple was sheer genius: the inexorable rhythm and the grave harmonies of the chant intensify enormously the stark despair of Judas.   And here Elgar's rhapsodical quasi-recitative melodic style suits perfectly Judas's desperate quick-changing moods. His restraint in avoiding the crucifixion scene itself, so that the shout of 'Crucify Him!' is heard through the ears of Judas and the cry of Christ on the cross through the orchestra, the bitterness of grief at Golgotha is felt through the hearts of Mary and John and the mocking and the wounding seen in retrospect through the eyes of the mystic chorus—all this yields the greatest music in the work.   The Golgotha scene, so short, so quiet, is marvellous in the awestruck intensity of its opening and in the exquisite tenderness of Mary and John.   The angelic chorus in 'At the Sepulchre' sings a strain of touching simplicity, with none of the banality that sometimes taints Elgar's simple tunes.

'By the Sea of Galilee' is dramatically and musically the least satisfactory of the Acts.   The conception of showing Mary Magdalene's past life in a dreamlike fantasy was bold, but the music falls short of the idea.   It is hard in music to differentiate between the real and the simulated, and in trying to present Magdalene's wickedness in her memory only Elgar has diluted it too much—it is, in any case, difficult to be depraved in six-eight time.   Mary Magdalene proves herself a tiresome creature, more especially as she appears twice.   The weakness of construction of this Act is the interpolation of Peter's episode in Caesarea Philippi between Magdalene's conversion and her forgiveness.   Peter's affirmation of Christ as 'the Son of the Living God' (cue no. 113) might either have been cut altogether or transferred to the opening of Part II, where its propinquity to Peter's subsequent denial of Christ would underline the irony. Canon Gorton [1] points out that it is only after Peter's confession that the Church is given the power of forgiving sins, which is immediately

---

[1] C. V. Gorton, *The Apostles: an Interpretation* (Novello).

Conflict between Theology and Drama—Leitmotives

exemplified in Magdalene's absolution. Theological and dramatic demands thus tug in opposite directions. In its present place Peter's declaration interrupts Magdalene, who, in the white heat of her conversion, should make her offering and be absolved. Here she needs some sustained song of fervent joy to counterbalance her necessarily hesitant music of desolation. Her resolve, 'Thy face, Lord, will I seek' (cue no. 109), at the end of 'In the Tower of Magdala' is only long enough to raise expectations that are not fulfilled. The Act culminates in a pedestrian *ensemble* for chorus and soloists, 'Turn you to the stronghold.'

So it is that Part II of this oratorio is finer than Part I. The scenes in and outside the temple, Golgotha, and the sepulchre are charged with imagination, dignity, and sheer musical beauty.

The Apostles is built from leitmotives: nearly one hundred fragments occur often enough to merit names in Jaeger's detailed analysis.[1] Often their use is imaginative and informative. The wailing chromatic version of the 'earthly kingdom' motive at Judas's end (cue no. 189); the way in which Magdalene's salvation is shown orchestrally by the 'sin' motive making an inner part to the 'ardent longing' and 'Mary's consolation' themes (cue nos. 125–6); the sudden foreboding struck by the 'passion' motive in 'And the Lord turned and looked upon Peter' (cue no. 164) and in 'But Peter follow'd Him afar off to see the end' (cue no. 159): these are examples of leitmotives used for their true dramatic purpose of bringing to mind the past or illuminating the future. But too often the motives are strung together, undeveloped, simply ticketing each word, whether or no the music gains by it. Indeed, the slavish use of leitmotive sometimes upsets the form of a section. Towards the end of the angel's cool, ethereal solo in the mountain appropriately comes the 'comfort' theme; but because the angel has the words 'For the Lord hath comforted His people' (cue no. 18) some twenty-five bars before, two bars of this theme are dragged in, anticipating and so spoiling its main appearance. The sketches[2] show how much surer was Elgar's

---

[1] *The Apostles*: analytical notes by A. J. Jaeger (Novello).
[2] B.M. Add. MSS. 47904–5.

Religious Choral Works

instinct than his judgment. In the Golgotha scene Mary sings three times a poignant phrase which ends:

After the first and third times the orchestra echoes her last bar; the second time, because the words are 'And of Thy people there was none with Thee,' the orchestra plays the 'loneliness' motive (bar before 196). Now in the sketch this bar is the same as the corresponding bar in the other two phrases, but Elgar ringed it round and wrote above it 'alone.' His original, purely musical, instinct was right. It is an intrusion to drag in this motive to point the moral, when it disrupts the musical flow that in itself expresses almost unbearably the loneliness of Golgotha. Elgar could make brilliant and imaginative use of leitmotives; there were times when he did not have the taste or the courage to omit them.

Elgar took great trouble with his libretto. Many versions exist. Originally he intended a solo for Christ at prayer on the mountain, and an episode to show His healing powers; both these were cut. Of the sequence of ideas presented in the work he wrote:

Mary Magdalene is the sinner who truly repents, not in old age, but in the flower of life. A manifestation of Christ's supernatural power was necessary to my plan: I chose the miracle of the walking on the waters in preference to the transfiguration because all the Apostles were present at the former. Judas, the type of sinner who despairs, is given prominence not from any melodramatic reason but because the lesson to be learnt from him is needed more at the present day than at any other time.

From the sketches of the music it would seem that Elgar seldom discarded, seldom altered his first idea. He expanded his original ideas by letting in new music at the seams. One exception to this is the chorus, 'Turn you to the stronghold.' This was apparently an

The Evidence of the Sketches—'The Kingdom'

afterthought, added when the bulk of the work was in proof; [1] and there are some passages published which differ from the sketches.

The Apostles was in Elgar's mind at least as early as November 1896, the year of *King Olaf* and *The Light of Life*. There is a sketch bearing this date of the opening of Magdalene's fantasy, marked *Apostles*, and enclosed within it, as if of the same date, are some bars from the Lord's Prayer in *The Kingdom*, the dawn music (cue nos. 35–6), Peter's motive, and a good deal of 'By the Wayside,' including the four chords (isolated, out of their context) of 'How much less man.'

The Kingdom, the second oratorio in the trilogy, deals with the Church in Jerusalem and the descent of the Holy Spirit. In the first Act the disciples and the holy women remember in fellowship the teachings of Christ, and Matthias is chosen to replace Judas. In 'At the Beautiful Gate' the two Marys sing of the pity of Jesus for the infirm before going into the temple. The third Act is divided between 'The Upper Room' and 'Solomon's Porch': the Holy Spirit comes to the disciples, their speech amazes the Jews, and Peter exhorts the Jews to be baptized. In 'The Sign of Healing' Peter heals the man that was lame and the disciples are arrested for their teachings; Mary sings her evening song. In the final Act the disciples and the holy women are reunited in the upper room and make their communion. The work ends with the Lord's Prayer.

There is a longish prelude that makes much use of themes from *The Apostles* and states several important new ones. The opening *ensemble* is one of Elgar's most satisfying, even if not most original, peaceful and unpretentious, and ending with a very lovely 'Amen.' The short second Act and the opening of the fourth, both 'At the Beautiful Gate,' have that combination of pathos and intimate sweetness that some find attractive and others repellent. Some of the most

---

[1] 27th May 1903. Jaeger, who was seeing the work through the press, refers to 'plans upset so dreadfully' by 'new chorus (17 pp.)'—the exact length of 'Turn you to the Stronghold.'

28th May 1903. Elgar writes: 'Part I ends with the new chorus.'

Religious Choral Works

original and sheerly beautiful pages in all Elgar's choral writing are at the beginning of the third Act, at the awaiting of the Holy Spirit. There is rare tonal poetry in the women's semichorus breaking a *ppp* accompaniment to the swaying orchestral theme, which by a slowly and scarcely moving bass under twisting enharmonic chords creates an atmosphere stilled yet expectant, in the middle of which the un-accompanied mystic chorus, 'I will pour forth of my Spirit,' is blinding in its brightness. The rest of the Act falls below this high level, even to prosiness in the squat treatment of 'He, who walketh upon the wings,' and an occasional blatancy of manner. The duet of John and Peter (cue no. 137) is curiously out of keeping with the rest of the work. It is in the melodious but undistinguished style of *The Light of Life* and may date from that period, though for this con-jecture there is none but internal evidence. The gem of the work is the Virgin's soliloquy, 'The sun goeth down,' which, being reflective, gains rather than suffers from the thematic quotations. But here again must be called in question the judgment of the librettist. The arrest of the Apostles by the Sadducees is announced in the con-tralto recitative, referred to in Mary's soliloquy, and described in the last Act by Peter, each time with attendant discordant motives. The repetition in narrative weakens the end of the work. Could not Mary's reference have been omitted, so allowing no roughness to dis-turb the tranquillity and radiant conviction of her song?

It is in Elgar's treatment of Peter that the basic weakness of *The Kingdom* lies. Grown enormously in stability since his failure in *The Apostles*, and in power since the descent of the Holy Spirit, Peter is the central figure and has several weighty solos; but musically he never assumes the stature that the text gives him. This is because nearly all his words are set to leitmotives already familiar from *The Apostles* or the prelude and early part of this oratorio, merely restated and not developed as Peter himself has been. New strength cannot be given to a character by a patchwork of second-hand material, and Peter succeeds only in bringing to mind assorted images which do not cohere to give him the authority and force which are his due. At one point only, where he calls for repentance and baptism, does he become a commanding figure. Here, in the new phrase 'In the

Comparison of 'The Apostles' and 'The Kingdom'

Name of Jesus Christ,' the words and music fit hand in glove with
that naturalness that characterizes so much of *Gerontius*:

Ex. 4

In the name of   Je-sus Christ

Later in the work (cue no. 131) Peter sings this same phrase, but
with the additional words 'of Nazareth' set to a couple of notes
clumsily tagged on—which illustrates the occasional infelicity of the
vocal writing.   Though the scoring throughout is of great beauty,
the orchestral *sforzandi* which mark important words in the narrative
are liable to smother them altogether.   The sketches[1] make clear to the
eye what the ear suspects, that the orchestra flourishes at the expense
of the voice.   Frequently the orchestral part is written in ink, the
vocal in pencil—for example, in Magdalene's fantasy; and in the first
sentence of *The Apostles* the vocal parts 'Because he hath' and 'To
preach the Gospel to the poor' are in pencil, the accompanying leitmotives in ink.   The sketch of Mary's soliloquy has the word
'patience' (cue no. 162) both times an octave lower; Elgar was more
occupied with the orchestra's 'loneliness' motive, and that soar of a
seventh in the voice was an afterthought.[2]

The Apostles is a grander work than *The Kingdom*.   Nothing
blazes out of this score as fiercely as the dawn, the morning psalm, the
rich *ensemble* at the end of 'The Ascension.'   There is nothing of
dramatic value comparable to Judas's betrayal.   But *The Kingdom*,
except for Peter's music, has greater continuity as a whole.   The
quality of the music is more on a level, even if the peaks may be a little
lower than those of *The Apostles*.   The serious defect in both works
lies in their structure.   At times Elgar handles his leitmotives artistic-
ally, but at other times he sacrifices musical flow for literary aptness,
thematic development for textual elucidation. Distinguished members
of Elgar's Church have praised the insight into her doctrines exemplified by this method, but oratorios are works of art, not sermons, and

[1] B.M. Add. MS. 47906.
[2] Jaeger's postcard dated 29th July 1906 indicates that it might well have
been his suggestion.

* E   127

Religious Choral Works

must be judged by artistic, not theological, criteria. That Elgar's religious sincerity occasionally betrayed him into an aesthetic fallacy is seen by his remark [1] (oddly enough about *Gerontius*, to which it does not apply): 'If the words are sufficiently interesting, the music will do.' There is much in these works that sounds manufactured, but there is much too of unrepeatable originality. Their peculiar quality is their power to concentrate into highly emotional music the mystery and beauty of Elgar's religion. The mixture of the ethereal with the sensuous and the spiritual with the grandiloquent may by its emotionalism pall, and may even sicken those who are not in accord with its sentiments, but it evokes an atmosphere overpowering in intensity. In none of Elgar's other works do the best and the worst in him jostle each other so closely, which may be why those who are temperamentally in tune with the oratorios tend to rate them too high and those who are not too low. Perhaps an awareness of things spiritual is most strongly felt at moments of stillness, such as the night scenes in both works, where the soprano voice hangs poised in a kind of ecstasy, the orchestral opening of *The Apostles* which wafts up in aspiration, and the gentle, drooping chords of acceptance which end *The Kingdom*.

Of the third, unfinished, oratorio in this trilogy a good deal can be deduced. It was to begin with the strife—Elgar used the word antichrist—and end with the judgment and the Heavenly Kingdom. Elgar's friends heard many titles for it: the one written on the file of sketches [2] is *The Last Judgment*. There is a memorandum that the last trumpet was to be the shofar and to herald eternal dawn. A good deal of the libretto was compiled. The prologue was to be from Daniel vii. Scene ii deals with Cornelius the centurion from Acts x. Revelation was to be drawn upon. Jotted down with question-marks are the words 'Cornelius,' 'blind man,' 'Peter imprisoned,' 'Antioch.' The libretto for the episode of Simon Magus is written. Of the music little exists (despite the fact that in

[1] Letter to Jaeger, 7th May 1900.
[2] B.M. Add. MS. 47905.

THE COMPLETION OF 'GERONTIUS'

A friend arrived at Birchwood to find Elgar putting the last notes to a score. Saying that the moment was historic, he took this snapshot. The work was *Gerontius*

The Unfinished Oratorio—'Gerontius'

1906 he told Jaeger: 'It's partly written!'), though probably much was in Elgar's head. One scrap, which later he intended to use in the Third Symphony, and which obviously had some special significance for him,[1] has in one sketch the heading 'Intro' and, in another 'The Judgment.'

Ex. 5

The Dream of Gerontius is Elgar's greatest work. Enigma is more fanciful, the Violin Concerto more sumptuous, Falstaff more logical, but Gerontius is the greatest. Though The Apostles and The Kingdom were written after it, they are not in the nature of a revelation as is Gerontius. The magnitude of its subject is matched by the beauty and perception of its music. It has the hall-mark of a great work of art—inevitability. One may wish that certain things in the symphonies and The Apostles were not as they are; Gerontius stands almost untouchable. Even those whose temperament is alien to the thought and mood of the work cannot fail to admit its greatness. Whatever his creed, for the duration of a performance the listener becomes, in imagination, one with Gerontius. Its style is most individual, most personal to Elgar, and yet it has a degree of universality that is instantly recognizable. It is the one work that contains all his greatest characteristics and none of his weakest, and is consistently inspired throughout. A performance of Gerontius is a profound and moving experience. Even though when it was written The Apostles, the symphonies, the concertos, and Falstaff were yet to come, the words Elgar wrote at the end of the manuscript need no revision: 'This is the best of me. For the rest, I ate, I drank, I slept, I loved, I hated as another. My life was as a vapour, and is not.

[1] See page 81.

Religious Choral Works

But this is what I saw, and know. This, if anything of mine, is worth your memory.' [1]

The poem of the text is by Cardinal Newman. It tells of the death of Gerontius (the name is derived from the Greek γέρων, an old man) and the experience of his soul as it approaches his God. Around the deathbed the priest and his assistants offer the prayers of the Catholic Church. After his death an angel escorts the soul of Gerontius to the veiled presence and he hears on the way the singing of demons and angelicals. Before the judgment the angel of the agony intercedes for him. After his judgment he joins the souls in purgatory who, with the angel and the choir of angelicals, sing as he is delivered to his night of trial. Elgar showed considerable insight in selecting parts of the poem, which was too long as it stood. A few other verses were actually set to music and then discarded. Even so, Elgar wrote to Jaeger that he was afraid the 'conversations between the angel and the soul are wearisome.' What is skilful is the way in which the music-ally intractable material of the second to fifth verses of 'Praise to the Holiest' (as printed in the vocal score) is speedily and lightly disposed of by some of the angelicals under a continuous chant of praise by the others: this would, had he given the words equal weight, have been unduly protracted.

From the composer's own words we know that *Gerontius* had simmered in his mind for eleven years before its production. Cer-tainly some of the themes existed before the writing of the actual work began: the 'prayer' theme was written in Sinclair's visitors' book in April 1898 to illustrate one of the moods of the bulldog, Dan. The middle section of 'Praise to the Holiest' underwent some revision: the melody later used in *The Music Makers* for 'To the old of the new world's worth' was discarded from 'And that a higher gift than grace.' The chief theme of the angel of the agony had as early as 1899 been associated with Judas—another indication that *The Apostles* was already in his mind at that time. Jaeger wrote: 'Nobody could dream that it was not originally inspired by these very words of New-man's.' [2] The sketches [3] for *Gerontius* show a curious method which

[1] Ruskin, *Sesame and Lilies*.   [2] 22nd May 1900.
[3] B.M. Add. MS. 47902.

Text, Sketches, and Alterations of 'Gerontius'

Elgar sometimes used, that of writing a kind of précis (in notation and words) showing the disposition of material and keys of an extended movement. The whole of 'Proficiscere' from cue no. 68 to the end of Part I was summarized in this way. Similar plans were made for the Prelude to *The Kingdom* and the slow movement of the First Symphony. Jaeger, as usual, made comments on the new work. Elgar refused to give the soul a 'dramatic' song to replace what Jaeger called 'the whine' at 'Take me away,' though he must have made some alteration, for Jaeger wrote: 'You have improved the whine somewhat'; and he did adopt Jaeger's idea for 'a *few* gloriously great and effulgent orchestral chords' to suggest 'the *momentary vision* of the Almighty.' Jaeger had charged him with 'shirking' the 'supremest moment.' This had touched Elgar on the raw, particularly when Jaeger had gone on to say 'it wanted a Wagner or a R. Strauss' to 'dare attempt it.' Elgar added the bars which now stand between cue nos. 118 and 120—'I'm glad I did it after all. I had in my original sketch marked it out so.' He also wrote: 'The *souls* chorus will *follow* the "Take me away."' As far as can be deduced, originally cue nos. 125–6 came at cue no. 118, followed by cue nos. 120–5, which went straight into cue no. 126.[1]

Gerontius himself is Elgar's most completely realized character. In a letter to Jaeger, which Basil Maine quotes, he explained his ideas.

Look here: I imagined Gerontius to be a man like us, not a priest or a saint, but a *sinner*, a repentant one of course but still no end of *a worldly man* in his life, and now brought to book. Therefore I've not filled *his* part with church tunes and rubbish but a good, healthy, full-blooded romantic, remembered worldliness, so to speak.

The part of Gerontius is finely written, with a greater appreciation of the sensuous beauty of the solo voice than Elgar sometimes showed, particularly in the sweeping, burning fervour of 'Sanctus, fortis.' This song of faith shows one of those tiny but significant details by which Elgar makes graphic the character of Gerontius. The first eight bars of 'Sanctus, fortis':

---

[1] The references are in the letters between 20th June and 12th July 1900.

Religious Choral Works

are repeated at its end; but then the first beats of the second and seventh bars are silent. Two crotchet rests reveal in a flash the physical effort that reciting his Creed has been, and those two gasps for breath make one feel in one's own body the exhaustion of the dying man. There is, for Elgar, unusual sensitivity to verbal rhythm throughout the work. For the angel's farewell, as in so many earlier works, words are fitted to an instrumental tune, but there are musical phrases which, to quote Byrd, are 'framed to the life of the words.' This, for example, has a sublime naturalness that makes it impossible, once heard, to dissociate words from music:

and so has this:

where the basses doubling at the great gap of three octaves the angel's voice lift it off this earth. Such things haunt one.

The choruses of the assistants, particularly the remote beauty of the Kyrie eleison as it steals into Gerontius's fevered cries, are of a simplicity more chaste than is to be found in *The Apostles* or *The Kingdom*. Though never archaic, the atmosphere of Part I is steeped in the timeless, changeless ritual of the Catholic Church, which Part II dispels by the more natural beauty of its Elysian Fields, so that the

Vocal and Orchestral Writing

distant voices on earth before the soul's judgment plunge one back into the cloistered world. Jaeger and Ernest Newman pointed out how this echo from earth apprehends eternity: Gerontius's soul has undergone great new experiences, yet his friends are still at his death-bed. A small chorus of picked women's voices is a favourite medium of Elgar's and is always beautifully handled. *The Apostles* and *The Kingdom* have their angels and mystic chorus, high up in the clouds like Raphael cherubs, and here in *Gerontius* the angelicals lightly sing the 'Praise to the Holiest' before the full chorus closes in on them, to split again into two choirs which overlap wave upon wave, tossing the melody from one to another as if from *decani* to *cantoris*. Antiphony or complex interweaving is most often Elgar's choral texture; but as the priest and the assistants speed the soul of Gerontius (cue no. 75) the chorus, in twelve parts, and the orchestra are fused together to diffuse the sound equally over the whole *ensemble*, so that the swaying crotchet movement was likened by Jaeger to the swinging of golden censers.

Although the vocal parts have unwonted beauty, it is the orchestral accompaniment which puts *Gerontius* head and shoulders above all previous English oratorios. The orchestra truly tells 'every marvellous shade of compassion for the human lot, every tinge of the tenderness and wistful longing which the transitoriness of life transmuted into music in his sensitive mind.'[1] The orchestra continually illumines the words with points of colour. The devitalized atmosphere of 'strange innermost abandonment' is horrifying in strings dissolved into fifteen parts and one pulsating harp note. But most astonishing, and most revealing of Elgar's intimacy with orchestral colour, is the way he makes one flute—the 'tender, soothing flute'—by a sudden crescendo in its low register at the words 'deep hideous purring' suggest the coarse depravity of the demons.

Gerontius is extremely chromatic (though the choruses are less so than the solo parts), but it is of a strength to withstand period changes. The power of the angel of the agony's solo remains undiminished by more recent harmonic developments. Elgar's characteristic of

---

[1] Walford Davies, quoted by Dunhill in *Sir Edward Elgar* (Blackie).

Religious Choral Works

slipping one simple chord into an ornate chromatic progression is nowhere more effective than in the 'death' motive:

Ex.9 The thought of death and judg - - ment was to me most ter - ri - ble

where the chord that strikes cold at the word 'terrible' is an innocent major triad in its first inversion. Some of the part-writing is wonderfully touching. The drooping fourths in this passage are exquisitely managed:

Ex. 10

Should teach His breth-ren and in-spire

The 'Amen' at the end of *The Kingdom*'s first chorus has the same fall, and so has the final chorus of Purcell's *Dido and Aeneas*, which shares with the last choruses of Bach's St Matthew Passion and *Gerontius* the same quality of culmination and emotional fulfilment. All the march tunes Elgar wrote, some bad, some good, all broad and flowing, are sublimated into the great processional theme, 'Go forth in the name,' swinging majestically over its steady bass. The vision which burns so brightly through the work flickers a little at the demons' chorus, which has nothing of the veracity of the angelicals'. Newman's words at this point do not bear much repetition, the choral devices have worn less well than elsewhere in the work, and the only moment which compels is the orchestra's theme at cue no. 43. One could wish that Elgar had given the demons an orchestral interlude. The words and voices hamper. The middle section of the Second Symphony's rondo is more eloquent than this of 'horror and dismay.'

Structurally *Gerontius* is firmer than *The Apostles* and *The Kingdom*. The plan of solos and choruses is built round the great climax of

Harmony and Leitmotives

'Praise to the Holiest.' The priest's 'Proficiscere' is balanced by the angel of the agony's intercession; the contrapuntal writing for the assistants by that of the souls in purgatory; 'Sanctus, fortis' by 'Take me away.' And the continuity of the work is immensely increased by the use of leitmotives.

These motives have greater intrinsic value than those in *The Apostles*. Their significance is less in the weight of their associations than in their qualities of evocation. It is possible, when listening to *The Apostles* (however well one knows it), to forget what some of the motives represent. There are a bewildering number, and some are fragmentary in length and have only an arbitrary relationship to the idea. But in *Gerontius* the motives evoke atmosphere, so that one feels an emotional response before bothering to think what Jaeger called them. Take, for example, the angel's words at cue no. 56 in Part II: 'Yes, for one moment thou shalt see thy Lord.' At that great thought the accompaniment burgeons into flowing harmonies which have already been used for 'A presage falls upon thee' at cue no. 26 in Part II and which therefore carry added meaning. But even if they had not they would still express perfectly this particular moment. Elgar's method in *Gerontius* is more one of subconscious self-quotation than deliberate use of leitmotive and the fabric of the music is never torn apart for the sake of it. It is significant that in Jaeger's analyses far more themes in *The Apostles* have specific names than in *Gerontius*, which is a much less didactic work. Elgar's letters to Jaeger confirm that what was part and parcel of the inspiration in *Gerontius* needed conscious thought in *The Apostles*.

My wife fears you may be inclined to lay too much stress on the leit-motive plan because I really do it without thought—intuitively, I mean. For instance, I did not perceive till long after it was in print that (p. 34) 'In Thine *own Agony*' and the appalling chords introducing and dismissing the *Angel of the Agony* were akin, but they are, aren't they? [1]

But about *The Apostles*:

You are a brick not to grumble at my correction: it's very important because I'd clean left out the 'earthly kingdom' motive at the important temptation point—copied from an early sketch instead of the complete one.[2]

---

[1] Basil Maine, *Elgar* (Bell).   [2] 5th August 1903.

Religious Choral Works

The Apostles and *The Kingdom* contain much fine music, but as complete wholes they do not approach *Gerontius*. In the last resort the explanation is simply that Elgar's genius burned more fiercely in *Gerontius*. But analysis sometimes helps to show how this reveals itself. The poem, *Gerontius*, is one of continuous thought, and as such is admirably suited by continuous musical fabric. The libretti of *The Apostles* and *The Kingdom* describe certain events, a series of separate pictures in the manner of a triptych, whose subjects are related but not sequentially developed. *The Apostles* and *The Kingdom* are episodic: that is not in itself a stricture; but to apply continuous musical treatment to an episodic libretto is a misjudgment. They are formally weak because Elgar tried to bind together things that would not cohere: by over-reliance on leitmotive he not only weakened the structure of independent sections but produced monotony instead of unity.

Elgar said that Mendelssohn's music, not Wagner's, suggested to him the use of leitmotives.[1] Certainly *Gerontius* was not the first English choral work to which Wagnerian principles were applied. Parry had done so in his *Prometheus Unbound* and *Job* (in which Elgar played as a violinist in 1893). But it *was* the first English work to make these principles viable. To Herbert Thompson, when he praised *Gerontius*, Elgar said simply: 'Well, it's my religion.'[2] The sincerity and conviction behind the work are unmistakable. Far more important is the fact that Elgar's imagination was fired by an intensely human and dramatic story at just the time when his technical skill had reached maturity. The result is imperishable music.

---

[1] Article by Jaeger in the *Musical Times*, October 1900.
[2] *Yorkshire Post*, 2nd March 1934.

CHAPTER XII

SONGS AND CHURCH MUSIC

ELGAR wrote no excellent and not a few bad solo songs. The dead weight of his period nowhere hangs more heavily round his neck. His choice of texts was lamentable, and as he was insensitive to word values and his accompaniments add nothing, the songs for the most part have neither fastidious detail nor convincing atmosphere. The Victorian drawing-room ballad plainly left its mark upon such songs as 'Like to the damask rose,' 'The Poet's Life,' 'In the dawn,' 'Come, gentle night,' and 'Pleading,' and there are echoes of Tosti in these and other songs at cadences, in phrase constructions, in the accompaniments (particularly in the doubling of the vocal line in the piano part with the barest of harmonies), and in the predictable modulations. 'The chariots of the Lord,' published as late as 1914, is a nasty piece of pretentiousness. It is not that they are technically bad as songs, for most of them are extremely singable, but that musically they are barren. Elgar was no instinctive song writer like Warlock or Quilter, and the example of Parry's *English Lyrics* was lost on him.[1] His place is certainly no higher than, for instance, Cowen's or Maud Valérie White's. It is, after all, only reasonable, for England in the first decade of this century could produce a handful of exquisite song writers, but only one *Enigma*. 'Rondel' and 'The Shepherd's Song' have an innocent sprightliness, and 'Queen Mary's Lute Song' and 'Speak, music!' are prettily fashioned, but the archness of 'The

---

[1] In fact, he wrote to Jaeger, 26th April 1908: 'One word as to my treatment of the words, not only in this op. but always. I hold that *short* syllables may be sustained occasionally for the sake of effect just as an actor does. There is one dear good man against whom I wd not *think anything* but the greatest admiration and that is Parry. But he almost if not quite annoys me in the way he sets the words which swarm in our language—two syllables, both short, the first accented, e.g. petal. Set in an ordinary way a poem sounds like reading a newspaper paragraph.'

Songs and Church Music

Pipes of Pan' is hard to stomach. His unison patriotic and community songs, such as 'Follow the Colours,' 'A War Song,' and those written for *The Pageant of Empire*, come from the same stock as songs like 'The Deathless Army.' They are catchy, but simple from vacuity and not from the blunt expression of noble thought that characterizes Parry's 'England' or Holst's 'O England, my Country.' The four songs in *The Fringes of the Fleet*, Elgar's only collaboration with Kipling, have a not unpleasant raciness; while Stanford's sea songs are reminiscent of the folk ballad, these would be at home in a Forces concert.

Compared with Elgar's other songs the five for contralto and orchestra in the cycle *Sea Pictures* are strikingly successful. Occasional infelicities of phrasing and accentuation do occur, but in each of the songs the atmosphere has been so unerringly caught that it would be churlish to complain of detail. In the middle of 'Sea slumber-song,' for instance, he evokes the feline grace of a deep-sea swell by floating a monotonous vocal part over strings rocking gently in octaves, low harp chords, and bass drum and gong, hit with a sponge-headed stick, added to timpani. The second song, 'In haven,' to words of Alice Elgar's, has the transparent texture of some of the *Enigma* variations; particularly subtle is the way in which Elgar strengthens and colours the vocal line by doubling a note here and there in the wood-wind. 'Sabbath morning at sea' is longer and more ambitious, and reaches a fervent climax at which a phrase from the first song recurs. The chords over the tonic pedal which open it are identical, except for the pedal note, with the chords that end the polka *Helcia* written for the asylum in 1883—an example of how a passage may be salvaged out of a composer's memory. 'Where corals lie,' the best-known song of the set, derives a piquancy from the ambiguity of key: the opening figure might be D major or B minor; the verse makes it apparent that it was B minor; but the song ends in D major, only doubling back to B minor in the orchestra's final bar. This ambiguity, the tonic pedal point, the small compass of most of the soothing vocal part, the simple rhythm of the accompaniment and its enchanting sound of harp and divided strings, give the song an enticing dreaminess to 'Lure me on to go And see the land where

Songs with Orchestra—Church Music

corals lie.   The last song, 'The Swimmer,' which incorporates part of the first, is the weakest of the set.   The opening recitative is not more than melodramatic, and the verve of the big tune when it comes is wrecked by its four-squareness.

The six choral songs with orchestra, *From the Bavarian Highlands*, are companionable, fresh, lively, tuneful, well made—and almost devoid of Elgar's personality.   Even the *allegro piacevole*, 'On the alm,' and 'Aspiration,' two moods which usually touch off a personal response, are blank in character, and 'The Marksman' might have been written by any of a dozen composers.   Of the six the 'Lullaby' is the most endearing.

The *Te Deum* and *Benedictus*, for festival, not ordinary, occasions, opens splendidly but lapses into commonplaces whenever praise is exchanged for prayer.   The 29th Psalm is straightforwardly set, with points in common with *The Spirit of England*, and the harvest anthem, 'Fear not, O land,' is pleasantly joyous; but the 48th Psalm has some poor moments.   There are a couple of good hymn-tunes, one for the 1902 coronation, the other published in 1909 as a carol, though it had graced the Elgars' 1897 Christmas cards to words in praise of Malvern.

The part-songs fall into several groups, each seemingly written with different performers in mind.   In the first are pastoral serenades for women's voices, two violins, and piano, of a lilting melodiousness, and of much the same weight as similar songs by Bishop or German. 'Fly, singing bird,' 'The Snow,' and 'Stars of the summer night' are from the early Malvern days, written most likely for one of the ladies' choirs with which the Elgars were associated.   'A Christmas greeting,' though later in date and quoting *Messiah*, has the same sort of cheerful and effective slightness.   In the second group there are the test pieces for male-voice competitions, such as 'Zut! Zut!' and 'The Reveille,' demanding technique and little else.   Then there is the group of unaccompanied part-songs, harmonically clean and in the main homophonic, in the English tradition of Henry Smart, many of whose songs the young Elgar must have known through the Worcester Glee Club.   'O happy eyes' and 'Love,' the one with words by Alice Elgar, the other dedicated to her, and the carol 'Good-morrow' are attractive examples of this style.   The best songs in this

Songs and Church Music

group are the five for men's voices with words from the Greek Anthology. These excellent songs combine the sturdy qualities of the plain part-song with gently humorous grace in 'It's oh! to be a wild wind' and 'Whether I find thee,' with scene-painting in 'After many a dusty mile,' with a broader choral style in 'Feasting I watch,' and with fire but terseness in 'Yea, cast me from the heights of the mountains,' one of the most striking of Elgar's short compositions.

The last and longest group is for mixed voices and gives the impression of having been written, not for Mrs Elgar's choral societies, not for competition festivals (though at these they are often sung), not for glee clubs, but out of the need to say something which could be said in no other way. All these songs have this in common: the finest words (and in most of the part-songs the choice and under-standing of the words are commendable) evoke the finest music, which pierces to the emotional heart of each poem. There could hardly be four songs of a more different atmosphere than the settings of Shelley's 'O Wild West Wind,' Tennyson's 'There is sweet music,' Byron's 'Deep in my soul,' and Rossetti's translation of Cavalcanti's 'Go, song of mine,' yet all these could have been written by no one but Elgar, for in them his personality is as strong as in the major works. True, there is no great depth in the words or music of the ingenuous little 'Angelus,' the placid 'How calmly the evening,' or the romantic 'Evening scene' and 'Weary wind of the west,' but in all of them the mood has been dissolved in the music and they are written with a loving care which makes them grateful to sing. In the biggest part-songs the union between words and music, so lacking in the solo songs, is stronger still. Here the impulse of the poem shapes the music, so that in 'Love's tempest' a change from the impersonal to the personal brings a new harmonic slant on to an otherwise strophic song, and 'O Wild West Wind' is a vigorous modern application of madrigal technique, where each new thought has a new musical idea, with just enough repetition to bind the whole together.

Elgar feared that he sometimes scattered over vocal parts directions more fitted to the orchestra, but his close attention to detail often lightens or points a phrase—the three *staccato* quavers near the begin-ning of 'The Shower' are one instance, the murmured *legato* bass

The Part-songs

echoing each non-*legato* line in 'After many a dusty mile' is another—and the frequent stress marks over individual chords deserve scrupulous attention in performance. In the unaccompanied part-songs particularly he takes advantage of the different texture afforded by chordal and contrapuntal writing, either by alternation, as in 'Love's tempest,' or by intermingling, as in 'O Wild West Wind.' For in the adventurous use of texture, colour, and interplay of sonorities these songs are markedly original. In the middle of 'Deep in my soul' sopranos and basses move in stark octaves between which altos and tenors add dark, soft clusters of notes; the eight-part 'There is sweet music'—less heart-easing but more seductive than Parry's setting—exploits the contrast of men's and women's voices; the six-part 'Go, song of mine' sets sustained sound against transitory, using a bare F$\sharp$ from the tenors as a pivot round which to move from the chord of B minor to that of E$\flat$ minor. The same song shows how skilfully Elgar uses colour as a point of climax, for the first four lines of the poem are built up to and fall away from the one brightly spaced chord in the passage, at the word 'dust.'

Most of Elgar's part-songs sound best when sung by biggish choirs. Many of those in four parts are subdivided. Purity of single line was not his. Comparison of his carol 'I sing the birth' with Holst's 'Jesu, Thou the virgin-born,' written twenty years before, shows how mildly pleasant is Elgar's handling of free solos interspersed with a burden in parts, and how compelling is Holst's. On the other hand, Holst never put bi-tonality to more expressive service than Elgar in 'There is sweet music'—and this was in 1908—even if G major and A$\flat$ major oppose each other more fiercely on paper than in performance, as they are alternated rather than combined. Elgar is at his best when he is rich and complex, piling up bold climaxes, adding colour to colour, drawing out resonances, weaving threads of close shades; then, for individuality, strength, and certainty of effect he has no superior among English part-song writers.

CHAPTER XIII

SHORTER INSTRUMENTAL WORKS

ELGAR's first work of importance and the first work of his to be performed at a festival was the concert overture *Froissart* (1890). Written
on the score is a quotation from Keats, 'When Chivalry lifted up her
lance on high,' and the name and spirit of the music is taken from a
conversation in Scott's *Old Mortality* which speaks of the 'true
chivalrous feeling' of the historian Froissart in describing the 'death
of the gallant and high-bred knight, of whom it was a pity to see the
fall, such was his loyalty to his king, pure faith to his religion, hardi-
hood towards his enemy, and fidelity to his lady-love!'

The music matches the prose in its romantic fervour, and pours out
tune after tune with an abandonment which might be thought simply
the impetuosity of youth until it is remembered how many of the
mature works begin with a similar spate of ideas: already Elgar's
ample invention bulges out of sonata form. In fact it is astonishing
how well formed and individual is the personality behind this music,
how phrase after phrase can be matched against a couple of bars in a
later work, and how familiar are the melodic features—sequence,
crotchet-quaver rhythm, upward-thrusting arpeggios, and leaps of
sixths and sevenths. The development, which follows, weakly, a
Brahmsian pattern (the only working-out section of Elgar's that does)
is gauche and relies for effect too much on *tremolando* strings and step-
wise modulating harmonic sequences, but the recapitulation is deftly
managed in that it starts straight off with the main theme, and what
was the introduction becomes a brilliant coda.

The scoring is competent and effective and shows a clear grasp of
orchestral values, though few of the idiosyncrasies that make up Elgar's
mature style of orchestration. Altogether, the overture is predictive
and besides that has some independent value, for it is excitingly alive
and evokes precisely the desired mood.

The *Serenade* in E minor for strings (1893) is a significant work. It
was produced in the same month as *The Black Knight*, but while that

sometimes shows the fumblings of inexperience, this, in its slender way, is as polished as it could be. It is revealing to compare the outer movements of this with Thyri's song from *King Olaf*, produced three years later. There is similarity in mood and idiom, but while that is stilted this is spontaneous. The *Serenade* is a slight but charming work.

The first movement is bound together by the opening dotted figure in the violas and has two pensive themes, the first curving up to and away from the flattened seventh of the key. The middle movement is considerably more than *salon* music, though unmistakably by the same composer as the *Chanson de nuit*, and the mixture of jubilant and elegiac feeling in its sustained string tune is prophetic: it is half-way up the scale between the *Chanson* and the great slow movements of the symphonies. The last movement sets off fluently but soon returns to material from the first movement, and after one joyous *crescendo* fades away in reminiscence of the initial dotted figure. Elgar himself held this work dear and in 1904 said he liked it as much as anything he had written.[1] The ideas for the *Serenade* were probably taken from the three string pieces played at Worcester in 1888.[2] The manuscript of these cannot be traced, but the titles—*Spring Song*, *Elegy*, and *Finale*—are apt enough for the *Serenade* of 1893.

Cockaigne (*In London Town*) (1901), the second and most frequently played of Elgar's three concert overtures, is a splendid piece, a picture of the London of procession and pageantry. The composer wanted it to be 'honest, healthy, humorous, and strong but not vulgar,'[3] and revealed a programme which accounts for the episodic nature of the work.

It opens with a bustling *scherzando* which gives way to a broad singing melody representing the Londoner. A snatch of tune which has the same smell of fresh grass (and the same rhythm) as the little passage that leads into Shallow's orchard in *Falstaff* takes us into a London park, where a pair of lovers sing a yearning *dolce* second subject with a pendant of exchanged confidences. Next on the scene comes a cocky street urchin, represented by the opening of the Londoner theme played in diminution (see example 15, page 154), the

---

[1] R. J. Buckley, *Sir Edward Elgar* (Bodley Head).   [2] See page 13.
[3] *Letter* to Richter, 30th August 1901.

Shorter Instrumental Works

device Wagner used to show the relationship between his master-singers and their apprentices, though Elgar is said to have had the idea from Delibes's *Sylvia*. The Londoner theme, high and sweet on fluid strings, leads from exposition to development, in place of which come a couple of brass bands. The first, a military band (the clarinet hints of its approach through the lovers' talk), has tremendous *panache*, a big fat tune for trombones, and a drummer who twirls his drumsticks as he plays—those trills can mean nothing else. The second band, more amateur in execution (did Elgar mean to suggest the Salvation Army?), plays a timid, strait-laced version of the same tune, comically in the wrong key. The lovers seek quietness in a church whose atmosphere is suggested in a *più tranquillo* passage, and go out into the street again as the opening theme approaches. In the recapitulation the positions of the characters are juggled with so as to leave the climax to the end. The lovers arrive more quickly on the scene, the urchin precedes his more dignified parent, there is a brief blare from the band, and to end comes the Londoner theme, *nobilmente* and powerful, as broad and flowing as the Thames itself.

The overture is scored with the most glittering virtuosity, and is a good craftsman's blend of that same emotion that touches our national pride in the *Pomp and Circumstance* marches, the jocularity that often passes for humour in our native Londoner, and the sheer 'English good fellowship' that Elgar himself admired so much.

Cockaigne is brilliant; *In the South* (1904) is sumptuous. This concert overture has an admitted programme as had the other, and is as frankly episodic in design, but whereas that involved character and incident, this is pictorial. The manuscript bears quotations which show the direction of the composer's thoughts.[1] There was a double image in his mind: the golden countryside of Italy and its glorious history. The idea for the whole work is contained in these lines from Tennyson's poem *The Daisy*:

> What hours were thine and mine,
> In lands of palm and southern pine,
> In lands of palm, of orange-blossom,
> Of olive, aloe, and maize and vine.

[1] Ernest Newman, *Elgar* (Bodley Head).

'In the South'

On the manuscript too is a quotation from Byron's *Childe Harold*:

> . . . a land
> Which *was* the mightiest in its old command
> And *is* the loveliest . . .
> Wherein were cast . . .
>   . . . the men of Rome !
> Thou art the garden of the world.

The overture starts straight off with a spirited tune (see example 18, page 154) that springs upwards in fifths and had already done duty five years before as 'Dan triumphant (after a fight)' in Sinclair's visitors' book. Idea after idea pours out in rich profusion: seven or eight themes from the exposition alone might be given. But it is irresistible to quote one incidental fragment (of a kind which meanders through all Elgar's most English music—even in Italy he could not forget his three rivers):

in comparison with this oboe figure from *Promenade* No. 5 of about 1878:

As in *Cockaigne* the place of a development is largely taken up by sections of fresh material. The first, harmonically bold, depicts 'What Roman strength Turbía showed In ruin on the mountain road' in an upthrusting tune and a massive, delayed cadence. The second is a serenade sung by a solo viola in the manner of an Italian *canto popolare*, with an enchanting silvery accompaniment of divided strings, harps, and glockenspiel. At the end of a straightforward recapitulation the main theme of the overture, swung into waltz rhythm by being at once augmented and speeded up, and combined contrapuntally with another theme from the exposition, brings this warm, blithe, and vigorous work to a close.

Shorter Instrumental Works

The *Introduction and Allegro* (1905) is written for string quartet and string orchestra. The quartet is used as an *ensemble*, as individual soloists, as part of the orchestra, and to add points of colour to the scoring in much the same way as Elgar often uses wood-wind in a full band. Although there is one conspicuous passage in direct antiphony, on the whole the interplay of the forces is subtle and not the simple one of weight against brilliance as in the old *concerti grossi*.

The Introduction presents three ideas. The first of these is an incisive descending triplet figure given out in a resonant and gripping *tutti*. The second has a favourite string rhythm of Elgar's, ♩♩♩, conspicuous too in the first movements of the Violin Concerto and the First Symphony, and wistfully rises and falls within a great curve: over this in the manuscript Elgar wrote 'smiling with a sigh.' The third (see example 22, page 157) is a lyrical melody for solo viola, of which the drooping third clung to Elgar's memory from some Welsh songs he had heard in the distance in the Border country. 'The work is really a tribute,' he wrote in a programme note, 'to that sweet borderland where I have made my home.'

These three ideas, sharply contrasted in mood, are presented in the fantasia-like Introduction; the Allegro proper swings off with the second of them, now less tentative and in the major. In due course comes a second subject, a real bowed-instrument pattern with pattering repeated notes (like the weird scherzo of the Cello Concerto), played in antiphony between soloists and *ripieno*. The theme which opened the Introduction, and now has a *con fuoco* melodic continuation, brings the exposition to an exultant close.

In place of a development there is, as Elgar put it, 'a devil of a fugue,' on a new dancing subject. However, it is not quite as new as it first sounds, for before it has gone far it is partnered by a curving theme that turns out to be part of the bass:

Ex. 12

of the main Allegro theme as it was presented in the Introduction, to which it later became a melodic pendant. If two themes share a

'Introduction and Allegro'

common counterpoint can they be entirely unrelated? The tempo picks up to *più animato*, the cut and thrust of the strings becomes fiercer, the tension is screwed tighter, and the whole thing works up to a climax. Now as a rule Elgar makes his climaxes by piling on dynamics and orchestral colour. Here the medium denies him those luxuries, and this climax is made by a closer weaving of the texture, by manipulation of the actual thematic material, and by a dash of astringency in the harmony. It is a climax of compression, not, as is his custom, of spacious spreading. It forces its way on to a dominant pedal and there relaxes; then follows a complete recapitulation of the Allegro. As a magnificent coda comes the 'Welsh' tune of the Introduction, richly and strongly harmonized.

This piece fits into no recognized category of form. True, there is a full recapitulation of the Allegro, but this is crowned by a theme which has made no appearance except in the Introduction, and there is no development section as in a sonata-form movement. Yet formally it is a beautiful thing. Wayward, improvisatory, elusive though it sounds, far more of its appeal comes from the balance of its material than in many of Elgar's apparently more strictly organized movements. His problem was always how to cope with the wealth of ideas that each work found in him: ideas and shape did not always match in movements that owe allegiance to sonata form; in the *Introduction and Allegro*, where he gave his fancy full rein, the loveliest thing about it is its equipoise.

The writing for strings is superb in its power and variety. Power comes from the quaver rest before the attack of big chords (at cue no. 6), from triple-stopping spread, not divided (at cue no. 12), from the grace-notes which increase sonority and stress the rhythm (at cue no. 30), and from the calculated use of open strings with their bright and character-giving overtones (at cue no. 15). For subtlety there is the magical sound of pure and *ponticello tremolo* bowing mixed at the unison, muted and *pianissimo*, just before the fugue; and the smack of that one *pizzicato* chord at the very end after the sonority of full bowing. But above all there is the sweep of strings in octave or unison to exhilarate the ear, either brilliant in passage work (at cue no. 28) or gloriously full in the athletic two-part writing after cue no. 27.

Shorter Instrumental Works

This two-part writing is indicative of a tendency throughout the work to a more linear thought than is usual in Elgar. The work's shapeliness, together with this slight stiffening, tempers its sweetness with strength and makes it a delight even to those who do not generally appreciate their Elgar.

The two *Wand of Youth* suites (1907–8) were developed from some early sketches written for a children's play (see page 106). They are admirable descriptive pieces, concise, swift in setting a mood, brimful of gaiety, rather like young irresponsible relations of the *Enigma* Variations. The brisk Overture of the first has something of the dispatch of 'G.R.S.,' though it makes room for a fat *cantabile* tune which is markedly like one in the finale of the Violin Concerto; both have a leap of a seventh which is one of Elgar's fingerprints. The Serenade and 'Fairy Pipers' are subdued, with pretty little tunes over delicate accompaniments. 'Slumber Scene' makes a virtue of a necessity (the original bass player could manage only the open strings) and has a lovely cadence. The Minuet is a gentle Purcellian pastiche. The 'Sun Dance' is the most developed piece, and the wood-wind writing is deft and glittering. 'Fairies and Giants' end the suite in a sort of joyous tarantella.

The second suite has only six pieces. The opening of the March is curiously unassertive, though the central major part is captivating in its jauntiness. 'Little Bells' and 'Moths and Butterflies' are both dainty dance-like pieces; the first has a middle section characteristic in its wistful use of the melodic minor, and in that on its repeat a solemn horn counterpoint is added to it. In the 'Fountain Dance' the arpeggios rise and fall with graceful artifice over a drone bass. 'The Tame Bear' and 'The Wild Bears' end the suite, one made plaintive by oboe, awkward by syncopation, pathetic by minor seventh and plagal cadence; the other playful and uproarious—'pantomime bears' as Dunhill called them—with tambourine, triangle, and xylophone.

The two suites have throughout something of the light touch of Tchaikovsky's ballet music, and indeed comparison with the *Nutcracker* suite is illuminating. The two marches; 'Moths and Butterflies' and the 'Dance of the Sugar Plum Fairy'; the opening of 'The

'Wand of Youth' and 'Nursery' Suites

Wild Bears' and the middle of the 'Dance of the Flutes'; 'Fairy Pipers' and the 'Arab Dance'; and the waltz melodies in the 'Sun Dance' and the 'Waltz of the Flowers'—all give examples of texture, mood, and occasionally definite features which are extraordinarily alike. But even if their dates did not make it clear that much of the *Wand of Youth* was written before the *Nutcracker*, Elgar's suites would be no mere copies. His orchestration is more colourful, his invention runs as freely, and his pieces have in turn more bite, more delicacy, and more warmth; though Tchaikovsky's are of course better for dancing.

The *Nursery Suite* (1931) is a collection of little characteristic pieces of considerable charm if slight content. The Aubade which opens it (and brings to mind the opening of the *Serenade* in E minor) contains a hymn-tune which Elgar wrote as a youth for his Worcester church. The waltz of 'The Sad Doll' has a harmonic progression reminiscent of the *Rosenkavalier* waltzes: a kind of Strauss bowdlerized for use in the nursery. The fifth piece, 'The Wagon Passes,' is a coup of musical imagery: the snatch of melody, the wagoner's whistle, is heard over a rhythmic *ostinato* which becomes deafening as the wagon lumbers past and fades into nothing as we watch it out of sight. Mussorgsky had used the same pictorial device in his *Bydlo*, but the Russian's theme is melancholy compared with the insouciance of the Worcestershire wagoner's. 'Dreaming' exudes the warm tender romanticism of Schumann, yet has an Elgar fingerprint in the sudden harmonic sideslip, *lento pp*, which occurs twice. 'Envoy' recapitulates some of the previous pieces in between violin *cadenzas*, and the suite ends with a return to the Aubade.

The two slight pieces called *Dream Children* (1902) were inspired by Lamb's essay and particularly by this passage: 'And while I stood gazing, both the children gradually grew fainter to my view, receding and still receding till nothing at last but two mournful features was seen in the uttermost distance. . . . "We are nothing; less than nothing, and dreams. We are only what might have been."'

These pieces are in that vein of wistful tenderness that was Elgar at his most poetic. The first is not untouched by longing as violins in octaves strain towards new keys over a tonic pedal. The second is

Shorter Instrumental Works

marked *allegretto piacevole* and has the same limpid sweetness as Elgar's other music with that direction. The scoring for small orchestra is a miracle of delicacy and soft colouring.

Apart from trifles, Elgar's only works for keyboard are the Organ Sonata and a Sonatina for piano. The latter was written for his niece and is Gurlitt *à la mode* of Elgar. The Organ Sonata (1896) is less certain in its touch than the other early instrumental works, *Froissart* and the *Serenade*, for its four movements are not well matched. The first is a sort of instrumental counterpart of the cantatas, starting off as for *The Black Knight*, and sharing the nature of its second subject with the ladies of *King Olaf* of the same year. The second movement is a pleasant but uncharacteristic *allegretto*. The third falls midway between Elgar's *salon* and serious requirements and does not quite satisfy either. The fourth is more interesting because of its effective quotation from the third movement and because of a passage which may have been the seed of 'O ye priests' in *The Kingdom*.

There remain five short orchestral pieces which make as a group a compendium of aspects of Elgar's mind and style, for each isolates one characteristic. The devotional, aspiring character of his long string tunes, built of recurrent patterns, is at its simplest in the main theme of *Sursum corda* (1901). The *Romance* (1910) for bassoon and orchestra is more in the mood of the reflective parts of the oratorios, and like them and the Violin Concerto of the same year is full of the minute fluctuations of tempo that make the solos so flexible. Gravely and richly handled discords and chains of suspensions go to make the string *Elegy* (1910). The violin part of *Sospiri* (1914)—the piece might almost be an accompanied *cadenza* and was written for Reed—plays musingly around the interval of a seventh over, at one point, very soft *tremolando* strings and harp.

CHAPTER XIV

SCORING AND MAJOR ORCHESTRAL WORKS

ELGAR'S use of instruments is brilliant and individual. His characteristic orchestral sound is both rich and sparkling.

He conceived his music in instrumental terms. This is plain from his words and from his manuscripts. 'I find it impossible to imagine a composer creating a musical idea without defining, inwardly and simultaneously, the exact means of its presentation . . . orchestration, in its highest sense, is the art of composing for an orchestra.' His words from a Birmingham lecture are confirmed by the evidence of the first manuscript sketches of the Second Symphony, which, although mere fragments, have the scoring indicated: clearly marked is the *fortissimo* horn arpeggio in the seventh bar of the first movement.[1]

Though Elgar first became known through his choral cantatas it was an orchestral work, *Enigma*, which proclaimed his importance. His orchestral expertness was evident from the beginning. Even his early unpublished pieces charm by their aptness when heard on the instruments for which they were written. Most press notices of the early cantatas have praise for the orchestral accompaniment. It is, in fact, to the orchestra rather than to the chorus in these works that one looks for distinction.

He learnt orchestration in the hard school of experience. He had not one lesson, but wrote for immediate performance. At first his family and young friends, then the asylum band, then the amateur orchestras of Worcestershire came under his baton and played his arrangements and his compositions. The fact that until his late thirties he never conducted a professional orchestra is very probably the reason why professional orchestras have such respect and affection for his music: he *had* to know how to achieve his effects by the easiest

---

[1] 'I never *have* had to alter anything [after performance],' he wrote to Jaeger, 12th July 1898.

Scoring and Major Orchestral Works

and simplest means. Orchestral players love Elgar 'because he is such fun to play.' 'There must be consideration for the players,' he wrote in his Birmingham lecture on orchestration, and 'orchestral instruments must be kept in the players' hands, they are intimate things. Solos must be prepared.' Reed told a story of a 'dry-as-dust' musician, trying to catch Elgar out, pointing to a bass clarinet doubling *pp* for bars. Unabashed, Elgar pointed in turn to a coming solo for the instrument; the doubling was deliberate, for warming up. He himself played violin, viola, bassoon, and trombone in some measure, and led the Worcester Philharmonic and Festival orchestras for some years. Tovey [1] gives an example of the 'enormous efficiency of Elgar's scoring.' An orchestra of students, only one of whom was not reading from sight, found on first rehearsal of *In the South* that the work carried them away and 'seemed to play itself.' Elgar knew his instruments: his father had sold and tuned them; he himself had handled them, played them, conducted them, even *made* a double-bass, and he treated them as 'intimate things.'

His orchestra is large but not extravagantly so. In *Enigma* he asks for two each of wood-wind with piccolo and double bassoon, four horns, three trumpets, three trombones and a tuba, strings, varied percussion, and organ *ad lib*. To this he adds a pair of cornets for *Cockaigne* and a third flute, cor anglais, bass clarinet, and harp for *In the South*. For his First Symphony he adds to the *In the South* mixture one more harp, but makes a note that 'the strings should be as numerous as possible, and it is desirable that the wood-wind and horns should be doubled.' For his Second Symphony he adds to this one E♭ clarinet, whose function is mainly to strengthen the flutes. The Violin and Cello Concertos have much the same orchestra as *Enigma*, *Falstaff* the same as the First Symphony. He admitted to hankering after four saxophones—an instrument whose tone he considered 'beautiful and expressive'—for *Caractacus*, but expense and rehearsal difficulties gainsaid him. The straight trumpet for the shofar in *The Apostles* and the tabor in *Falstaff* (which may be played on the *tamburo piccolo* without snares) are his only excursions into the exotic.

[1] Tovey, *Essays in Musical Analysis*, vi (Oxford).

Familiarity with Instruments—Size of Orchestra

For one of his Peyton Professorship lectures at Birmingham Elgar took as his text Mozart's G minor Symphony. In his notes for this he wrote that the limitations of the instruments 'sometimes have disastrous results: it being impossible to find any note that will "fit" the chord, the horns have to be silent: so it happens that the musical climax is often not the climax of tone.' In the score he himself used for preparing this lecture he marked a case where the climax is weaker than the preceding bar owing to the compulsory absence of the second horn. This was a lesson which Elgar learnt well. His own scoring ensures that the musical climax and the climax of tone are one. It is common enough in the scores of any composer of Elgar's period to find a melodic climax bolstered up by fuller orchestration of its harmony. But Elgar applies this principle not only harmonically but melodically and to almost every phrase he writes. If the cellos have a sweeping theme the oboe will double the six notes of climax in it:

If the clarinet has a short curving phrase the flute will top it:

In the First Symphony, where cellos, horns, clarinets, bass clarinet, and cor anglais take over the theme at cue no. 8, oboes and first violins reinforce the highest notes. Comparatively seldom does Elgar double a melody wholly and solely in one other instrument, but the high notes of his phrases are emphasized with extra colour and force. Even tiny *crescendi* and *diminuendi* are achieved by the number of instruments playing as well as by their intensity. Elgar phrases with his orchestra.

He uses a couple of notes from an extra instrument not only to mark the top of a phrase but also to give more bite to rhythm. Syncopation in an oboe will be pointed by a flute:

Scoring and Major Orchestral Works

and a complicated syncopated pattern for cellos and violas is clarified by being outlined on bassoons and having the main beats doubled by horns and plucked violins:

Rhythm as well as tone guides Elgar in doubling his themes: the weightier notes only are doubled, so that the foundations are reinforced but the decorative detail is uncluttered. Trombones give a strengthening quaver to horns and trumpets:

Cor anglais outlines a theme given to lower strings, horns, and clarinets:

Elgar matches the weight of his instruments to the rhythmic importance of each note.

Where a tune *is* doubled, seldom will it be by one instrument for

Selective Doubling of Instruments

all its length. In the First Symphony, at cue no. 66, the melody is played by the first flute. Nearly every note is doubled, but by violins *arco*, violas *pizz.*, solo violin, and clarinet, each having no more than a couple of notes in succession, so that behind the flute is a colourful kaleidoscope of tone. In the next example, where violins carry the argument, a horn doubles the main beats of the bar, the oboes the downward, and the clarinets the upward figure:

Ex. 19 Cockaigne

Elgar's themes stand out in sharp perspective from his orchestra because one instrument pencils the line, and others put in light and shade.

In his Mozart score Elgar marked particularly a passage in the development of the last movement where the strings exchange the main theme in close imitation. He drew attention to the fact that each entry was marked by *one* note being doubled in the wood-wind. This again gives a clue to Elgar's own scoring methods. The top, *sforzando* note of string passage work is brightened by oboes and clarinets:

Ex. 20 1st Symphony

Two notes from a trombone reinforce a cello and bass entry five bars before cue no. 15 in the First Symphony.

This picking out of one or two vital notes by a second instrument frequently shows another characteristic of Elgar's, that of mixing

Scoring and Major Orchestral Works

plucked strings with brass, edging blunt tone with sharp. Impact is given to the grunt of trombones by the *pizzicato* strings in *Cockaigne*:

Another example comes from *Gerontius* at the words 'Go forth upon thy journey, Christian soul,' and yet another at the solemn words 'Because already in thy soul the judgment is begun,' where horns intone *pianissimo* the 'judgment' theme picked out by four vibrating harp notes. In the First Symphony, at cue no. 149, harps pile brilliance on to trumpets, and at cue no. 99 one note from a harp touches up the plaintive oboe, cor anglais, and clarinet.

In his Mozart score Elgar scribbled at the beginning of the first movement's development section: 'Sustained chords again mark change of harmony.' In this case bassoons sustained the chords: in Elgar's scores it is the horns that frequently slide the strings over a harmonic change. In the first interlude from *Falstaff* the horns play but four notes, each tied over a barline, carrying one phrase over to another, joining the harmony. In the 'Romanza' from *Enigma* one horn note tied over a bar-line smoothes the opening sweep of strings. Elgar makes much use of the blending quality of the horns.

Notes tied over a bar-line are often used by him for deliberate effect in writing for strings as well as horns. In the First Symphony, during the first statement by full orchestra of the big A♮ tune, every bar-line except five (out of eighteen) has one or other string group tied across it. The direction here is *molto sostenuto*. In the same movement, at cue no. 19, observe the notes tied over the strong beats in a passage marked *pianissimo teneramente* which floats imperceptibly along. 'Slumber Scene' from the first *Wand of Youth* suite has much the same bowing. *Froissart* provides an early example in the half-dozen

Writing for Strings

bars before letter K. Wherever Elgar wants a sound of great smooth-
ness he writes so that one group of strings has a sustained bow while
the others change before a strong beat, so avoiding that fraction of
silence when all bows change together. Is it mere chance that the
'Welsh' melody in the *Introduction and Allegro* begins like this?

Ex. 22

The strings are the heart of Elgar's orchestra. His great *cantabile*
tunes lie perfectly on their instruments. There are a remarkable
number of string solos in his works—the veiled viola solo in the
Prelude to *Gerontius* springs to mind—and he treated his second
violins (he had been a second violin himself) to an unusually full
share of the juice in any work. Two characteristics of his string
writing are his frequent subdivisions into more than two groups and
the doubling of a part at the octave: Part I of *Gerontius* at cue no. 70
exhibits both. An entirely new effect in writing for strings is the
accompaniment to the *cadenza* in the Violin Concerto, where a chord
is 'thrummed with the soft part of three or four fingers across the
strings,' producing a wonderful shimmer which may well have been
suggested by the Aeolian harp Elgar kept in his window at 'Plas
Gwyn.' Elgar had himself anticipated this effect in *The Apostles* in
the presentation of the 'prayer' theme at cue no. 15, where strings play
pizzicato triplets of double-stopping marked *ppp mistico*.

The two notes for solo clarinet at the end of the First Symphony's
slow movement show how well Elgar knew the technical and
expressive capabilities of his wood-wind instruments. He demanded
virtuosity from his brass and sensitivity from his percussion; in the
'Romanza' from the *Enigma* the timpani roll must be played with side-
drum sticks,[1] and the gong in *Sea Pictures* must be struck with a
sponge-headed stick.

Throughout all his scores minute directions are given to every

[1] The practice of playing this with two coins was, according to Dunhill,
started by Richter's timpanist.

Scoring and Major Orchestral Works

detail of nuances, phrasing, bowing, and tempi (see, for instance, example 23, page 159). Performers sometimes complain that his care was excessive and leaves nothing to the interpreter, but Elgar, who admitted this to be true in the case of vocal music, knew his own mind about orchestral, as this letter to W. G. McNaught of Novellos about some part-songs shows: 'Would you give yourself the trouble to look over a proof with an eye—two eyes—to expression-marks and stage directions? I overdo this sort of thing (necessary in orchestral stuff) as I put down all my feelings as I write and then haven't the heart to take 'em out.' [1] In his music, dynamics are as much part of the musical thought as melody or rhythm.

His orchestral sound is often compared with Wagner's. It is true that both the composers indulged in large orchestras, but once the similarity is admitted the differences of detail are the more strikingly apparent. For where Wagner's tone is fully saturated, Elgar's glistens and glints. Elgar himself said that he learnt more about orchestration from Delibes than Wagner, though few of Elgar's characteristics colour the music of *Sylvia* and *Coppélia*. Meyerbeer, whom Elgar admired, is another matter. Page after page of *Les Huguenots* yields familiar sights to the Elgar student: the same flicks of wood-wind and *pizzicato*, the same selective doubling, the same apparently overcrowded page which on analysis shows every note in its right place. What in Meyerbeer was a technical device became in Elgar a consistent personal style. It is significant that while he was their conductor the Worcestershire Philharmonic played Chabrier's *España*, Delibes's *Sylvia* and *Le Roi s'amuse* suites, Massenet's march from *Le Cid*, and an excerpt from Berlioz's *The Childhood of Christ*. From Wagner he inherited orchestral opulence; from the French composers, orchestral clarity. His style owes as much to the Parisian theatre pit as to Bayreuth.

The subtleties of his scoring are almost non-existent in *Froissart*, gradually creep into the cantatas, and in *Caractacus* emerge as a fully synthesized style. There is little difference in the handling of the orchestra in *Caractacus* and *Enigma*—though all the world of difference

[1] 4th January 1908.

Wagner, Delibes, and Meyerbeer—'Enigma'

in every other way—and it is not surprising that Elgar wrote to Jaeger about the cantata: 'I think it is the best scoring I ever saw! and the worst written.'[1] It makes the appearance of *Enigma* a little less startling to have watched the gradual assimilation of Elgar's orchestral technique throughout the earlier works.

The *Enigma* Variations (1899) announced to the world that England had a composer of distinctive style, a poetic turn of thought, and great orchestral skill. It remains the work of Elgar's which is most often performed in this country and which travels best abroad.[2]

The theme is original and as productive as a gold-mine. There are two phrases: the first in G minor, pathetic in its falling intervals and mute first beats; the second serenely travelling in thirds in G major (see example 14, page 153). The first phrase:

Ex. 23 Andante

is repeated after the second, melodically exact, to make a ternary theme, but in the third bar violas and cellos surge in with a counter-theme which never fails to catch at the throat. How seldom can Elgar resist a new inner part at a repetition! 'R.B.T.'s' perky oboe theme has a bassoon bubbling away under its second appearance and 'W.N.' has a few extra chuckles thrown in as she says good-bye.

The variations are very free and none maintains intact the structure of the theme, though 'C.A.E.' is very close. In two variations, 'Intermezzo' and 'Romanza,' thematic connection is untraceable. 'H.D.S.-P.' and 'Nimrod' use only the first phrase of the theme, 'Troyte' uses the second phrase with the briefest mention of the first at the very end. 'R.P.A.' adds a rich counter-melody to the first phrase

[1] 25th February 1899.

[2] In a letter to Bennett, dated 10th December 1904, Elgar mentions Rimsky-Korsakov and Glazunov as 'saying the Variations were such a success that they would be repeated.'

Scoring and Major Orchestral Works

and smooths out the rhythm of the second. 'G.R.S.' strips both phrases to their essentials and alternates them abruptly. 'W.M.B.,' 'W.N.,' and 'Ysobel' use both parts of the theme in their original order but rhythmically transformed; 'B.G.N.' draws a curving cello tune out of it. 'E.D.U.' gives himself sixteen bars' introduction, reintroduces 'C.A.E.' and 'Nimrod,' and rounds off the work in tremendous style. This last variation originally ended just after cue no. 76. Jaeger suggested an extension of the coda. Elgar at first demurred—the difficulty was that he had already blazed out the main tune in the tonic at cue no. 68—but wrote it nevertheless, and liked it when done.[1]

The abandonment of the structural ground-plan—though unlike Strauss's *Don Quixote, Enigma* keeps the caesura between variations—makes possible immense variety. The swift and sudden changes of mood are as right here as they can be disconcerting in the symphonies. For each variation has its own personality as far removed from the others as the tentative approach of 'H.D.S.-P.' is from the emphatic downrightness of 'W.M.B.,' the precise grace of 'Ysobel' from the upsetting high spirits of 'Troyte,' the shy flutterings of 'Dorabella' from the bragging gusto of 'E.D.U.' They are—and we should know it without the composer's admission—character pieces, and since each is short and complete in itself Elgar encounters none of the difficulties of keeping the music going that make the symphonic works sometimes sound as if they are chasing their own tails. His ability to perceive seemingly endless derivations from one theme is here put to the perfect use. Each variation is as pithy and polished as an epigram.

The harmony of the variations is surprisingly diatonic, either tempestuously as in 'W.M.B.' or suavely as in 'W.N.' Surprisingly, because it is more so than in Elgar's other music of the period. The tonality is clear and the progressions and modulations are of the simplest. Even so there is effective contrast, for, as Reed pointed out, the theme, itself in the minor, ends on a major chord so that succeeding variations in the tonic sound deceptively distant; the fifth, sixth, and

---

[1] The original ending was published in *Music & Letters*, April 1935.

'Enigma'

seventh variations are in the subdominant key; and the ninth, 'Nimrod,' which is the centre-piece of the set, is treasured and placed apart in E♭ major, the final G of the previous variation hanging in the air for a moment's suspense, then settling warmly into its new key. Elgar's sequential suspensions, so hard-worked in the cantatas, come in this engaging guise:

Ex. 24

Many transformations of the theme are made rhythmically, leading to such niceties as the implied syncopation of 'W.N.' and the balance of 'B.G.N.'s' drawn-out version of the theme. The chief delight of these pieces lies in their poetry—but the technical skill in them is astonishing: tucked away in 'W.M.B.' one finds a perfect bit of canon.

Though Elgar was forty-two when he wrote it, *Enigma* is a young man's music. It has impulsiveness and charm and an almost Gallic sparkle and delicacy. There is none of the sentimentality of the cantatas in it, and not much of the wistfulness, the twisted chromaticism, the yearning *rubato* of the later Elgar, or even of its contemporary, *Gerontius*; yet it lacks nothing of sensibility. It is a masterpiece of pure delight, whose freshness will not fade.

The advent of a symphony from Elgar in 1908 could not but arouse much speculation. From his past music and from the example of his contemporaries a symphonic poem or other illustrative music might have seemed more probable, but he chose to assault the pinnacle of the symphony itself, and though its aesthetic value may rise or fall as taste changes, historically his first is the earliest English symphony that will assuredly live. He denied that it had a specific programme beyond that of human experience, but Colles, writing

Scoring and Major Orchestral Works

a month after its production, referred to the difficulty of the listener when Elgar used certain themes which were for him 'connected with sundry ideas—for the most part moral qualities, such as aspiration, courage, love, and hatred . . . without reference to the musical context.' Elgar hinted at some extra-musical idea in a letter to Neville Cardus. 'You do not see that the fierce quasi-military themes are dismissed with scant courtesy; critics invariably seem to see that a theme grows, but it appears to be a difficulty to grasp the fact that the coarser themes are well quashed!'[1] So it is reasonable to regard as a symbol of moral and spiritual virtues the motto theme which opens the work, which appears at points in the first and last movements, whose first four notes can be traced in many of the themes, and which triumphs at the end of the Symphony.

This theme is austere but grand, slow-moving, by step or big leap, in an unusual balance of seven-, ten-, and six-bar phrases, and marked *nobilmente*. It makes an introduction to the first movement, whose nervously excitable exposition lets loose a leaping *appassionato* first subject and finds a moment's serenity in the F major theme of its second. The development is ingenious, for some of the derivations are not disclosed until the recapitulation. For instance, the relationship of the tenuous violin figure at cue no. 19 to the first subject is not seen until the recapitulation, when it becomes its bass (though in the sketches[2] it appeared in the exposition marked 'alternative bass'), and its relationship with the motto theme is not revealed until the coda. Similarly, not until cue no. 36 is it quite clear that the arabesque figure between 21 and 22 is an embroidery of the bar at 9 (though in one sketch the bars between 9 and 10 are immediately repeated in the exposition with this arabesque). The weakness of this movement— and it is met with in others—is that the tonal climaxes are made by inflating frail melodies with more volume and intensity than they can stand. The delicate phrase from the second subject, five bars after cue no. 11, is blared out, augmented, shrill, and coarsened, twice by the full orchestra, at cue nos. 17 and 44, to end the exposition

---

[1] Quoted by Cardus in the *Manchester Guardian Weekly*, 2nd March 1934.
[2] B.M. Add. MS. 47907.

First Symphony

and recapitulation. Even granted that Elgar had some undisclosed programme which he thought justified it here, this procedure must be counted part of his style, for the first movement of the Second Symphony provides an exact parallel, when the second subject is treated in the same manner at the corresponding point; and the main climax in the Violin Concerto's first movement, though in the development, is made, as before, by shouting out at the top of the orchestral voice what was originally a shy, tender tune. The climax is made, but the mood is violated. Elgar, in common with some other late-romantic composers, showed at times scant regard for the character of his material in his treatment of it.

The second movement is an ebullient scherzo (though marked only *allegro molto*), opening with scampering strings and coming shortly to a march tune with a swagger to it. The trio, which comes round twice, is delectably scored and has that carefree atmosphere which infects all Elgar's open-air music. 'Play it,' he said, 'like something you hear down by the river.' After its second return the main scherzo tune slows itself down and emerges, transformed by new rhythm, new harmony, and in a new key, as the gravely exultant subject of the slow movement. The pitch of the notes is identical except that the seventh bar of the slow movement slips down a semitone in one of Elgar's sudden reticences. This movement is wonderfully sustained, throbbing with emotion in poised, controlled themes. There is a moment of singular beauty when, after the second subject has been played by violins, the lower strings take it while the violins and harp make above it such a sense of movement that the tune seems to have taken wings. This effect, from accompanying string triplets, Elgar loved and used often, and as early as the Larghetto in the *Serenade*, from which, very distantly, this Adagio is descended. It ends, unusually, with a new theme, that has the quality of benediction in it (and is like the music to which Magdalene asks and Christ bestows forgiveness in *The Apostles*). This is the only part of the Symphony for which there is evidence that it might have been written earlier. The sketch in short score is headed 'Sunday, August 21, 1904' and is in C major, though at the end is Elgar's signature with the date 1908 and the words 'The rest is silence.'

Scoring and Major Orchestral Works

The tonality of the Symphony is curious. It begins and ends in A♭ major. Through the first three movements a strong pull has been felt towards the distant key of D: the first movement is wrenched into D minor after its introduction, the second movement is in F♯ minor, and the third in D major; their common theme is ambiguous enough to accommodate both. The last movement begins in D minor, but its second subject is recapitulated in G♭ major, and in the middle there is a great chunk in the same key to tilt the scales well over before the motto theme comes back gloriously in A♭ major. 'Chunk' is the word, for this last movement is structurally the poorest of the four, and its joins are clumsy. One or two moments, particularly the factitiously stealthy introduction, sound contrived, and the main subject of the Allegro chugs along without the natural exhilaration that propels some of Elgar's other tunes, similarly obsessed by a single rhythm.

Though sometimes the very complexity of the scoring is distracting, some of the orchestral sounds in this Symphony are ravishing. What could be more romantically beautiful than the muted brass triplets which end the slow movement, or the sweet mingling of melodic strands over harp accompaniment in the middle of the last?

The Second Symphony (1911) has no opening motto theme like the first, but the second full bar of the first subject is sometimes taken to represent the 'spirit of delight' of the Shelley quotation which stands at the Symphony's head, for its gentle presence is felt at the end of the Larghetto and in the closing pages of the work. The whole first movement of this Symphony is 'tremendous in energy,' as Elgar himself said, impetuous, a little imperious, and wholly ardent. The two themes of the second subject are lyrical, the one shifting waywardly from key to key, the other a sweet, yearning tune for cello, but they do not stem the current which sweeps mightily through the movement from beginning to end. The development is mainly occupied with an extended, highly organized theme for cellos over a pedal point. This strong, ominous tune, and the violin thirds swaying in octaves which introduce and accompany it, are derived from the first full bar of the first subject, which is itself woven into the

Second Symphony

alternate bars of the accompaniment. The nature of its derivation, remote and subtle, is that the augmented triad of the first subject made in passing by a purely decorative melodic chromaticism, an F♯ for an instant over B♭ and D, is in the development isolated, seen as a harmonic, not melodic factor, and as such generates a great new tune. It is an illuminating glimpse of Elgar's way of seizing a non-essential detail and, by looking at it from a new angle, making it more productive than anything else in his exposition. The approach to the recapitulation is by way of part of the first subject, which when it arrives is compensatingly shortened. Elgar often makes a nice point by slightly altering his recapitulations, sometimes changing the order of the themes, so that *Froissart* and *Cockaigne* exchange a quiet lead into the development for a showy ending. Also in this way is brought about a magical moment in the first movement of the Violin Concerto, when the wistful second subject is insinuated into the seventh bar of the recapitulation, touching and transforming part of the first subject with its own exquisite sadness.

Though the slow movement of the Second Symphony is not named a funeral march, it is a great solemn elegy. It is enclosed by silken interlocking sixths for strings, and its three themes are loaded with dignity. The first comes in full twice; the second time the muffled impressiveness of the accompaniment is increased, and weaving in and out is the thin, sad sound of an oboe. This first theme, like the D♭ major one in the slow movement of the Violin Concerto, is one of Elgar's few where the harmony commands the melody. More often his active melodies take the lead, but here, in the fourth and fifth bars, it is the change of chord under the held notes that propels the tune along. The second theme, for strings *dolcissimo*, like many of Elgar's, is one where texture is as important as curve. The string threads are each incomplete without the others, and the rich loveliness of the passage is made by their warp and woof. (The First Symphony gives a similar example, in the second subject of the first movement, of a tune made entrancing by the tendrils of the accompaniment.) The third theme, diatonic and major, brings fortitude and consolation, and its top note is thrillingly doubled by the trumpet.

The rondo opens with a fleet-footed, will-o'-the-wisp section, full

Scoring and Major Orchestral Works

of cross rhythms, *staccato* strings, and whistling wood-wind scales. This alternates with a ponderous string tune in typical one-bar metre and with a passage haunted by this little wood-wind figure, in itself insignificant, but one of those fragments that breathe the scent of Severnside to those who know it:

The mood is suddenly darkened by the cello tune from the development of the first movement, again anchored by a pedal note and now made grim and powerful and savage by repeated notes in wood-wind (unusual for Elgar) and percussion. The opening figure of the rondo swirls round it, disclosing a hitherto concealed relationship with it in its second and third bars—both figures involve the arresting augmented subdominant. Elgar once [1] compared this passage with the lines in Tennyson's *Maud*:

> Dead, long dead,
> Long dead!
> And my heart is a handful of dust,
> And the wheels go over my head.

He did not say whether he found direct inspiration in this or whether the two passages seemed to him parallel, but his own is most certainly antagonistic to the 'spirit of delight.' After it has gone its way, the music picks up simply its former mood.

The last movement is compact and clear in design. It steers a straight course from first to last; if it is uncharacteristic in that, its three big tunes *are* characteristic, with one-bar repetitions, aspiring leaps, and sequences. It is the movement in which Elgar came most easily to terms with sonata form, its pace is swift though unhurried, and its character is generous yet magisterial.

Both symphonies are complex, spacious in their design, and long—too long for present taste. Both enshrine the opulence and splendour

[1] W. H. T. Gairdner, *W. H. T. G. to his Friends* (S.P.C.K.).

Violin Concerto

of their age. Both are magnificently scored for orchestra. Both have immense vitality, which is at once their strength and their failing, for though their drive unifies them it can also exhaust. Walford Davies put his finger on this when, writing to Elgar about the symphonies, he spoke of their 'ceaselessness' and 'the mere aural fatigue which naturally results.' [1] Both symphonies depend very much in performance on the right tempi and the right feeling for their length, for they can all too easily strut instead of stride. Except for the slow movements, the second is the finer of the two. It is more soundly constructed and more consistently inspired, and it scores heavily over the first in the superiority of its final movement. The restless stream of the First Symphony is in the second not only a wider but a deeper flow.

To listen to the Violin Concerto (1910) is at times like eavesdropping on a private conversation—or even a confessional—so inward is its quality. The violin part is difficult but has no empty virtuosity: the rhapsodic figuration is a flowering rather than an ornamentation. The special nature of the Concerto comes much from the fluctuations of *rubato* peculiar to Elgar, the minute quickenings and dallyings, the *animati* and *tenuti*, the impulses and the hesitancies which an unsympathetic interpreter can make sound mannered or perverse, yet whose secret must be won, for it is an essential and consistent part of his style, and naturally is most fully enjoyed by a soloist in a concerto, and at best in the *cadenza*. In the *cadenza*, in the central part of the slow movement, and in the second subject of the first movement—such an artless strain of repetitions—there is particularly that rapt and wondering concentration by which Elgar bestows beauty on simple things.

His liking for a group of ideas instead of a single subject is shown at its clearest and most characteristic in the first movement, where the four such motives of his first subject never reappear in their original order: in the violin's exposition and in the recapitulation the third and fourth are reversed in position, and the second is altogether omitted

[1] 6th October 1911.

Scoring and Major Orchestral Works

from the recapitulation. The opening of the Second Symphony and the Eastcheap scene in *Falstaff* are other occasions where Elgar favours a subject whose motives can in the course of the work be split off, used independently, and juggled with to make new patterns and permu-tations. In *Falstaff* the fragmentary nature of the theme, 'made up of short, brisk phrases' was Elgar's own comment, is emphasized by the contrasted orchestration, but in the Concerto and Symphony the melodic flow is such that the first impression is of one sweeping, continuous subject.

The slow movement of the Concerto opens with an ingenuous pastoral air. After the orchestra has played it, the soloist repeats it; and here is a point. Elgar commonly makes his orchestral intro-ductions do duty afterwards as accompaniments. In the cantatas the voices more often than not immediately and dully double the tune. In the opening of Part II of *Gerontius* and in 'By the Wayside' in *The Apostles* a large piece of orchestral introduction becomes an accom-paniment, not immediately, but shortly. But in this movement the violin charmingly deceives, beginning as an inner part and joining in unison with the orchestra only at the fourth bar. Very like it is Mary's evening song in *The Kingdom*, where the voice comes out of its orchestral veil only half-way through the original tune. This slow movement is less sustained, more rhapsodical, less stately, more meditative and self-communing than those in the symphonies.

Elgar is credited with saying that he wrote the last movement just for the *cadenza*, and if he meant that he purposely designed it to show the *cadenza* to the best advantage, he was perfectly right. For until the *cadenza* is reached the movement is strongly anticipatory, and is in fact an exposition and recapitulation with no working-out section. A theme, now augmented, from the slow movement heralds the long coda, and brings about, in an impassioned *nobilmente* which is the crux of the movement, one of those revelations of hidden relationships that are Elgar's speciality. This had already been suggested in the slow movement itself, where the theme (a), wafted over the strings at cue no. 47, was worked after 55 to the movement's climax at 56, trans-forming itself as it went to recall two motives from the first movement. Here in the last movement the passage is repeated: the connection is

Violin Concerto

confirmed. Three motives, (a) from the slow movement, (b) the first motive (less angular in interval but unmistakable), and (c) the third motive of the first movement's first subject, are linked in a continuous stream of melody and their underlying unity is for a moment glimpsed, illustrating Elgar's words that all the material for one work came from the same 'oven.'

Ex. 26

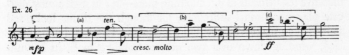

A brief return to the last movement proper dies suddenly away and there comes the *cadenza*, whose amazing loveliness would alone keep Elgar's name alive. The strings throb mysteriously in the *pizzicato tremolando* of his own invention, while the violin recalls themes from the first movement as one might live again memories too dear to be allowed to fade. Then the violin spins away as in the introduction to the movement, and the slow movement theme swings upwards in two-bar sequences which recall the early cantatas. Here and in the several phrase-sequences in the other two movements the effect is less hum-drum because the interval of sequence, which is not strict, is a third or one greater, while in the cantatas it was nearly always a second; though there is one passage at Q in the first scene of *The Banner of St George* which in shape and behaviour is amusingly like this at cue no. 111. Such is the importance of context!

The length of the Concerto has sometimes told against it. Albert Sammons, who was temperamentally its ideal interpreter, spoke of this to Elgar, who suggested that a cut might be made in the last movement; but when he heard it so played his disappointment was obvious. Sammons never made the cut again.

It is possible to compare the two symphonies, for they have much in common, but not the two concertos. The Violin Concerto is much more succulent than that for cello of eleven years later. This was written at the same time as the chamber music, and, whether or not that has any bearing on it, the orchestra, though of the same size as in

Scoring and Major Orchestral Works

the Violin Concerto, is lightly used and its tone pared down, so that
the cello never has any difficulty in speaking through it.

In the Cello Concerto the form of each of the four movements
is simplicity itself. The first opens with a commanding recitative
for the soloist, whose last note glides into a long, sinuous tune which
gently uncoils itself, and the first part of the movement is nothing more
than five restatements of it. Nothing more—but in itself a most delicate play upon tonal inflections, for though the theme looks and
sounds like a snake it behaves like a scorpion. First heard unharmon-
ized, winding down over two octaves from F♯ to E, its key un-
pronounced, it has a hidden harmonic sting in its last two bars, which
sends it first to E minor, where the theme starts restlessly on the supertonic; then to B minor, where the F♯ is at peace as the dominant; then
back to E minor, but shifts the theme down a tone to begin strongly,
twice, on the tonic; then back again to its troubled supertonic F♯.
So the six statements move from vagueness through disquiet and tranquillity to confidence and back to disquiet, by the least rhetorical of
means and with their lulling crochet-quaver movement undisturbed.
An episode follows which shares the twelve-eight signature and some
of the rhythmic idioms of the love-duets in *Caractacus*, but how much
more deeply tender is this idyll than that! Four restatements of the
first theme are recapitulated, but now the rhythm of the episode moves
disturbingly underneath and the cello breaks in at the climax with a brief,
moving counter-melody; then the movement winds away and fades.

The first three chords of the introduction, now *pizzicato*, bring the
second movement, a kind of *moto perpetuo*. To this, the high *tessitura*
of the cello part flitting through false relations with frequent harmonics,
the *pizzicato* accompaniment, the occasional low chords for divided
strings or muted horns, and the trailing wisps of clarinet all give a
fantastic atmosphere. The one melodic feature which is thrown up is
typical in its wide, swinging leaps, its *rubato*, and its two-bar construction.

The third movement is pure song, straight from the heart. In
it time is stilled and there is no sense of forward movement, for the
melodic patterns shun full closes—the movement ends on the dominant—and overlap each other with no check, and are drawn even

Cello Concerto

more tightly together by the sequences: it is a moment out of time into which is compressed a lifetime of feeling. There are only two phrases: the one questingly opens and ends the movement, the other is repeated; the second, more impassioned time, it is a semitone lower, not higher, so that the effect is not to increase the excitement but to deepen the longing.

The last movement, like the first two, starts with a *cadenza*-like recitative, which serves to show that its main theme is related to the opening of the Concerto. After the two subjects are presented, the cello sets off on what sounds like a new episode, but almost at once it is joined by a violin counter-melody which is a melodic skeleton of the first subject, augmented—an example of Elgar's way of linking the old and the new by a counter-melody. In this last movement the old Elgar rears his head in the swaggering gait of the main tune, the impatient crashes on the weak beats, the rattling brass semiquavers. But the mood is short-lived. There comes an accompanied cadenza, plangent and aching, which merges into the slow movement, ending in a quotation from it of six bars. This, surely, is a perfect quotation, as inevitable here as in its original context. The cello then repeats its first recitative, full and eloquent, and with the main theme of the movement the work ends brusquely.

This Concerto is shorter in length and lighter in weight than the Violin Concerto; but it is more original because while that modified an established form, this creates its own and must remain unique. Elgar was always most at ease when he allowed his ideas to shape their own designs, and for that reason this shares with *Gerontius* and the *Introduction and Allegro* an integration which is not so apparent in the symphonies. Although one can point to many of the same finger-prints, this Concerto is free from their tension and overwhelmingly energetic drive, and it is selective where they were prodigal. The note of resignation heard in it is new; the sense of valediction is painfully strong, and, as it turned out, prophetic. But if the spirit is haunted by an autumnal sadness, it is the sadness of compassion, not pessimism.

For his symphonic study *Falstaff* (1913) Elgar went not to *The*

Scoring and Major Orchestral Works

Merry Wives of Windsor but to the *Histories*. In his own analytical note [1] he stresses this point, talking of the 'caricature' in *The Merry Wives* and refuting the idea which he thought to be then prevalent that Falstaff was merely a 'farcical character.' In his enthusiasm he went too far the other way, and his conception of Falstaff was a romantic, idealized one: the words of the eighteenth-century essayist Morgann, which chimed with his own thoughts, were 'a knight, a gentleman, and a soldier'—he emphasizes them persuasively in his analysis. His attitude towards Falstaff is subjective—one of admiration for his humanity, indulgent tolerance of his peccadilloes, and sympathy for his degradation—not the objective one of Shakespeare, who neither praises nor condemns but simply creates. The character of Elgar's Falstaff is less than the complete sum of Shakespeare's. If it were not so his symphonic study might be a more acute piece of literary criticism; it does not follow that it would be better music. For what Elgar has selected from Shakespeare is precisely that which appealed to his own nature, which therefore he could best handle, which most keenly inspired his imagination; which, incidentally, is the very stuff that music feeds on: Falstaff at his most swashbuckling, at his most innocent, against his English countryside and on his deathbed.

The opening music of Falstaff and the prince is courtly, urbane, with a twinkle in the eye and a touch of charade—Elgar might perhaps have been thinking of the mock play in Act II where the two impersonate the royal father and son, as well as of their conversation in the prince's apartments. The first Interlude, a dream-picture of the young Falstaff, has a fair and candid beauty and a hint of regret. With the whole wealth of Falstaff the man to choose from, who but Elgar would have cared for the boy and for 'what might have been'? The Interlude in Shallow's orchard has all the scents and sounds of Shakespeare's countryside, never more freshly and touchingly translated. Falstaff's end is as sweet in Elgar as in Shakespeare. He sinks to death in the same music in which he sank into slumber behind the arras. His themes falter and fade. Across his mind flicker

---

[1] Edward Elgar, *Falstaff* (Novello).

'Falstaff'

memories of Gloucestershire fields, the Boar's Head, and his prince. A gentle clarinet and a *pianissimo* brass chord tell that he 'went away an it had been any christom child.' These are the things in *Falstaff* that grip the memory and show the greatness of Elgar. Falstaff in notation is a little less profligate than Falstaff in letterpress: if not exactly virtuous, he is never bawdy. There is a theme in the tavern episode which to Elgar represents the Falstaff who described himself as 'a goodly, portly man, of a cheerful look, a pleasing eye, and a most noble carriage.' But how melancholy is this cheerfulness which sways through chromatic four-part harmony in low compass, topped by doleful violas and cor anglais! Tovey, before reading Elgar's analysis, attributed this theme to 'blown up like a bladder with sighing and grief.' Was Elgar being extraordinarily subtle in so portraying the incurable optimism of a character doomed by stage tradition (as every spectator in the Globe knew) to a bad end?

Elgar's definition of the work as a study is vindicated in that he has picked and chosen his scenes to create moods and illustrate character rather than to re-create events (though he keeps the fights and makes technical use of them). He disregards the actions that took place at the Boar's Head and gives instead an impression of its cheerful bustle, even ignoring the chronology of Shakespeare's events, for in *King Henry IV* there is no scene at the tavern before the robbery—the plotting takes place in the prince's apartments. How well he knew what music can and cannot do is shown by his substitution of the dream Interlude for the comic business of finding the bill when Falstaff slept behind the arras. His published analysis shows that the relationship between the music and the plot is close. But though its inspiration was literary, the musical design, which is one long movement, stands firmly on its own feet. The first section, 'an apartment of the prince's,' presents four out of the five main Falstaff themes and that of the prince's 'courtly and genial mood.' The two fights, at Gadshill and Shrewsbury, provide by their action the opportunity for technical working out, and the 'honest gentlewomen's' theme is the germ of a scherzo which has a trio and a short reprise when Falstaff returns to the Boar's Head after the theft. The two Interludes, which are independent enough (though too short) to be played out of their

Scoring and Major Orchestral Works

context, are reflective pauses. The last scene, near Westminster, has a feeling of recapitulation about it: the king's approach is suggested by a variant of his 'courtly and genial' theme as it was at Gadshill, and this theme is presented in full for the first time since the first scene. So, although manifestly programme music, *Falstaff*'s musical form has elements of exposition, development, and recapitulation, and takes in on the way a scherzo and two lyrical pieces which add up to a slow movement.

The apparatus of working out which Elgar uses here belongs to the fugue rather than the symphony. The treatment the themes receive is that of augmentation, diminution, *fugato*, and combination. It is a most flexible and intelligent way to write a musical character study. How better can Falstaff be shown, waiting in ambush at midnight at Gadshill, than by his chief theme tiptoeing *staccato* in diminution? Or his discomfiture when he in turn is robbed than by his 'boastfulness' theme diminished and worked in *fugato*? his expansiveness at the Boar's Head than by his 'boastfulness' and 'noble carriage' themes in combination? his conquests than by his 'cajoling' and the 'honest gentlewomen's' themes in combination? his confident, vaunting words on hearing 'Harry the Fifth's the man' than by his 'boastfulness' theme in augmentation? or his bursting loyalty and glorying in the favour of his prince, now king, than by a seemingly new, gracious, full-hearted string tune (see example 36, page 192) immediately shown to be a counterpoint to his own chief theme?

Foreigners often refer to Strauss, and particularly to *Till Eulenspiegel*, in connection with *Falstaff*. Like *Till*, *Falstaff* asks to be met half-way and frankly needs the commentary Elgar supplied with it. It has its touches of realism, notably the bassoon solo recitatives (about which it is not at all necessary to know that over them in a manuscript sketch [1] Elgar wrote 'hic! hic!') and the orchestral snores that lead into the first Interlude. What sharply distinguishes *Falstaff* from *Till* is that there is not a trace of caricature in it. In fact, the work owes little enough to Strauss and is entirely characteristic of Elgar—too much so to be Shakespeare's Falstaff. A couple of tiny points are worth

[1] B.M. Add. MS. 47907.

'Falstaff'

comparing with earlier works. The 'cheerful, out-of-doors, ambling' theme at Gadshill is a type of tune, moving by a pattern of alternate long and short notes and with an illusion of sequence, that can be found in all periods of Elgar's music. Compare a few bars out of it:

Ex. 27ᵃ

with this, written for the wind quintet when Elgar was about twenty-one, and used up in 1930 for the *Severn Suite*:

Ex. 27ᵇ

And compare the opening of the triumphal march in *Falstaff* with the first few bars of *Caractacus*—same key, same rhythm, same atmosphere.

The craftsmanship of *Falstaff* is superb: all Elgar's technical resources are at their best. It is less of a personal document than either the symphonies or the concertos, and so, to those who find Elgar's personality uncongenial, less embarrassing. A good case can be made for its being his finest orchestral work; he himself thought so. Certainly it is one of the world's great pieces of programme music. It has the fertility of his earlier works without their diffuseness, their generosity without their extravagance. It has culled chivalry from *Froissart*, comedy from *Cockaigne*, and characterization from *Enigma*, and its bouquet is ripe and mature.

CHAPTER XV

CHAMBER MUSIC

THE String Quartet and Piano Quintet, though written during the same months and in the same place, are not alike in character. The Quartet is nervously active or gently pitying; the Quintet is confidently virile or luxuriantly romantic.

The Quintet (1918) is an uneven work with a glorious Adagio flanked by less distinguished Allegro movements. In the first movement Elgar's sense of flow deserted him. It is begun and ended by a Moderato embodying two separate ideas. The main Allegro, instead of driving along to offset this rhapsodical passage, is cut up: the first subject ends abruptly in the tonic; the second subject is introduced by a modulation in three bars from the tonic to the dominant which sounds like a chance improvisation; the recapitulation comes swinging back splendidly, but an *allargando* and a loosening of the rhythm spoil the reappearance of the theme introducing the second subject, which has no sooner got going than it collapses weakly on to longheld string notes and an 'oompah' piano part. The second subject itself is in Elgar's weakest melodic vein, a short figure waving about in nearrepetition and helped not at all by its commonplace presentation. But despite these faults the movement has an unmistakable air of grandeur. The design is big even if individual features are blemished.

If ever a movement of Elgar's ought to be headed *nobilmente* it is this Adagio. It is most assured and ripely lovely music. Though not a note of it could have been written by anyone but Elgar, it is, of all his movements, the one most like Brahms both in its spacious atmosphere and in tiny technical details. The way the second phrase of the opening theme is extended on itself; the way in the first two bars the bass is tied over the barline under a change of chord; the texture of the writing for piano against held string notes; the crossing of duplets and triplets in the piano just before the end: these points are as Brahmsian

176

Quintet

as are typically Elgarian the chromaticism at cue no. 30, the enharmonic slip from the dominant seventh of C♯ into C major at cue no. 40, and the lingering interrupted cadences which follow it.

The Quintet is cyclic, for both the themes from the opening Moderato of the first movement reappear in the last, one as an introduction, the other, the octave piano motto theme, in the development, where it sheds light on two others. At the end of the exposition or at the beginning of the development (there is no clear line of demarcation) comes a new theme:

Ex. 28

Soon afterwards a statement of the motto theme in the extended form it took in the first movement shows a relationship between the two:

Ex. 29

The new theme immediately follows, its intervals enlarged, but with a cello counterpoint which also acknowledges the motto theme:

Ex. 30

At once comes a ghostly presentation of the second subject from the first movement, with yet again the same figure:

Ex. 31

Of course, the intervals are not exact; the drop of a sixth is a fingerprint of Elgar's and the similarity between the themes may be just

Chamber Music

coincidence. But it is their contiguity that makes the similarity noticeable, and in this working-out section Elgar chooses to gather together the motto theme, one idea from the first and one from the last movement, and through a nebulous atmosphere just lets the family likeness be discernible.

The Quintet is a big work and also a baffling one, which does not quite measure up to the standard the composer obviously set himself. Inconsistency of style is its demerit. Every now and again there is an incongruous reminder of Elgar's early *salon* style. The piano is the worst offender. The writing for it is nowhere adventurous, and in the first movement shows plainly that Elgar did not understand it as he did the strings. At the very opening it is given a theme beyond its power to sustain, and in some of the big climaxes the writing is clumsy in its attempt to get maximum sonority from the instrument. Bernard Shaw's comment on the piano writing in the chamber works, though wrapped in blarney, was pertinent:

There are some piano embroideries on a pedal point that didn't sound like a piano or anything else in the world, but quite beautiful, and I have my doubts whether any regular shop pianist will produce them: they require a touch which is peculiar to yourself, and which struck me the first time I ever heard you larking about with a piano.[1]

Elgar's confessed wish to write a quintet in which the piano was one of five may account for the fact that often it is given nothing more than obvious accompaniment, yet its position is indeterminate, because in both the Allegro movements it is put in direct opposition to the strings at climaxes in concerto fashion. Perhaps he never really got 'to like the piano better.'

The three movements of the Quartet (1918) are refined and precise. The texture is at times almost Mozartian in its purity, and the middle movement has a veiled intensity that brings to mind the first movement of Mozart's G minor Quintet: both have as an important feature those anacruses leaping on to a discord, though the minor ninths of Mozart are fiercer than the diminished sevenths of Elgar. Elgar's movement has that winsome quality and quiet-minded reflectiveness, with yet a

[1] Letter to Elgar, 8th March 1919.

Quartet—Violin and Piano Sonata

disturbing undercurrent of melancholy, that is an atmosphere peculiarly his own, often, as here, found in music with his direction *piacevole*.

The first movement reverses Elgar's usual plan of tension and relaxation in sonata form. The symphonies start off with a sweeping exposition at a steady pace and with tremendous impetus, and in the developments the pace slackens as fragments are presented in isolation; here the opening is tentative, capricious in tempo and mood, and the working-out section builds up by figural development to the climax of the movement. The last movement too is formally of interest. For the only time Elgar uses *Bogen* as an alternative to sonata form: immediately after the development the second subject is recapitulated before the first subject, which returns at the end just before a coda which draws on both.

The Quartet is real chamber music in its intimacy and excellent craftsmanship: none of its ideas is too expansive for the medium, and the music has the vitality of a sensitive, highly strung nature. The Quintet may be a bigger work, but it is less near perfection than the Quartet.

The Violin and Piano Sonata is the most lyrical of the three works written in 1918. A feature of both the outer movements is that they have proportionately very short developments and long recapitulations: in the first, part of the development is repeated just before the coda, and in the last, at the corresponding point, the tune from the middle of the slow movement is recalled, now in augmentation. The first part of the slow movement, 'Romance,' has an exotic sound; as a young man Elgar wrote several pieces whose music was less Spanish than their titles, but in this and in one theme in the Quintet the flavour is certainly un-English. His environment may have had something to do with this,[1] and with the pastoral serenity found in the music of this period, which was written in his Sussex woodland retreat.

The importance of these three works as the nexus of a modern English school of chamber music is considerable. At the same time, they are conservative, especially harmonically. They break no new

[1] See page 209.

Chamber Music

ground and are considerably less modern than, say, *Gerontius*. They give the impression that Elgar was no longer questing, no longer driven by unfulfilled ideas, but was creating out of a mind that had been fully stretched and was now satisfied, and therefore not working under such high pressure. The invention is no less ready, but less urgently propelled. Though the Quartet has something of the old nervous energy, the Quintet and Sonata spread themselves with a leisurely ease—which made for more contented music, but was not auspicious for the future.

CHAPTER XVI

MUSIC OF POMP AND CIRCUMSTANCE

ELGAR had a unique place in the ceremonial life of his country, for though he held no official position until the end of his life, from the beginning he unashamedly poured out, side by side with his other works, music hymning the country's greatness, catching the ear of the people, and earning him the niche of a musician laureate. Queen Victoria's Diamond Jubilee produced the first works of the kind, the *Imperial March* and *The Banner of St George*. From then on no national occasion found him wanting.

It has at times been fashionable to disparage Elgar's popular music.

I like to look on the composer's vocation as the old troubadours or bards did. In those days it was no disgrace for a man to be turned on to step in front of an army and inspire them with a song. For my part, I know that there are a lot of people who like to celebrate events with music. To these people I have given tunes. Is that wrong?

Of course it was not; and Elgar's own apologia, recorded in the *Strand Magazine* in May 1904, is as good as any. He had a natural *penchant* for the spirit-stirring drum and the royal banner. Though war is no longer glorious and his marches suit better the military parades of peace-time, it is no mean thing to have written a tune so adopted as a national symbol that, in its fifty-first year, it was not only played at the coronation of a queen but was sung by the fifteen survivors of a Grimsby trawler while waiting, with the sea breaking over them, to be rescued from their sinking ship. His five military marches, *Pomp and Circumstance*, were an avowed attempt to treat the march to a full-dress uniform without forgetting its functional purpose. They and his other marches, some so named, others—especially in the cantatas—unnamed but of obvious derivation, are nearly all of the type that have a section of crisply vigorous or grandly processional rhythm alternating with a broad, agreeable tune, first in a related key and then in the tonic. The first *Pomp and Circumstance* march

Music of Pomp and Circumstance

(which begins on E♮ though its key is D major, as Elgar gleefully pointed out to 'Dorabella') and the fourth are like this; the third and fifth have the *cantabile* central tune, but the opening of the third is brusque and dark, and the bread in the sandwich of the fifth is a gay jig. The second has no bland middle tune, for the trio is brisk; the opening, for all its alert rhythm, is minor in mood as well as mode.

Elgar was no culprit for writing music like this, except, perhaps, that lesser composers might have written it equally well while Elgar could have been using the time to write something which lesser composers could not—though there is no guarantee that he would not have used it to fly a kite. The fact that he wrote 'Land of Hope and Glory' or—far worse—*The Crown of India* can no more damage *Gerontius* than *The Battle of Vittoria* can damage the Ninth Symphony. But the critical problem is not so simple as that. What one cannot do is to treat Elgar's pomp and circumstance manner as a watertight compartment of his style: unpalatable to the purist or admirable in its proper place, popular music, if one takes a healthy enjoyment in a plain tune. For this manner is not reserved for the march, the song, and the ceremony. To some degree it permeates all his music. The dichotomy was not, as in Sibelius, to whom there is a superficial resemblance, complete. In Sibelius's symphonies there is no trace of the *Romance in D♭* or *Valse triste*: the two sides of his nature are distinct and do not intrude upon each other. But Sibelius himself said of Elgar that he wrote 'pages of magnificent music and then, without warning, lapsed into a few bars of vulgarity, only to recover himself as if he had never written a bar below his best.'[1] Elgar's problem, like Kipling's, was how to reconcile the drummer-boy and the poet within him. One example which shows the interrelationship of the two styles is that it is possible to trace the descent of the opening progression of Elgar's greatest sustained tunes from his facile, on-the-surface type. The 'sumptuous banquet' tune in *The Black Knight* begins on the mediant and passes, slightly decorated, through the subdominant to the dominant over a bass moving in thirds with it in the harmony I, ^{7}Vc, Ib. The 'bringer of light' motif from *The Light*

---

[1] Gerald Abraham (ed.), *Sibelius* (Oxford).

The Poet and the Drummer-boy

of Life has precisely the same framework. The melody and bass which begin the 'comfort' motive in *The Apostles* are again the same, but expanded by decoration and interpolated chords and with the harmony altered to I, II, III. The tune of 'Nimrod' has the same melodic outline, but the second bass note makes the interval of a sixth with it, for IVb has been substituted for the ⁷Vc of the first example. The opening of 'Softly and gently' from *Gerontius* has the identical framework as 'Nimrod.' All these tunes begin alike. In the progressive deepening of their character, technically achieved by substitution or addition of chords and passing-notes, can be seen not only the gradual growth of one style into the other, but also how close fundamentally the two are.

Furthermore, fingerprints often appear in the major works which have their origin, stylistically, if not always chronologically, in his popular manner. Brass rattling its way up or down part of a chromatic scale is as familiar a sound at cue no. 16 in the First Symphony as in the *Coronation March*. The bluster of bass passing-notes comes at 'The Lord hath chosen him' in *The Apostles* as well as at 'Be brave if your cause be right' in *The Banner of St George*. Marching crotchets form the bass of such august moments as the opening of both symphonies and the final climax of the *Introduction and Allegro*, as well as the trio of many a march. Accompanying parts start off sleekly in thirds and sixths under the 'light and life' motive in *The Apostles* and in 'At the Beautiful Gate' in *The Kingdom*, as well as under tunes like 'The Flag of England' in *The Crown of India* and the trio of *Pomp and Circumstance* No. 3. The syncopation ♪♪♪, a frequent idiom of Elgar's, is commonly the only rhythmic interest in the expansive tunes of his march trios (it is prominent in 'Land of Hope and Glory'), and in the tunes which are connected by their words with patriotic feeling (two of the *Spirit of England* themes show it). But it is also found, slightly disguised, in many of the tunes of the same stock but better breeding like 'A presage falls upon me' in *Gerontius*, where the first quaver is tied to the preceding note, and Prince Hal's theme in *Falstaff*, where the figure is augmented and the last note tied to the succeeding one. The occasional interest given to this trio type of tune by an upward thrust of passing-notes in the tenor, such as in the

Music of Pomp and Circumstance

Empire March, is found too in the finest of all this class, the great
processional 'Go forth' in *Gerontius*. The swaggering thump on the
off-beats, a feature of *Pomp and Circumstance* No. 3, is one of Elgar's
most persistent rhythmic mannerisms. It comes with vigour where
the cellos take over the first subject in the opening of the First Symphony, with revelry *con fuoco* at the Boar's Head, and with magnifi-
cence in the Second Symphony's funeral march, while its echo can be
heard in the first bar of the Violin Concerto and in the harmonization
of the 'judgment' theme on the first page of *Gerontius*.   Linked with
this, and springing from the same need of the march to sound each
pulse-note, is his habit of marking emphatically in the accompaniment the beats of any sustained note in voice part or tune.   *The
Music Makers* abounds in examples: one occurs between cue nos. 35
and 36 at the words 'Or one that is coming to birth.'   The lead into
a big tune commonly calls it forth: the two bars before 'Go forth in
the name' in *Gerontius* and the six bars before the recapitulation in the
first movement of the Second Symphony show it plainly.

Mannerisms which he adopted from his popular style can be pin-
pointed so. What must be less specific is how successfully he
integrated his popular and his symphonic styles in his big works.   In
Froissart and *Cockaigne* the problem is not very great, for here the
militarism is frankly idealized as chivalry.   An example of their
perfect integration would seem to be the last movement of the Cello
Concerto.   Here are the two-bar phrases, the first bar made of two
detached notes, the second of a brisk rhythmic group, so reminiscent
of *Pomp and Circumstance* No. 1; here can be found the off-beat
swagger, the brassy punctuation chords, the plodding quaver bass,
the trombone semitone runs—all the insignia of his ceremonial
manner, yet transformed by a charity and a tolerance that leave far
behind the brash perkiness of pomp and circumstance.   In *The Spirit
of England* sentimentality was heated to compassion and in *Falstaff*
bravado was turned to proper pride.   He was not always as successful.
The finale of *Enigma* has not quite shed the bumptiousness of the
military march, and in *The Music Makers* he tried to express in one
style what properly belonged to the other.   Often his neatly matched
phrase-lengths become monotonous.   Many a four- or two-bar

The Integration of the Two Styles

phrase in the major works seems shaped for tramping feet; Elgar's predilection for the popular at times limits his sensitivity. The mannerisms will not stand exaggeration, and when rhythmic idioms from his pomp and circumstance manner occur at climaxes of an oratorio the disparity of style is noticeable. For instance, in *The Kingdom* the off-beats of the 'supplication' theme, which was first played by two violas, clarinet, and muted horn, are at the words 'Of his own will, God brought us forth' (cue no. 116) blared out by brass; and the 'new faith' theme, originally as gentle as falling dew, at the end of the same Act (cue no. 121) has each beat stamped out by full orchestra. Such things reduce the courts of heaven to the size of a parade-ground.

It has been argued in defence of Elgar that he believed as sincerely in his popular as in his great music. That was undoubtedly but unfortunately so. It occasionally led him to accept as heaven-sent whatever his spontaneous invention suggested. That his invention was at worst capable of the trite and the trivial cannot be denied, and his taste was no touchstone for appropriateness, no certain diviner of worth. He could write and revel in the honest heartiness of pomp and circumstance and the sweet commonplaces of *salon* music, but where in his deeper works his popular style is either not eliminated or not fully integrated, his music can jar and grate and suddenly displease. To invest the superficial with the significance of a profundity or to deck true excellence with gaudy trappings is not only inartistic but false. Elgar's discrimination was not always acute enough to compel him to reject the obvious and to search and select and ultimately sift what was irrefutably right.

Yet perhaps the conclusion of the whole matter is that his vulgarity is the over-exuberance of a vital, fertile genius: his music is never open to the charge—which he would have despised—of being scholarly or academic. Constant Lambert [1] told how, on the one occasion they met, Elgar, speaking of his early days and influences, talked exclusively of Italian opera, as he had heard it from touring companies. His flamboyance has a touch of grand opera about it, entirely alien to his

---

[1] 'Elgar and the Theatre,' *Referee*, 4th March 1934.

Music of Pomp and Circumstance

geographical surroundings. His full-blooded style was a welcome transfusion into contemporary English music, which suffered from anaemia and which had no other figure of his stamina. Had he been more fastidious, he might well have been less great. The broad appeal of his music to his countrymen is surely due, as Parry said, to the fact that he touched the hearts of the people. This he did by drawing on his popular style, at best refined and concentrated, in all his music.

Besides marches, Elgar wrote occasional music for the theatre, the war, and royal events.

In the same way as the bassoon *Romance* seems to have been run up from remnants of *The Kingdom*, so the *Coronation Ode* (1902) uses many themes that would not be out of place in *Caractacus* or *King Olaf*. The chorus in 'Britain, ask of thyself' would suit equally well the hosts of Caractacus and Claudius, and the recitative is of the hail-fellow-well-met type, of triplet and Scotch snap, that Elgar adopts for the armed forces. The next number is even more in the style of the cantatas. In the chorus added for the queen at the 1911 coronation Elgar's flexible approach to scansion (by no means always a virtue of his) is pleasant. The poem has three verses, of which all the lines are in identical metre. Unexpectedly he makes welcome what is an ordinary enough tune by the variety of his phrase-lengths. Even 'Daughter of ancient kings,' which is the weakest number (though how characteristic is that melodic minor rising cadence), is phrased 2+2+3+2. The most impressive, opening chorus holds something of the place in Elgar's choral music that *In the South* does in the orchestral, for it has the same grand overture style. To end this chorus and again to end the ode Elgar uses the trio from *Pomp and Circumstance* No. 1. Good enough though it is in a march, it is not strong enough to bear a nation's pride. It is, however, worth noticing that Elgar did not set the words quite as badly as custom has allowed them to be sung.

The Crown of India, a masque produced on the occasion of the royal visit to India in 1912 (though in 1903 its introduction illustrated the 'sinful growth' of the bulldog Dan), reaches rock-bottom in Elgar's

Odes, Masques, and Mélodrames

occasional music. It is pompous and it is trivial, but then Mogul emperors, 'John Company,' and nautch-girls, with St George thrown in, are not the best inspiration. Much of it is declamation over necessarily scrappy bits of music, and of the interludes only the title-march is at all good, and that is overshadowed by the *Coronation March* (1911), which is of the same kind but better. The offertorium for the same coronation, though there is overmuch syrup in its chromaticism, is on quite another plane, and so is the short, gracious ode in memory of Queen Alexandra (1932).

From his incidental music for the theatre a slight minuet from *Beau Brummell*, one dance from the ballet *The Sanguine Fan,* and nothing at all from *King Arthur* was published. He wrote a handful of songs and dances for the children's fantasy play *The Starlight Express*—the excerpts from *The Wand of Youth* are the best of them. The fanfare and wisp of song from Yeats's *Grania and Diarmid* can have no existence apart from the play, but the funeral march well deserves an occasional hearing.

Of the war pieces, *Carillon* (1914), *Polonia* (1915), *Une Voix dans le désert* (1915), and *Le Drapeau belge* (1917), only *Carillon* has stood the test of time, and was still able to stir some feeling with Laurence Binyon's new words for it written during the Second World War, when Cammaerts's original poem inciting the Belgians to revenge was outdated. The four notes from tonic down to dominant sound, as might a chime, right through the work, pulsating beneath and between the declaimed verses; the three-beat bars thrust the accent on to each note in turn. *Mélodrame* such as this might easily have been only superficially effective, but this music has a reckless, fiery surge and, at moments, the gentleness of 'Novissima hora est,' which one phrase melodically resembles. *Une Voix dans le désert* and *Le Drapeau belge* are recitations over music of the same type, but shorter and poorer. Two of the ideas in the latter, one harmonic and one rhythmic, sound like chips off the block of *For the Fallen* of the year before. *Polonia* is an orchestral prelude which borrows tunes from Poland, Chopin, and Paderewski.

The finest work by Elgar as musician laureate is *The Spirit of England* (1916–17), which comprises three poems from *The Winnowing-Fan*

Music of Pomp and Circumstance

by Laurence Binyon, set for tenor or soprano solo, chorus, and orchestra. The theme is the sacrifice demanded by the First World War, and the music has a dignity and a breadth that make it less ephemeral than Elgar's other war music. The direction *grandioso* occurs more than once in the score, but there is not a trace of the grandiloquence that the sentiment might unhappily have aroused, though the first movement is less distinguished than the other two. In this the demon music from *Gerontius* does duty for the enemy. The second and third movements, *To Women* and *For the Fallen*, contain music of a high order. *For the Fallen*, which is the longest of the three and is traditionally performed on Armistice Day, falls into four sections. There is a solemn and restrained opening; an ironic march of gay rhythm and sad harmony, 'They went with songs to the battle'; a wonderful *in memoriam* passage with a keening accompaniment and the exquisite falling cadence, 'At the going down of the sun'; and a recapitulation of the opening. It detracts not one whit from this noble movement to know that the tune at cue no. 1 and the modula-tion introducing it were first used in 1902 to illustrate a mood of Dan, Sinclair's bulldog.

CHAPTER XVII

STYLE AND QUALITY

ELGAR's early style is to some extent influenced, very naturally, by the music with which he grew up. This consisted largely of the oratorios of Mendelssohn, Spohr, and Gounod, which, with those of their imitators, were then at the height of their very considerable popularity. Mendelssohn formed the staple fare of the Three Choirs Festival during Elgar's teens and twenties, and Spohr's *The Last Judgment* was performed in 1874, 1876, 1880, and 1885, as well as other music of his during the same period. (Elgar first played in the orchestra in 1878, but it would have been strange if he had not attended performances, and most probably rehearsals, of earlier festivals.) Gloucester did Gounod's *Redemption* in 1883 and followed it with *Mors et Vita* in 1886 and *Messe solennelle* in 1889, but Gounod's influence was already widespread by then, and Elgar's unpublished *Salve Regina* of 1876 owes something to it. Of his two published settings of O *Salutaris* one is very like Gounod except for an 'Amen' of which Spohr would have been proud, and the other sets off as fair Mendelssohn. Mendelssohn's chief bequest to Elgar's early style is a particular type of melody, sweetly docile or placidly pious, never less than respectable in Mendelssohn, but in Elgar, who had not Mendelssohn's natural refinement, a trifle fulsome. Such tunes as Mendelssohn's two-part song 'Greeting' have a large progeny in Elgar's music, and the end of *King Olaf*:

Ex. 32   Strong-er than steel   is the sword of the Spi-rit

Style and Quality

seems to have sprung Minerva-like from *Elijah*:

Ex. 33 Now by this I know that thou art a man of God

From Gounod Elgar probably acquired his taste for consecutive root-position triads. At the end of *The Redemption* ('Is one with the Father in everlasting Trinity') there is a curious anticipation of the 'prayer' motive in *The Apostles*: both melodic lines move up by step over, in Gounod, triads of B♭ major, G minor, E♭ major, C minor, and so on, and in Elgar, more adventurously, E♭ major, A minor, F major, B minor, and so on. The likeness is the more marked because in both cases the accompaniment is of repeated chord triplets. There are other early reflections of Gounod, mainly in the religious music, though one such is the C major episode in the Allegretto of the Organ Sonata. Conspicuous in Elgar's oratorios is the flattened sixth of the key, particularly at cadences ('He will remember their sin no more' in *The Apostles*), which was among the common currency of Spohr and Gounod. Passages like 'Each the father's heart embraces' in *The Black Knight* and 'As torrents in summer' in *King Olaf* equal in tasteless sentimentality Sullivan's 'O pure in heart' (*The Golden Legend*) and Spohr's 'Blest are the departed' (*The Last Judgment*), though Elgar used the same unaccompanied part-song style with more distinction in the *Coronation Ode* and *The Spirit of England*.

Elgar's chromaticism is to some extent derived from that of Spohr. Spohr favoured cadences of chromatically descending consecutive thirds or sixths over a dominant or tonic pedal. The middle of 'Thou only hast the words of life' in *The Light of Life* shows an early Elgar adaptation of this, and in the later oratorios, particularly *The Apostles*, he carried what is essentially Spohr's procedure much further. Mary Magdalene's wandering chromatic chords over pedal notes, the cadence which ends the introduction to 'By the Wayside,'

Early Musical Environment

and the cadence which first introduces the 'new faith' theme in the prelude of *The Kingdom* are examples of Elgar's development of Spohr's sliding chromaticism. Allowing for Elgar's greater strength and complexity, the assimilation of Spohr's influence is clear in a comparison of character, melodic line, harmonic progression, and doubling of parts between this from *The Last Judgment*:

Ex. 34

and this from *The Apostles*:

Ex. 35

This is not, of course, to say that Elgar's style is nothing but an aggregate of influences. In the enervating atmosphere of the music current in his formative period, which at its worst achieved no more than a flabby fluency, any but a strong original talent was unlikely to survive. But what may sometimes be felt as a strain of excessive emotionalism in his sacred music would not have been discouraged by his environment. Both his indebtedness to his early background and his individual superiority to it are seen by comparing 'When thou art in tribulation' from *The Apostles* with Gounod's 'They are blessed, the poor in spirit' from *The Redemption* or Stainer's 'That whosoever believeth in Him' from *The Crucifixion*. Elgar falls naturally into the same technical idiom, triple time with gentle suspensions, to express the same idea, spiritual consolation, but illumines it with an

Style and Quality

unearthly radiance quite beyond the power of a Gounod, not to mention a Stainer.

What is remarkable is how from such unproductive soil, and with so few of the conventional advantages, his personal style emerged so early, was so distinctive, and remained so consistent. It became necessary to coin the word 'Elgarian' to epitomize the indescribable but immediately recognizable manner and quality of his music. This is of course partly due to his oft-repeated turns of speech. There is his liking for the interval of the seventh, often coupled with the sixth, one rising, the other falling (see *Enigma*, example 23, page 159). Colles went so far as to say: 'One or other of them (but most frequently both together) is certain to come as the point of the tune, at the moment when the composer says: this is what I really mean,' and concluded: 'It might almost be said that his whole output is a series of variations on one melody which was the essence of his being.'[1] Elgar's frequent leaps on to accented passing-notes make his tunes (and often inner parts) strong but pliable, moving by alternate spring and step, tension and release.

Ex. 36

The above example is from *Falstaff*; the end of the exposition of the Second Symphony's last movement shows the same shape; and the stretch of the seventh and the accented dissonance combine with a pang in the Cello Concerto's peroration. Reed noted as characteristic the imperative upward surge of strings in *Froissart*, and compared it with the *Serenade*; the following examples, taken from *Froissart*, the *Serenade*, *Chanson de matin*, the funeral march from *Grania and Diarmid*,

[1] *The Times*, 1st April 1939.

Melodic and Rhythmic Fingerprints

the First Symphony, *Enigma* (B.G.N.), and *For the Fallen*, in that order:

Ex. 37

show how engrained in his mind was this melodic shape, rising by ever-widening intervals as though reaching for the sky. Often his themes make a great octave spring within themselves (for example, in the 'Londoner' and 'lovers' themes in *Cockaigne*). Characteristic too are the billowing curves which open the early *Serenade*, 'W.N.' and 'Romanza' from *Enigma*, and the Allegro of the *Introduction and Allegro*, and these also show the wide compass, essentially instrumental, that his themes cover. His music is energized by accentuated rhythm and fluctuating *rubato* and dynamics, making it sometimes restless and feverish but always alive; there is hardly a note without an expression mark, hardly a bar without an ebb and flow of volume or speed (for which he invented his own signs, see example 45, page 200). All these things add up to give his tunes the swoop and soar, the ardour and the richness, the vehemence and the stress that are their hall-mark.

His themes are commonly made from one rhythmic pattern. *The Music Makers* opens with twenty bars of ♩♩ | ♩ . The second subjects of the first movements from the Quartet and Second Symphony are but repetitions of ♩. ♩♩♩ . A favourite pattern is a dotted crotchet and a quaver as, for instance, in the 'captives' motive in *Caractacus*, the main subject of the First Symphony's last movement (again for twenty bars the rhythm is unbroken), and two of the themes from *Falstaff* (a bit of one, as well as a similar boyish tune, is quoted on page 175). The shorter note always received due weight under Elgar's baton. 'Don't starve the quaver,' was his frequent plea. The lilting compound-time rhythm ♩♪♩ ♪ makes the themes of Olaf's 'grace and beauty' and of 'inexpressive lightness' in *Gerontius*, and can be found unbroken for great stretches in the *salon* piece *Rosemary*, in the first movement of the Second Symphony, and yet again, bar after bar, in the first movement of the Cello Concerto. The most

Style and Quality

striking example of Elgar's habit of making a long and in this case complex theme by repeating one short pattern is the main subject of the Second Symphony's last movement: a theme of eight bars, all but the last of which are ♩.♩ ♫♫ ♫ .

This fundamental habit of increasing length by repetition is most clearly seen in his sequences. Sometimes the sequence is of just a couple of notes within a melody, pulling it together, as do the fifth and sixth bars of the slow movement from the First Symphony. Usually, as here, the pattern of rhythm as well as of pitch is repeated, though in the *Enigma* theme (see example 23, page 159) the sequences of which it almost entirely consists are disguised by the rests and alternating rhythmic groups. Often a tune is made from a couple of bars which just shift up and down the scale in a melodic tonal sequence (see *Introduction and Allegro*, example 22, page 157). As frequent as proper sequences are passages made sequentially, within which the intervals are varied enough to propel the music along but not to destroy the character of the original, as often when the same rhythmic figure is preserved for many bars.

What makes Elgar's sequences individual is that more often than not they occur at a wider interval than that of a second. In melodic sequences he favours those a third apart, as in the 'new faith' theme from *The Kingdom*, which shows too the stressed second beat and the triplet, characteristic particularly of the cantatas but found in later works, as this and example 18, page 154, indicate:

Ex. 38

The cantatas and *Froissart* show another habit, that of moving not just a few notes but a unit of at least two bars in harmonic real sequence up or down by step, in rosalia, with lifeless and boring effect. How dangerous is it, however, to generalize, for it is precisely thus that the massive and superb sequence at 'Go, in the name' in *Gerontius* is built up (see example 56, page 211); here the exact repetition through three keys cumulates as does the majestic catalogue of angels and

Sequence—Modulation—Tonality

archangels, thrones and dominations, princedoms and powers, cherubim and seraphim. But on the whole in the mature works Elgar substitutes for the regularity of a good many of the early sequences ones which are inexact or do not move by step. In *The Kingdom*, at cue no. 79, 'He, who walketh upon the wings of the wind,' an eight-bar phrase in A♭ major is exactly repeated in A major, but separating the semitone statements, and so making them less square-toed, is one in E major. One type of sequence encloses the other at cue no. 13 in the Violin Concerto: five bars are repeated in exact sequence a minor third apart; the second bar sounds like a sequence by step of the first bar, but one interval is changed, so that the first beats of the two bars are a tone apart, the last beats a major third.

The potency of the sequence in Elgar's hands is as an instrument of modulation. The sequences of his maturity are the complement of his harmonic procedure, for their repeated pattern provides a connective thread in his swift modulations—or a screen on to which his ever changing harmonic lights can be projected—and by his flexible manipulation he sends them round the corner of whatever key he chooses. Consider this transformation of the 'Spirit of the Lord' motive from *The Apostles*:

Ex. 39

The pattern is repeated at the gap of a third; it is not quite exact, for the first interval in the melody is a semitone, in the repetition a tone; it is impossible to be dogmatic about the key of any given chord; the keys invoked are related to each other by the continuity of the pattern; and the passing abruptly through alien tonalities suggests mystery, which is what Elgar here wanted. The sequence, which happened to be for Elgar a natural way of thought, was one answer, and a good

Style and Quality

one, to the need of the particular stage of evolution harmony had reached by his period, when the utmost was being squeezed out of the major-minor key system and its potentialities for modulation.

Elgar is a tonal composer, for though he writes long stretches where it is impossible to pin down the key, so that apparently tonality is weakened and obscured, yet it is precisely this that opens up a harmonic hinterland beyond the immediate foreground. A modulation that enormously enlarges the background to a theme occurs in the slow movement of the First Symphony: when first heard this theme is in A major; it swivels on a bass note B into G major, then back to A; on its repetition it is in D♭ major, and it swivels as before on the supertonic, but this time makes an enharmonic change on it which topples the melody over by a semitone into C major—and by doing so expands its territory:

Again, in the last movement of the Second Symphony between 142 and 143 the first four bars are repeated, but by treating a melodic E♭ as a D♯ the second time the tonality rises for five bars from B♭ major into B major, from which the countryside looks fresh and new. The flow and propulsion in a characteristic passage of Elgar's owes much to his swift and fluid key changes, implied as often as established, together with his mobile, pliant bass line and his sinuous inner part-writing (often doubled at the octave), making glancing chromatic dissonances. At times he deliberately strikes a balance between keys: he will put chords (usually spread into arpeggios) implying different keys into direct antithesis. The four bars after cue no. 4 in *The Music Makers* each in turn suggest the keys of F, D, C, and A (three of the chords are dominant sevenths); in *The Apostles* at cue no. 21 a

Wagner

dominant seventh in the key of D major oscillates with B♭ major (the bars are derived from the motive 'Christ, the man of sorrows'); in *Gerontius*, dominant sevenths in the keys of E, C, and D are in turn pitted against a first inversion E♭ major triad—an inspired musical interpretation in balance, of the angel's 'I poise thee, and I lower thee, and hold thee.'

To attempt to refute or to deny Elgar's harmonic indebtedness to Wagner would be simply perverse. Elgar inherited from Wagner the full evocative vocabulary of chromaticism, decorated by suspensions, appoggiaturas, altered notes, and passing-notes, often concurrently in several parts; of delayed or eliminated resolutions, of free handling of high-powered chords, by which to express in dissonance from the most delicate to the most intense every degree of romantic emotion. It would be easy to point out progressions that Elgar had 'cribbed' from Wagner. One may perhaps see traces of the Wanderer's motives in Peter's or in Gerontius's 'O Jesu, help.' It is hard to miss the echo of the 'spear' motive at the opening of the First Symphony, or for the angel of the agony not to recall the agony of Amfortas. The 'Loge fire' motive (in its shape in the Prelude to *Götterdämmerung*) hints at the opening of the 'sleep' motive in *Gerontius*, and Herzeleide's motive at moments in the slow movements of the Second Symphony and the Cello Concerto—and the list could go on and on. Yet, when one hears these things, one recognizes Elgar's voice, not Wagner's. There are in the cantatas a few things which are not all of a piece and suggest undigested Wagner, such as Odin's motive in *King Olaf*. It cannot be disputed that without Wagner Elgar would not have written in quite the way that he did, but in Elgar's mature works, though much of their harmonic language he surely learnt from Wagner, there is no question of imitation: the thought is Elgar's own. His own comment to Jaeger in 1897 is not without humour: 'I forget if I told you I am appreciating your Wagner letters very much: go on—go on. It is nice to be told I am a sheep—but after all a bell-wether *is* something.' [1] The test of Elgar's originality is the wonder he can invoke by the most simple diatonic

---

[1] 18th October 1897

Style and Quality

music: consider the opening to Part II of *Gerontius*. One may admire the modernity of his harmony—his assured chromatic part-writing, his striking consecutives (the bass fifths which begin the rondo of the Second Symphony, for example), his resourceful modulations—and perhaps grow a little sated with it all in time; but that he can take an ordinary string of sixths or thirds and by setting them in contrary motion, reflecting them as if in a mirror, produce something as new-born as the opening of the Second Symphony's Larghetto or the orchard theme in *Falstaff* is proof of the creative imagination of genius.

In certain moods Elgar tends to avoid the exactness of the major seventh of the key at cadences, particularly in the minor. This shapes his melodic line: the character and melting loveliness of this cadence from *Gerontius*, which is immediately repeated sequentially, comes from the fall and rise in the sopranos from D to C♮ and back:

Ex. 41

and in the same way and in the same work the phrase from the 'Sanctus,' 'God is Three, and God is One,' dips gently to a flattened seventh and sixth before its end. The 'Spirit of the Lord' motive which opens *The Apostles* swings solemnly from A♭ major to F minor in ten chords, and the fact that not one has a determining G or E♮ in it deepens their mystery. The openings of Part II of *Gerontius* and the slow movement of the Violin Concerto are made serene and peaceful by plagal cadences. His pastoral music he often builds from the falling melodic minor scale and so saddens it a little, as when the sheer beauty of the countryside brings an ache as well as a delight. The 'pastoral' motive in *The Apostles* hovers round the minor seventh and sixth, and the theme evoked by a shepherd and his home-made music in *In the South* runs down in C minor from E♭

The Flattened Seventh

through D, C, B♭, and A♭ to G. A couple of bars from the orchard Interlude in *Falstaff* are hazy in their tonality because of their melodic scale, further blurred by parallel fourths and fifths:

and Reed noticed something in them 'strangely akin' to the wagoner's tune in the *Nursery Suite*—which moves from A up to natural Cs and Ds and down to natural Fs and Gs. 'Sadly merry' Elgar called his *Falstaff* Interlude, and how better can be described the touch of pathos which his minor intervals give to his country music? Sometimes a plain dominant chord is made minor, as in this pitying and tender half-close from *The Kingdom*:

and in the cadence of example 3, page 124. Elgar's fondness for the flattened seventh showed itself early, for in Op. 10 the *Mazurka* has a *pianissimo* tune which begins C♮, B♭, A, over a held D minor chord, and the *Sérénade mauresque* has a few bars rocking between A minor and E minor triads. The move away during Elgar's lifetime from the clear-cut major-minor tonality was of course partly dependent on the weakening of the leading note's function. It seems unlikely that the revival of folk-song or Tudor music fostered this characteristic in Elgar, for he was uninterested in either, but as a Roman Catholic

Style and Quality

he would from boyhood have been familiar with plain-song. His usually chromatic harmony takes a personal flavour from the flattened sevenths, melodic minor falls, and plagal cadences which at least in part give to his soft and gentle moods their pensive quality. Stronger than pensive, even anguished, is the effect in Magdalene's music in *The Apostles* of the D♮ and C♮, melodically emphasized, in the first two bars, which, although they have a signature of two sharps, sound more like E minor than B minor. And the disturbance of these flattened sevenths is violent in two places: the chord (in fact, the same in both) of the angel of the agony in *Gerontius* and of Golgotha in *The Apostles*. In both there is a leap to the minor seventh of the key which falls through the minor sixth to the fifth, but under the minor seventh at the octave is the major seventh, in direct and bitter contradiction.

The half-shy, half-impulsive moments in Elgar's music often come from a chord escaping from the prevailing tonality either to double back at once, as in the Violin Concerto:

or to turn right aside, as in the Second Symphony:

This was from the first a personal fingerprint. Even in the early anthem 'Jesu, meek and lowly' a cadence in A minor is deflected on to a six-three triad of G major. Always the unexpected chord is

Chromaticism and Counterpoint

itself simple; its aloofness comes from its alien context, it is lingered over in a sudden hush, and its effect is of a withdrawal, a shrinking for an instant into a secret self, that is the essence of Elgar the dreamer.

Elgar's chromaticism, though extensive, is usually dependent on semitonal movement of at least one part. A study of the motives of the religious choral works illustrates this. Reed compared the four bars before the letter K in Scene II of *The Black Knight* with those in Magdalene's scene in *The Apostles* at the fifth bar after 87. Both show a typical Elgarian progression, by semitone, often in parallel thirds or sixths, that nine times out of ten will sound sweet or pathetic, according to the context, but the tenth time cloying or whining. At worst, five bars before cue no. 220 in *The Apostles*, for instance, where chromatically descending melody, chromatically descending sixths in inner parts, diminished sevenths, and chords tied over the bar-line are all combined in sequence over a pedal, the proportion of the reaction may be inverted. What saves Elgar's music from sagging far more often than it does is the girders of his counterpoint.

It is one of his happiest gifts, this flow of natural and vital free counterpoint. He constantly refreshes the repetitions of his themes by slipping into them a new strand. The bent showed itself early, naïvely but definitely, in *Mazurka*, Op. 10. In the works of his prime, familiarity can never cheat of surprise and wonder the humour of the little horn and cello aside, thrown off with such apparent unconcern, under each repetition of the 'urchin' in *Cockaigne*; or the joyous lift given to the second subject of the Second Symphony's first movement when violins sweep over the top of it; or, in the same symphony, the bleak thread of oboe adding personal to monumental grief in the recapitulation of the Larghetto. His music is full of such gratuitous hidden treasures. It is as though the themes through sheer joy of life put forth spontaneously a new shoot. In fact Elgar knew well the value of it, for in his score of Mozart's Fortieth he scribbled against the bassoon in the recapitulation: 'New part added for poetical effect.'

Elgar believed in inspiration. Ideas came to him at any moment, some to be used at once, others to be stored in his pocket-book.

Style and Quality

When he was asked to contribute to a symposium on inspiration for an article in *The Chesterian*, his reply was more revealing of his character than of his music: 'I am obliged to you for your letter of Sept. 20th. I am not acquainted with *The Chesterian*, whatever that may be; but in any case I cannot undertake to furnish a memorandum on the subject you name.'[1] But had he not already given his answer to R. J. Buckley in 1904? 'Music is in the air—you simply take as much of it as you want,' and to Maine he broke off in a technical discourse to say: 'All this is beside the point because I *feel* and don't invent.' More informative of Elgar's working methods is Sanford Terry's account:[2]

In every movement its form, and above all its climax, were clearly in his mind. Indeed, as he has often told me, it is the *climax* which invariably he settles first. But withal there was a great mass of fluctuating material which *might* fit into the work as it developed in his mind to finality—for it had been created in the same 'oven' which had cast them all.

Yet even though Elgar planned the climax and the form first, the preliminary sketches for his big works suggest that he could never resist an afterthought. And how precious some of these afterthoughts are! Such a one was the fifth and sixth bars after cue no. 143 in *Falstaff*, two bars pasted on to the manuscript sketch[3], their place marked with an arrow in red pencil, obviously a sudden wayward blossoming: two bars like a spurt of compassion for the dying Falstaff. His rhapsodical mind was unsuited to consistently developed argument. 'You won't frighten me into writing a logically developed movement where I don't want one by quoting other people,'[4] he wrote as early as 1899 to Jaeger. The trait is shown in his letters and lectures, where he always permitted a minor point to divert him from the main issue, and his taste for lavishness comes out in Sir Barry Jackson's account of *The Spanish Lady*: 'The story was fined down to the uttermost dramatic limits in my version; but Sir Edward was

[1] *The Chesterian*, Jan.–Feb. 1928.
[2] Bound with sketches of the Second Symphony in possession of the Athenaeum Club.
[3] B.M. Add. MS. 47907 (see facsimile opposite). [4] 27th June 1899.

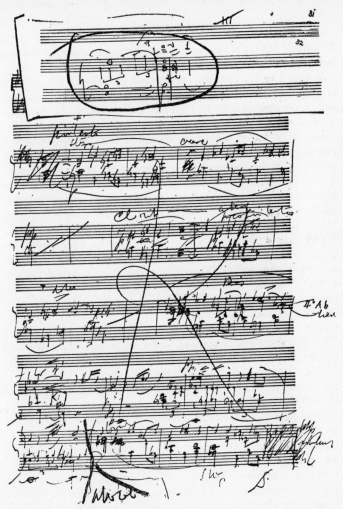

Facsimile of a page from the sketches for 'Falstaff.' (The large symbol like an 'R' is one Elgar apparently used to indicate that a fair copy of the page had been made)

Style and Quality

determined that the work should be on a grandiose scale; for he added incidents and complications without end.'[1] No professor took a blue pencil to his composition exercises or imposed discipline by pruning his ideas. With a composer whose lanes and byways are often more enticing than his high roads, might we not be the poorer if he had?

For Elgar has a method of symphonic development which is original. What he does in his developments is not to expound the properties of the material from his expositions or to set the main themes in contrast and conflict in the manner of the Viennese sym-phonists, or simply to reiterate them like the Russians, but, like Sibelius, to take snatches and fragments and make of them something new. Sibelius gathers his fragments and welds them into a solid mass. Elgar, quite differently, flits from one to another, never stating but always hinting, shedding a momentary gleam of light here and there: he reveals relationships between apparently unconnected themes. Often chronological sequence is waived, as it is his habit not to display the resemblances at first, so that with recognition comes astonishment and then illumination. In fact, the moment of illumin-ation is often not in the development itself but in the recapitulation. This is so in the First Symphony, where in the first movement several points of the development are clarified in the recapitulation, and in the Violin Concerto, where the melodic bond between three themes is established near the end of the last movement: the ideas are shown to be cognate after they have been separately presented. Sometimes he uncovers a tiny obscure detail, ponders over it, allows it to grow and produce what seems to be a new flower; but in its growth to unfold hidden relevance. The new theme in the Second Symphony's first movement and then the additional connection of the rondo's theme with that come about this way. This method of development is not confined to specific working-out sections or to movements in sonata form. The First Symphony reveals in slow motion such a relation-ship when its scherzo theme is transformed step by step for the slow movement. *Falstaff* gives an example of a 'new' theme afterwards

[1] W. H. Reed, *Elgar as I knew him* (Gollancz).

Method of Development

shown to be a counterpoint to a previous one, and the *Introduction and Allegro* connects two themes at first separate by running the same counterpoint with them.

Contrapuntal relationship is common. Sometimes a movement gives the impression that its themes must all move over the same harmonic ground at the same speed, so easily do they fit over each other, with never a tuck or bulge. In the second movement of the First Symphony a tune from the trio lingers carelessly above the return of the scherzo theme, and the scherzo on its second time round puts its own two themes in double counterpoint. Always the choice of the exact moment to reveal such a relationship is masterly. The end of both *The Apostles* and *Gerontius* is immeasurably strengthened by the revelation that the 'faith' and 'Christ's prayer' motives in the one, and the 'angel's farewell' and 'Lord, Thou hast been our refuge' in the other, all previously heard separately, lock together with splendid certainty. The last movement of the Second Symphony shows how important to Elgar was this relationship between themes. Forty-five bars before the end of the development (cue no. 152) he presents a theme derived from the second subject. Eight bars later he connects it with the first subject by working a figure from that contrapuntally with it. And then, at the recapitulation, as if to stress the relationship, he unexpectedly brings in a hint of it over the last bars of the first subject.

Elgar's developments, indeed whole movements, have a continual reaching forward and back, a fleeting allusiveness, that baffles and tantalizes a mind less perceptive, less nimble—and more logical—than his own. It is more fertile than cyclic form or a motto theme—though Elgar uses both as well—for besides creating unity within a work it is, by increasing the potentialities of the themes, a method of development. It plays havoc with the cogency and proportion of structure that are expected of a symphony, yet compensates by its intuitive and imaginative comprehension. It is as if imagery had taken the place of argument. Elgar's mind is poetical not only in what it expresses, but in its function, which is the perception of underlying resemblances. What was his *Enigma* if not just that?

Elgar's method of development, then, is personal and characteristic

Style and Quality

of his mind. This partly explains why, though he used principles of systematic leitmotives in his oratorios, the results do not sound much like Wagner's. For Wagner treated his leitmotives not only as symbols, modifying them as the dramatic action demanded, but also as musical subjects, developed in Beethoven's manner and spun into a symphonic web. Such motival development is not Elgar's most natural way. He frequently interlaces his leitmotives contrapuntally, but otherwise his treatment of them is more like that of mosaic: permutations of their order rather than modifications of individual ones. The introduction to Part II of *The Apostles* shows how his motives are arranged, chip by chip, in a new order to make a new pattern. It is much like the way in which the libretti were constructed, snippets from one Book being made into another, and his sonata-form first subjects, which sound continuous but can often be split up and the fragments rearranged, show the same tendency. Sometimes of course in the oratorios motives undergo metamorphosis, but as a general rule they are constant rather than variable, and one great difference between Wagner and Elgar lies in that fact. *The Apostles* and *The Kingdom* do not grow organically as *Tristan* does, and their form is the less strong because of it.

His mosaic method of construction is clearly seen in the sketches for his big works, which seem to have started from scraps and sections on individual sheets of paper with no intelligible indication of their order, but which ultimately were pieced together into his design. The sketches for the unfinished last works suggest that the scraps came into being easily enough but that the effort of final organization was too great: lack of concentration, not of inspiration, was what held back the Third Symphony and *The Spanish Lady*. There is something a little pathetic in Elgar's, after playing at being a country gentleman for some dozen years, having to take up again the labour and discipline of composition. The amount of material written for *The Spanish Lady* indicates that the moment of organization would not have been far off—the four dances are virtually complete, and some of the songs nearly so—yet it is impossible to evaluate a full-sized opera in such a piecemeal state, nor would it be possible, as Elgar so tragically realized, for other people to make anything of his

The Unfinished Works—Musical Images

sketches. As far as one can see there would have been no radical change of style.[1]

In Elgar's music similar mental images frequently find similar musical expression. This is of course most apparent in his vocal works, where the words give a clue to the underlying thought. Often these cross-references are between works roughly contemporary. In *King Olaf* and *The Light of Life* (both produced in 1896) the idea of deliverance from dark, wintry days, actual in the cantata:

Ex. 46 Allegro

symbolical in the oratorio (the preceding words are 'I will deliver them out of the places where they have been scatter'd'):

Ex. 47 Allegro

in each case brings a chord on B♮ sliding through a dominant seventh on B♭ to an E♭ triad, under a long, suspended soprano F♮.

[1] For detailed accounts of the unfinished works see:

Sir Barry Jackson, 'Elgar's Spanish Lady,' *Music & Letters,* January 1943. W. H. Reed, *Elgar as I knew him* (Gollancz) (The Third Symphony). Articles on the Third Symphony by Ernest Newman in the *Sunday Times,* 22nd September and 27th October 1935.

Article on Elgar in Grove's *Dictionary*, 5th ed.

Style and Quality

Extraordinarily alike in shape and effect are the swelling orchestral passages descriptive of the breaking of light, actual in the dawn scene in *The Apostles* (cue no. 34), symbolical in the interlude before the soul is 'quicken'd by the glance of God' in *Gerontius* (cue no. 101, Part II). In *The Kingdom* (cue no. 164) and *Gerontius* (5th and 6th bars after cue no. 107), farther apart in years, the feeling of exhilaration implicit in the words 'glorious' and 'thrilled' bursts out in each case into a warm downward-curling phrase for violins.

These passages, separated by eight years, express grief, caused in *Caractacus* by threat of exile:

and in *The Kingdom* by Judas's betrayal:

Musical Images

Reed pointed out that the first five notes and their harmony of the motto theme in the First Symphony had exactly occurred at the end (cue no. 82) of *Enigma*. There are no words here to give the context, but the emotional significance of both is undoubtedly triumph. The idea of danger or evil is often conveyed by two root-position triads, one major and one minor, in juxtaposition. The Black Knight tells the king that he destroys only those in the bloom of life—'Roses in the spring I gather'; and 'roses' is harmonized by G major and F minor triads. The foreboding orchestral theme during the reading of the bad omens in *Caractacus* begins with a chord of B♭ major, then of A♭ minor over a pedal B♭. In 'The Sweepers' the look-out calls 'Mines reported in the fairway' over D major, B♭ minor, D major triads.

As in this last example, sometimes the similarities are found in works years apart in composition. The dance in *The Black Knight* and the theme at cue no. 5 in the first movement of the Quintet have affinity of atmosphere, though no more factual resemblance than that the first half-dozen melody notes from both are, but for one semitone, an inversion of each other, and that both themes are built with a minor supertonic in tune and harmony. The clue to the mental image may be found in Reed's suggestion that the Quintet subject was inspired by a legend. Near the village where it was written stood some withered trees, which local people would have it were the forms of Spanish monks, struck by lightning while performing impious rites. The words of the Black Knight's dance include 'danced a measure weird and dark.'

One thematic figure seems to have for Elgar a connotation of divine influence or presence, for over it in *The Light of Life* is written in the score 'And he worshipped Him';

Style and Quality

it recurs in connection with inspiration in *The Music Makers* (the curved line indicates the melody):

and again in the slow movement of the Cello Concerto, which has the receptive stillness of communion:

Of particular interest in Elgar's development are the instances where an idea from one work is put to finer purpose in a later one. *Geron-tius* was in his mind for some eleven years, during which time *King Olaf* and *Caractacus* were written. These chords introduce the invocation to the god Taranis in *Caractacus*:

and this progression occurs four times during the intercession for the soul by the angel of the agony in *Gerontius*:

Musical Images

Ex. 54

The admission of Christian faith referred to in *King Olaf* where the heathen Sigrid refuses to renounce her gods but says to Olaf, 'Bow thou to thy cross':

Ex. 55 Bow thou to thy cross ____ for woe ____ or weal ____

is blazed out in *Gerontius*:

Ex. 56 In the name of An-gels and Arch-an-gels; In the name of Thrones and Domi-nations;

a sequence in each case of four chords, the first two being the same.

Between *The Black Knight* and *Falstaff* was a span of twenty years. Compare these passages and their contexts. The first occurs just after the death of the king's children, when the Black Knight claims his victims:

Ex. 57 Lento
In the Spring, ____ in the Spring, ____ in the Spring, I ga ____ ther.

Style and Quality

the second introduces Falstaff's death scene as delirium swamps him and memory wanders.

Ex. 58[1]

In both the thought is of death. In both the melody rises an octave from F♯ in four bars resting on the first beats, under each of which (with one exception) is a dominant seventh. The square four-part chording, the repeated words, the conventional harmonic resolutions, and the *crescendo* rob the Black Knight of mystery and terror. In *Falstaff* the wandering threads of violins rise over swaying unresolved discords to a muted *pianissimo*: the sick mind leaves the body and the strength seeps away.

The same mental image produced at fifty-six the same technical approach as at thirty-six; the difference in the emotional content is a yard-stick by which to measure the distance between Elgar's early and late work. In few other composers is the distance between so great. The change in Elgar at about the age of forty from a composer of talent into a composer of genius is one of the most puzzling things in the history of music. In 1890 he made his début with *Froissart*; for nearly ten years he produced respectable works of talent; at the turn of the century came *Enigma* and *Gerontius*; then twenty years of genius; then all but silence until his death. The change is the more astonishing because such weaknesses as are present in the lesser works are seldom wholly eliminated from the greater. It was not so much a purging or a refinement as a supplement: a quickening of the imagination. One may try to account for it by the fact that because he was self-taught his rate of development was slowed down, or by the fact that he had first to slough off the conventional skin of the provincial

---

[1] Over a MS. sketch of this Elgar wrote, as he sometimes did when obviously pleased by a passage, 'good.'

Tastes in Music

England where his work was done. Or one may attribute it to the stimulus of his wife, with whose death ended his own creative life; it is significant how often for the next few years he calls himself in his letters a 'broken' man. But though she best knew how to make him productive she did not directly turn him into a genius, for all his second-rate as well as first-rate music was written after their marriage: it was ten years after her influence began before he wrote *Enigma*. Perhaps all these things contributed. At bottom it must remain as incalculable as when a stream which springs and flows underground surfaces in its own time and becomes a river.

Elgar's musical taste was quite clear. He enjoyed music which, like his own, had 'tune, rhythm, and colour.' [1] He had no patience with cerebral patterns; it must be 'music with blood flowing in it,' though he had his limits and proprieties: 'To think that Gloucester Cathedral should ever echo to such music,' he said of Scriabin's *Poème de l'extase*. 'It's a wonder the gargoyles don't fall off the tower.' [2] He never lost his affection for things he had heard and played in his youth. Reed recounted how in his retirement he liked to play Spohr, Rubinstein, and Ries, how 'the fun he got out of *L'Oiseau de feu* and *Petruschka* never put Mendelssohn, Gounod, Grieg, and Schumann out of court,' how he once insisted on playing the whole of *Faust* as a piano duet, and how familiar and dear to him were *Messiah* and *Elijah*, which he had played at the Three Choirs. Strauss he pronounced in a Birmingham lecture (1905) to be the greatest living composer, and this he very probably believed as well as its being a politic reply to Strauss's salute three years earlier; his private comment on Strauss in 1902 was: 'Truly great man, somewhat cynical in his music but a powerful genius.' [3] He liked particularly Wagner, Berlioz, and Liszt; he liked Schumann, with whose introspective moods and characteristic pieces his own music has something in common, and whose *Carnaval* has notes which are not played as *Enigma* has a tune which is not heard. Though Elgar often pointed

[1] W. H. Reed, *Elgar as I knew him* (Gollancz).
[2] Foss and Goodwin, *London Symphony Orchestra* (Naldrett).
[3] Letter to Arthur Johnstone, 7th June 1902.

Style and Quality

out the weakness of Schumann's scoring and that of Brahms (whose music he found dull at times), he would have no 'tinkering with it.' He liked Puccini's *Tosca* and had some reference to it in his mind for *The Spanish Lady*, for one sketch bears its name with a query. He got great enjoyment from Meyerbeer, whose *Coronation March* his own marches imitate just enough to flatter. He had little use for English sixteenth- and seventeenth-century music, though he made an exception of Purcell's 'When I am laid in earth,' and his lack of interest in polyphonic music was not due to ignorance, for Sir Richard Terry [1] found that his study of it was careful and profound. He was helpful when he could be to younger composers, but seemed not over-enthusiastic about their work.

For though equipped with every technical skill and spurred by an adventurous mind, Elgar was a traditionalist. It is his special historical position that while nationally he marked decisively a renaissance, internationally he is at the end of an epoch. It is difficult now, when Elgar is part of our life, to recapture the thrill and pride with which his great works were received by a public who recognized his European stature but could claim him as English. Unlike Parry and Stanford, whose greatest importance may well be their cultural and educational influence rather than their achievements, Elgar never divided his energies: his music alone is his memorial. By it he bestowed new fortune on English music. 'Of all English composers,' wrote Shaw,[2] doubtless meaning contemporaneous composers, 'Elgar is alone for Westminster Abbey.'

Englishness in music cannot be defined: nor can it be quantitatively measured. It is a fact that foreigners think less highly of Elgar than we do—the French in particular have never understood him—and it may be that a special affinity with his countrymen limits his appeal to others. Folk-song meant nothing to him, though he was a founder member of the Folk Song Society, and he once answered a tactless question with '*I* write the folk-songs of this country,' but

---

[1] 'Elgar as I knew him,' *Radio Times*, 9th March 1934.
[2] *Music & Letters*, January 1920.

Position in History—An English Composer

English he was by birth, upbringing, and inclination. His patriotism was strong and blunt. He wrote to Jaeger about *Caractacus*: 'I knew you would laugh at my librettist's patriotism (and mine), never mind: England for the English is all I say—hands off! there's nothing apologetic about me.'[1] It has been said that when Elgar was not praising God he was praising England. He came into his own when England was powerful, backed by the solidarity of Victoria's reign and invigorated by the exuberance of Edward's. Certain aspects of the period found a natural response in him. It was a time which encouraged the worst in his nature, when superficially patriotism, in the face of surface security, was crude and complacent: some of what he wrote was ephemeral. It was also a time when there was much that was worth praising, and the zest, the resplendence, and the expansiveness of English life were Elgar's too. Often he sang the songs of his time and place, and if the *Zeitgeist* of the Edwardian age is no longer ours, our understanding of it is the greater and our heritage the richer for his interpretation of it. Yet when praising England he is an extrovert, and his music is most abidingly English when he muses and broods over her, reflects her shifting skies in his *Introduction and Allegro*, paints the slow movement of his Quartet with her soft water-colours, conjures up the fragrance of her West Country orchards in *Falstaff*, or turns a triplet and a couple of dotted notes into the ripple of a river. These things are changeless and have no period. They are English because they touch us exactly as does the English countryside and its reflection in English painting and English poetry. Fenby confessed that when he was working with Delius in France, if he felt home-sick it was always Elgar's music that stole into his mind. His musical habit of thought, by allusion and implication, gives him seisin of a land whose outlines are soft, whose people tend towards suggestion rather than clarity, and whose speech is rich in imagery.

Professor Dent took too much upon himself when he wrote: 'For English ears Elgar's music is too emotional and not quite free from vulgarity. His orchestral works . . . are animated in

[1] 12th July 1898.

Style and Quality

colour, but pompous in style and of a too deliberate nobility of expression.'[1]   But there was too much truth in the charge for it to be ignored.   Elgar's music is exceptionally dependent on the quality of its performance.   If it is over-emphasized it can sound pontifical and pretentious, its chromaticism slimy and its orchestration ostentatious. Some temperaments will always remain averse to it, as they will to any strong character which is not directly to their liking; but Elgar's music has character strong enough to command admiration even from those who dislike it.   He did not excel in all spheres.   He wrote no love music—which distinguishes him from Wagner and Strauss—and, like César Franck's, his sinners are less convincing than his saints.   He was an idealist, a visionary, and a dreamer, and the directions that he made peculiarly his own—*nobilmente, mistico*, and *piacevole*—lie at the heart of his music.   One of the last great romantics, in him the bloom of full summer has ripened into the rich yet regretful fall of autumn.   Right through his music runs a philosophy, touched at times with wistfulness, at times a fervent threnody, yet always humane and with ultimate consolation, that is fundamental and enduring.   Who turns to it to be fortified and to be healed will not depart unsatisfied.   'I send you my stately sorrow,' he wrote to Ernest Newman [2] on the manuscript of part of the Adagio of the third, uncompleted symphony; 'naturally what follows brings hope.'   He had the faith to commit himself, to assert his convictions, to be fired by his aspirations, and to share his dreams.   Elgar was no composer for cynics.

Critics frequently say of a man that it is to his credit that he is never vulgar. Good.   But it is possible for him—in an artistic sense only, be it understood —to be much worse; he can be commonplace. . . .   An Englishman will take you into a large room, beautifully proportioned, and will point out to you that it is white—all over white—and somebody will say what exquisite taste.   You know in your own mind, in your own soul, that it is not taste at all—that it is the want of taste—that it is mere evasion.[3]

---

[1] Article on modern English music in Adler's *Handbuch der Musikgeschichte* (second ed., 1930).

[2] *Sunday Times*, 27th October 1935.

[3] Birmingham lecture.

'*Nobilmente,*' '*Mistico,*' '*Piacevole*'

Elgar's words present his aesthetic belief. His music is sometimes vulgar; it is never evasive. His faults were those of over-generosity, not of minginess. He wrote his own epitaph when he asked at Birmingham that English music should have 'something broad, noble, chivalrous, healthy, and above all an out-of-door sort of spirit.' One may question his taste, but his invention, his uniqueness, his creation of immortal beauty—in short, his genius—never.

APPENDICES

Op.	Title	Author of Words
I	*Romance* (vln. and pf.)	—
IA	*The Wand of Youth* (orch. suite No. I)	—
IB	*The Wand of Youth* (orch. suite No. II)	—
2(i)	*Ave, verum corpus,* arr. for C. of E. service as 'Jesu, word of God incarnate'	—
2(ii)	*Ave Maria,* arr. for C. of E. as 'Jesu, Lord of life and glory'	—
2(iii)	*Ave maris stella,'* arr. for C. of E. as 'Jesu, meek and lowly'	—
3	*Cantique* (organ or orch.)	—
4(i)	*Une Idylle* (vln. and pf.)	—
4(ii)	*Pastourelle* (vln. and pf.)	—
4(iii)	*Virelai* (vln. and pf.)	—
5	'A Soldier's Song,' renamed 'A War Song' (male voices)	C. Flavell Haywar
6	Quintets and short pieces (2 flutes, oboe, clarinet, and bassoon)	—
7	*Sevillana* (orch.)	—
8	String Quartet	—
9	Sonata (vln. and pf.)	—

²US NUMBERS

mposed	Published	First Performance	Dedication
⁷9 or arlier	1885	?	Oswin Grainger
⁷9 or arlier	1907	14th December 1907, Queen's Hall, London. H. J. Wood	C. Lee Williams
⁷9 or arlier	1908	9th September 1908. Worcester Fes⁻ tival. E. E.	Hubert A. Leicester
?	1902	?	—
?	1907	?	Mrs H. A. Leicester
?	1907	?	Rev. Canon Dolman, O.S.B., Hereford
?	?	15th December 1912. Albert Hall, London (orch. version)	Hugh Blair
?	?	?	E. E., Inverness
?	?	?	Miss Hilda Fitton, Malvern
?	?	?	Frank W. Webb
384	1890	17th March 1884. Worcester Glee Club	F. G. P., Worcester
⁷7–9	MS.	1st December 1934. Sheffield	Various
?	1884	1st May 1884. Worcester Philhar⁻ monic Society	W. C. Stockley
early	MS. des⁻ troyed by E. E.	—	—
early	MS. des⁻ troyed by E. E.	—	—

Appendix A—Catalogue of Works

Op.	Title	Author of Words
10	Three Pieces (small orch.).	—
(i)	*Mazurka*	—
(ii)	*Sérénade mauresque*	—
(iii)	*Contrasts* (Gavotte, A.D. *1700–1900*)	—
11	*Sursum corda* (strings, brass, and organ)	—
12	*Salut d'amour* (orch.)	—
13(i)	*Mot d'amour* (vln. and pf.)	—
13(ii)	*Bizarrerie* (vln. and pf.)	—
14	Eleven Vesper Voluntaries (organ)	—
15(i)	*Chanson de matin* (small orch.)	—
15(ii)	*Chanson de nuit* (small orch.)	—
16(i)	'Shepherd's Song'	Barry Pain
16(ii)	'Through the long days' (song)	John Hay
16(iii)	'Rondel' (song)	Longfellow, after Froissart
17	*La Capricieuse* (vln. and pf.)	—
18(i)	'O happy eyes' (S.A.T.B.)	C. Alice Elgar
18(ii)	'Love' (S.A.T.B.)	Arthur Maquarie
19	*Froissart* (orch., concert overture)	—
20	*Serenade* in E minor (strings)	—
21	*Minuet* (small orch., originally pf.)	—
22	Very Easy Exercises (vln.)	—

Works with Opus Numbers

omposed	Published	First Performance	Dedication
1881	1899	Played as a suite and separately from 1883 onwards. Appear variously as *Pas Redoublé* and *Intermezzo*. Complete suite 1st March 1888. Birmingham	Lady Mary Lygon
		?	
		12th December 1883. Birmingham	
		?	
894	1901	9th April 1894. Worcester Cathedral	H. Dyke Acland
889	1889	11th November 1889. Crystal Palace, London	à Carice
?	1890	?	—
?	1890	?	—
890	1891	?	Mrs W. A. Raikes
?	1901	14th September 1901. Queen's Hall, London	—
?	1901	14th September 1901. Queen's Hall, London	Dr F. Ehrke
?	1895	?	—
?	1887	25th February 1897. St James's Hall, London	Rev. E. Vine Hall
?	1896	7th December 1897. St James's Hall, London	—
891	1893	?	Fred Ward
894	1896	?	—
894	1907	?	C. A. E.
890	1890	9th September 1890. Worcester Festival. E. E.	—
892	1893	7th April 1893, Larghetto only, Hereford 5th March 1905, complete, Bechstein Hall, London. E. E.	W. H. Winfield
1897	1899	16th July 1899. New Brighton	Paul Kilburn
?	1892	—	May Grafton

Appendix A—Catalogue of Works

Op.	Title	Author of Words
23	'Stars of the summer night' (partsong with orch.)	Longfellow
24	*Études caractéristiques* (vln.)	—
25	*The Black Knight* (cantata for chorus and orch.)	Uhland, trans. Lo▪ fellow
26	Two Partsongs (S.S.A.A., 2 vlns. and pf.): 'The Snow'	C. Alice Elgar
	'Fly, singing bird'	
27	*From the Bavarian Highlands* (6 choral songs with pf. or orch.)	Bavarian folksongs ad▪ ted by C. Alice E▪
28	Sonata in G (organ)	—
29	*The Light of Life* or *Lux Christi* (oratorio for 4 soli, chorus, and orch.)	Adapted from the Scr▪ tures by Rev. Capel-Cure
30	Scenes from the *Saga of King Olaf* (cantata for 3 soli, chorus, and orch.)	Longfellow and H. Acworth
31(i)	'After' (song)	Philip Bourke Marsto▪
31(ii)	'A Song of Flight' (song)	Christina Rossetti
32	*Imperial March* (orch.)	—
33	*The Banner of St George* (ballad for chorus and orch.)	Shapcott Wensley
34	*Te Deum* and *Benedictus* (chorus and organ)	*Te Deum* and *Benedi▪*
35	*Caractacus* (cantata for 4 soli, chorus, and orch.)	H. A. Acworth
36	*Variations on an original theme,* 'Enigma' (orch.)	—

Works with Opus Numbers

...posed	*Published*	*First Performance*	*Dedication*
?	1892	7th April 1893. Hereford Philharmonic Society	—
?	1892	—	Adolphe Pollitzer
?	1893	18th April 1893. Worcester Festival Choral Society. E. E.	Hugh Blair
?	1895		Mrs E. B. Fitton
		12th March 1904. Queen's Hall, London	
		?	
?95	1896	21st April 1896. Worcester Festival Society (choral version)	Mr & Mrs Slingsby Bethell, Garmisch
?95	1896	8th July 1895. Worcester cathedral	Dr C. Swinnerton Heap
?5–6	1896	10th September 1896. Worcester Festival. Anna Williams, Jessie King, Edward Lloyd, Watkin Mills. E. E.	Dr C. Swinnerton Heap
?5–6	1896	30th October 1896. North Staffs. Festival, Hanley. Medora Henson, Edward Lloyd, Ffrangcon-Davies. E. E.	—
?95	1900	2nd March 1900. St James's Hall, London	—
?	1900	2nd March 1900. St James's Hall, London	—
?	1897	19th April 1897. Crystal Palace, London	—
?	1897	18th May 1897. St Cuthbert's Hall Choral Society, London	—
?897	1897	12th September 1897. Hereford Festival	Dr G. R. Sinclair
?97–8	1898	5th October 1898. Leeds Festival. Medora Henson, Edward Lloyd, Andrew Black, John Browning. E. E.	H.M. Queen Victoria
?898	1899	19th June 1899. St James's Hall, London. Richter	'To my friends pictured within'

Appendix A—Catalogue of Works

Op.	Title	Author of Words
37	Sea Pictures (5 songs for contralto and orch.):	
	1. 'Sea Slumber Song'	Hon. Roden Noel
	2. 'In Haven' (orig. 'Love alone will stay')	C. Alice Elgar
	3. 'Sabbath Morning at Sea'	Elizabeth Barrett Brown
	4. 'Where corals lie'	Richard Garnett
	5. 'The Swimmer'	Adam Lindsay Gord
38	The Dream of Gerontius (oratorio for 3 soli, chorus, and orch.)	John Henry Newman
39	Pomp and Circumstance marches (orch.): No. 1 in D	—
	No. 2 in A minor	
	No. 3 in C minor	
	No. 4 in G	
	No. 5 in C	
40	Cockaigne (In London Town) (overture for orch.)	—
41(i)	'In the Dawn' (song)	A. C. Benson
41(ii)	'Speak, Music' (song)	A. C. Benson
42	Grania and Diarmid (incidental music): Funeral March 'There are seven that pull the thread' (song)	Play by George Moo and W. B. Yeats
43	Dream Children (2 pieces for pf. or small orch.)	After Charles Lamb
44	Coronation Ode (4 soli, chorus, and orch.)	A. C. Benson

Works with Opus Numbers

mposed	Published	First Performance	Dedication
897–9	1900	5th October 1899. Norwich Festival. Clara Butt. E. E.	—
899–900	1900	3rd October 1900. Birmingham Festival. Marie Brema, Edward Lloyd, H. Plunket Greene. Richter	A. M. D. G.
901	1902	19th October 1901. Liverpool	A. E. Rodewald and Liverpool Orch. Society
901	1902	19th October 1901. Liverpool	Granville Bantock
?	1905	8th March 1905. Queen's Hall, London	Ivor Atkins
?	1907	4th September 1907. Queen's Hall, London	G. R. Sinclair
930	1930	20th September 1930. Queen's Hall, London	Percy C. Hull
?	1901	20th June 1901. Philharmonic Society, London. E. E.	Members of British Orchestras
?	1901	26th October 1901. Queen's Hall, London	—
?	1901	?	Mrs E. Speyer Ridgehurst
1901–2	1902	Irish Literary Society, 1902	Henry J. Wood
		18th January 1902. Queen's Hall, London	
?	1902	4th September 1902. Queen's Hall, London	—
901	1902	2nd October 1902. Sheffield Festival. Agnes Nicholls, Muriel Foster, John Coates, Ffrangcon-Davies. E. E.	H.M. King Edward VII

Appendix A—Catalogue of Works

Op.	Title	Author of Words
45	*Five Partsongs from the Greek Anthology* (T.T.B.B.):	
	1. 'Yea, cast me from the heights'	Anon., trans. Alma Stret
	2. 'Whether I find thee'	Anon., trans. Andr Lang
	3. 'After many a dusty mile'	Anon., trans. Edmu Gosse
	4. 'It's oh, to be a wild wind'	Anon., trans. Wm. Hardinge
	5. 'Feasting I watch'	Marcus Argentari trans. Richard Garn
46	Pianoforte Solo	—
47	*Introduction and Allegro* (string quartet and orch.)	—
48	'Pleading' (song)	Arthur Salmon
49	*The Apostles* (oratorio for 6 soli, chorus, and orch.)	Compiled from the Scriptures by E. E.
50	*In the South*, 'Alassio' (overture for orch.)	—
51	*The Kingdom* (oratorio for 4 soli, chorus, and orch.)	Compiled from t Scriptures by E. E.
52	'Christmas Greeting' (carol for 2 sops., male chorus *ad. lib.*, 2 vlns., and pf.)	C. Alice Elgar
53	Four Partsongs (S.A.T.B.):	
	1. 'There is sweet music'	Tennyson
	2. 'Deep in my soul'	Byron
	3. 'O wild west wind'	Shelley
	4. 'Owls, an epitaph'	? Elgar

Works with Opus Numbers

omposed	Published	First Performance	Dedication
?	1903	25th April 1904. Albert Hall, London	Sir Walter Parratt
1901	MS. now lost	2nd December 1901. St James's Hall, London	Written for Fanny Davies
904-5	1905	8th March 1905. Queen's Hall, London. A. W. Payne, W. H. Eaynes, A. Hobday, B. Patterson Parker. L.S.O. E. E.	Prof. S. S. Sandford, Yale University
?	1908	?	Lady Maud Warrender
902-3	1903	14th October 1903. Birmingham Festival. Albani, Muriel Foster, John Coates, Kennerly Rumford, Andrew Black, Ffrangcon-Davies. E. E.	A. M. D. G.
1903	1904	16th March 1904. Elgar Festival, London. E. E.	F. L. Schuster
1905	1906	3rd October 1906. Birmingham Festival. Agnes Nicholls, Muriel Foster, John Coates, William Higley. E. E.	A. M. D. G.
1907	1907	1st January 1908. Hereford	G. R. Sinclair and Hereford Cathedral Choir
?	1907	?	Canon Gorton Julia H. Worthington Dr W. G. McNaught Pietro d'Alba

Appendix A—Catalogue of Works

Op.	Title	Author of Words
54	'The Reveille' (T.T.B.B.)	Bret Harte
55	Symphony No. 1 in A flat	—
56	'Angelus (Tuscany)' (S.A.T.B)	Adapted from the Tusca
57	'Go, song of mine' (partsong, 6 parts)	Cavalcanti, trans. Rosse
58	*Elegy* (string orch.)	—
59	Song cycle (orch. acc.): 3. 'Oh, soft was the song' 5. 'Was it some golden star?' 6. 'Twilight' (1, 2, and 4 never composed)	Gilbert Parker
60	Two Songs (pf. or orch.): 1. 'The Torch' 2. 'The River'	Folksongs of Easter Europe, paraphrased b E. E. and Pietro d'Alb
61	Concerto in B minor (vln. and orch.)	—
62	*Romance* (bassoon and orch.)	—
63	Symphony No. 2 in E flat	—
64	'O hearken thou' (offertory, chorus and orch.), also pub. as *Intende voci orationis meae* for coronation of George V	—
65	*Coronation March* (orch.)	—
66	*The Crown of India* (imperial masque for soli, chorus, and orch.)	Henry Hamilton
67	'Great is the Lord' (anthem for 4-part chorus)	Psalm 48
68	*Falstaff* (symphonic study for orch.)	After Shakespeare, *Kir Henry IV* and *V*

Works with Opus Numbers

Composed	Published	First Performance	Dedication
?	1908	17th October 1908. Blackpool Festival	Henry C. Embleton
907-8	1908	3rd December 1908. Manchester. Richter	Hans Richter
?	1908	8th December 1910. Albert Hall, London	Mrs Charles Stuart Wortley
1909	1909	9th September 1909. Hereford Festival	Alfred H. Littleton
1909	1910	13th July 1909. Memorial concert of the Worshipful Company of Musicians, London	Worshipful Company of Musicians
?	1910	24th January 1919. Queen's Hall, London	—
?	1909	11th September 1912. Hereford Festival	Yvonne
1910	1910	10th November 1910. Queen's Hall, London. Kreisler	Fritz Kreisler
1910	1910	16th February 1911. Herefordshire Orch. Society	Edwin F. James
910-11	1911	24th May 1911. London Musical Festival. E. E.	In memory of Edward VII
1911	1911	22nd June 1911. Coronation of George V	—
1911	1911	22nd June 1911. Coronation of George V	—
911-12	1912	11th March 1912. London Coliseum. Marion Bealey, Harry Dearth. E. E.	—
1912	1912	16th July 1912. Westminster Abbey, London	Dean of Wells, J. Armitage Robinson, D.D.
1913	1913	1st October 1913. Leeds Festival. E. E.	Landon Ronald

Appendix A—Catalogue of Works

Op.	Title	Author of Words
69	The Music Makers (ode for contralto, chorus, and orch.)	Arthur O'Shaughnessy
70	Sospiri (strings, harp, and organ)	—
71	Two Partsongs (S.A.T.B.): 1. 'The Shower' 2. 'The Fountain'	Henry Vaughan
72	'Death on the Hills' (S.A.T.B.)	Maikov, trans. Ros Newmarch
73	Two Partsongs (S.A.T.B.): 1. 'Love's Tempest' 2. 'Serenade'	Maikov, trans. Ros Newmarch
74	'Give unto the Lord' (anthem for 4-part chorus, organ, and orch.)	Psalm 29
75	Carillon (recitation with orch.)	Émile Cammaerts
76	Polonia (symphonic prelude for orch.)	—
77	Une Voix dans le désert (recitation with orch.)	Émile Cammaerts
78	The Starlight Express (incidental music)	Play adapted from Algernon Blackwood's A Prisoner from Fairyland
79	Le Drapeau belge (recitation with orch.)	Émile Cammaerts
80	The Spirit of England (sop. or ten. solo, chorus, and orch.): 1. 'Fourth of August' 2. 'To Women' 3. 'For the Fallen'	Laurence Binyon from The Winnowing Fan

Works with Opus Numbers

Composed	Published	First Performance	Dedication
1912	1912	1st October 1912. Birmingham Festival. Muriel Foster. E. E.	Nicholas Kilburn
1914	1914	15th August 1914. Queen's Hall, London	W. H. Reed
?	1914	?	Miss Frances Smart. W. Mann Dyson, Worcester
?	1914	?	Lady Colvin
1914	1914	?	Prof. C. Sanford Terry Percy C. Hull
1914	1914	30th April 1914. St Paul's, London,	Sir George Martin, M.V.O.
1914	1914	7th December 1914. Queen's Hall, London	—
1915	1915	6th July 1915. Polish Victims' Relief Fund concert, London	I. J. Paderewski
1915	1915	29th January 1916. Shaftesbury Theatre, London	—
1915	1916	29th December 1915. Kingsway Theatre, London	—
1917	1917	14th April 1917. Queen's Hall, London	—
1916	1916–17	24th November 1917. Albert Hall, London. Agnes Nicholls, Gervase Elwes. E. E.	To the memory of our glorious men, with a special thought for the Worcesters
		4th October 1916. Birmingham. Rosina Buckman	
		3rd May 1916. Leeds Choral Union. Clara Butt. E. E.	
		3rd May 1916. Leeds Choral Union. Clara Butt. E. E.	

Appendix A—Catalogue of Works

Op.	Title	Author of Words
81	*The Sanguine Fan* (ballet based on a fan, by Condor)	—
	Echo's Dance, from above	
82	Sonata in E minor (vln. and pf.)	—
83	Quartet in E minor (strings)	—
84	Quintet in A minor (pf. and strings)	—
85	Concerto in E minor (cello and orch.)	—
86	Transcription of Bach's organ Fantasy and Fugue in C minor for orch.	—
87	*Severn Suite* (brass band)	—
	Severn Suite (arr. for orch.)	—
87A	Organ Sonata No. 2 (arr. from op. 87 by Ivor Atkins)	

WORKS WITHOUT OPUS NUMBERS,

Title	Author of Words
'The Language of Flowers' (song)	Percival
Chantant (pf.)	—
Rondel: 'The little eyes that never knew' (song)	Swinburne

Works without Opus Numbers

Composed	Published	First Performance	Dedication
1917	MS.	20th March 1917. Chelsea Palace, London	—
	1917		
1918	1918	21st March 1919. Aeolian Hall, London. W. H. Reed and Landon Ronald	Marie Joshua
1918	1918	21st May 1919. Wigmore Hall, London. Albert Sammons, W. H. Reed, Raymond Jeremy, Felix Salmond	Brodsky Quartet
1918	1918	21st May 1919. Wigmore Hall, London. As above, with William Murdoch	Ernest Newman
1919	1919	26th October 1919. Queen's Hall, London. Felix Salmond. E. E.	Sidney and Frances Colvin
1921-2	1921-2	27th October 1921. Queen's Hall, London (fugue only). 7th September 1922. Gloucester Festival (fantasy added)	—
1879 & 1930	1930	September 1930. Crystal Palace Brass Band Festival, London	G. Bernard Shaw
1932	1932	7th September 1932. Worcester Festival	
	1933	1933. Organ Music Society, London	

ARRANGED IN ORDER OF PUBLICATION

Composed	Published	First Performance	Dedication
1872	MS.	?	His sister Lucy for her birthday
c. 1872	MS.	?	—
1887	MS.	26th April 1897. Worcester Musical Union	—

Appendix A—Catalogue of Works

Title	Author of Words
Anthems, etc., in St George's Roman Catholic Church, Worcester	—
Dance Music in County Lunatic Asylum, nr. Worcester	—
Introductory Overture	—
Gavotte (vln. and pf.)	—
Allegretto on a theme of 5 notes, G.E.D.G.E. (vln. and pf.)	—
'As I laye a-thinking' (song)	'Thomas Ingoldsby' (Richard Barham)
'The Wind at Dawn' (song)	C. Alice Roberts
Four Litanies B.V.M. (unacc. chorus)	
Ecce Sacerdos Magnus (chorus and organ)	
O Salutaris Hostia (4-part chorus)	
'Queen Mary's Song' (song)	Tennyson
'The Poet's Life' (song)	Ellen Burroughs
'Song of Autumn' (song)	Adam Lindsay Gordon
'Like to the damask rose' (song)	Simon Wastell
'My love dwelt in a northern land' (S.A.T.B.)	Andrew Lang
Minuet (pf. solo, see Op. 21)	—
'Love alone will stay' or 'Lute Song' (later No. 2 of *Sea Pictures*, Op. 37)	C. Alice Elgar
Hymn-tune	R. Campbell's trans. of *Verbum supernum* and 'Hear thy children' in *Westminster Hymnal*
O Salutaris Hostai (in Tozer's *Benediction Manual*)	

Works without Opus Numbers

Composed	Published	First Performance	Dedication
1875–85	MS.	(Used at the church)	—
1879–84	MS.	(Frequently played at dances and concerts at the Asylum)	—
?	MS. now lost	1878, Public Hall, Worcester	—
?	1886	?	Dr C. W. Buck, Settle
?	?	?	The Misses Gedge, Malvern Wells
?	1888	?	—
1888	1888	?	—
?	1888	?	Father T. Knight, S.J., Worcester
1888	1888	9th October 1888. St George's Roman Catholic Church, Worcester	Hubert Leicester, Worcester
?	1888	?	—
1889	?	?	—
?	?	?	—
?	?	?	Miss Marshall
?	?	25th February 1897. St James's Hall, London	
1890	1890	13th November 1890. Tenbury Musical Society	Rev. J. Hampton
?	1897	?	—
?	1898	?	—
c. 1880	1898 & 1912	(St George's, Worcester)	—
?	1898	?	—

Appendix A—Catalogue of Works

Title	Author of Words
Sérénade lyrique (small orch.)	—
'To her beneath whose steadfast star' (S.A.T.B.)	Frederick W. H. Mye
'Dry those fair, those crystal eyes' (song)	Henry King
'Pipes of Pan' (song)	Adrian Ross
May Song (pf.)	—
'Come, gentle night' (song)	Clifton Bingham
'Always and everywhere' (song)	Krasinski, trans. F. Forty
'Land of Hope and Glory' (song from *Coronation Ode*, Op. 44)	A. C. Benson
'O mightiest of the mighty' (hymn)	Rev. S. Childs Clark
'Weary wind of the west' (S.A.T.B.)	T. E. Brown
Skizze (pf.)	—
'Speak, my heart' (song)	A. C. Benson
In Smyrna (pf.)	—
'Evening Scene' (S.A.T.B.)	Coventry Patmore
'How calmly the evening' (S.A.T.B.)	T. E. Lynch
'Is she not passing fair?' (song)	Charles, Duke of Orlean trans. Louise Stua Costello
'Marching Song' (S.A.T.B.)	Capt. de Courc Stretton
'Lo! Christ the Lord is born' (carol, S.A.T.B.)	Shapcott Wensley
Two Single Chants for Venite in D and G	—
Two Double Chants in D for Psalms 68 and 75	—
'They are at Rest' (elegy for S.A.T.B.)	John Henry Newman

Works without Opus Numbers

omposed	Published	First Performance	Dedication
?	1899	27th November 1900. St James's Hall, London	Ivan Caryll's orchestra
1899	1899	24th May 1899. Windsor Castle, before Queen Victoria	—
1899	1899	?	—
1900	1900	12th May 1900. Queen's Hall, London	—
?	1901	?	—
?	1901	?	—
?	1901	?	—
1901	1902	?	—
1901	1902	9th August 1902. Coronation of Edward VII	H.R.H. Prince of Wales
1903	1903	2nd May 1903. Morecambe Competitive Festival	—
?	1903	?	Julius Buths, Düsseldorf
?	1903	?	—
1905	1905	?	—
1906	1906	12th May 1906. Morecambe Competitive Festival	In memory of R. G. W. Howson
?	1907	?	—
1886 or earlier	1908	?	—
?	1908	24th May 1908. Empire Concert, Albert Hall, London	—
1897 or earlier	1909	?	—
?	1909	?	—
?	1909	?	—
1909	1910	22nd January 1910. Royal Mausoleum on anniversary of Queen Victoria's death	—

Appendix A—Catalogue of Works

Title	Author of Words
'The Kingsway' (song)	C. Alice Elgar
'A child asleep' (song)	Elizabeth Barrett Brownin
'Arabian Serenade' (song)	Margery Lawrence
'Chariots of the Lord' (song)	John Brownlie
'The Birthright' (S.A.T.B.)	George A. Stocks
'Fear not, O land' (harvest anthem, 4-part chorus)	Joel ii
Carissima (small orch.)	—
'Follow the colours' (male chorus adapted from 'Marching Song')	Capt. de Courcy Stretto
Rosemary (small orch.)	—
'Fight for the Right' (song)	William Morris
The Fringes of the Fleet (4 songs for 4 baritones)	Rudyard Kipling
'Inside the Bar' (song for 4 baritones)	Gilbert Parker
'Big Steamers' (song)	Rudyard Kipling
'The Wanderer' (T.T.B.B.)	Anon. adapted from Wit and Drollery, 166
'Zut, zut, zut' (T.T.B.B.)	Richard Marden
King Arthur (incidental music)	Play by Laurenc Binyon
Memorial Chimes for a carillon	—
Empire March (orch.)	—
Pageant of Empire (7 songs for solo or chorus)	Alfred Noyes

Works without Opus Numbers

Composed	Published	First Performance	Dedication
1909	1910	15th January 1910. Alexandra Palace, London	—
?	1910	?	Anthony Goetz
?	1914	?	—
?	1914	28th June 1914. Albert Hall, London	—
?	1914	?	—
1914	1914	?	—
1913	1914	15th February 1914. Albert Hall, London	Winifred Stephens
1914	1914	10th October 1914. Albert Hall, London	—
1915	1915	?	—
1916	1916	?	Members of the Fight for the Right Movement
1917	1917	11th June 1917. London Coliseum. George Parker, Harry Barratt, Frederick Henry, Frederick Stewart. E. E.	—
1917	1917	25th June 1917. As above	To the 4 Singers
1918	1918	?	—
?	1923	?	—
?	1923	?	—
1922–3	MS.	12th March 1923. Old Vic Theatre, London	—
1923	MS.	22nd July 1923. Opening of the Loughborough War Memorial Carillon	—
1924	1924	23rd April 1924. Opening Ceremony, British Empire Exhibition, Wembley, London	—
1924	1924	Exhibition, Wembley, London	

Appendix A—Catalogue of Works

Title	Author of Words
'The Herald' (S.A.T.B.)	Alexander Smith
'The Prince of Sleep' (S.A.T.B.)	Walter de la Mare
Civic Fanfare	—
Beau Brummel (incidental music)	Play by Bertram Matthew
Minuet from above	
'I sing the birth' (carol, S.A.T B.)	Ben Jonson
'Goodmorrow' (carol, S.A.T.B., for the King's recovery)	George Gascoigne
'It isnae me' (song)	Sally Holmes
Nursery Suite (orch.)	—
'So many true princesses who have gone' (ode for chorus)	John Masefield
Sonatina (pf.)	—
Adieu (pf.)	—
Serenade (pf.)	—
'The Rapid Stream' (unison song)	Charles Mackay
'When swallows fly' (unison song)	Charles Mackay
'The Woodland Stream' (unison song)	Charles Mackay
Mina (orch.)	—

Works without Opus Numbers

omposed	Published	First Performance	Dedication
?	1925	?	—
?	1925	?	—
927	MS.	4th September 1927. Hereford Festival, at the Mayoral Procession	Percy C. Hull
928	MS.	5th November 1928. Theatre Royal, Birmingham	—
928	1929		
?	1929	?	Rev. Harcourt B. S. Fowler
929	1929	9th December 1929. St George's Chapel, Windsor	—
930	1931	October 1930. Dumfries	Miss Joan Elwes
931	1931	23rd May 1931. Kingsway Hall, London	T.R.H. Princesses Elizabeth and Margaret Rose
932	MS.	9th June 1932. Marlborough House, London, unveiling of Queen Alexandra memorial	—
?	1932	?	May Grafton
?	1932	?	—
?	1932	?	John Austin
933	1933	?	—
933	1933	?	—
933	1933	18th May 1933. Worcester City Schools Musical Festival	Stephen S. Moore, Worcester
933	1934	Recorded 8th February 1935 and 7th January 1935 (the latter in an arr. by Haydn Wood)	—

Appendix A—Catalogue of Works

Title

Berceuse *Petite Reine* by Victor Bérand, arr. for vln. and pf.

'God save the King' for sop. solo, chorus, and orch.

Orchestration of 2 chorales from Bach's *St Matthew Passion*, arr. for 3 trumpets, 4 hor 3 trombones, and tuba

'Ye holy angels bright,' hymn to the tune Darwalls 148th, words by Richard Bax and R. R. Chope, orchestrated

Transcription of Bach's organ Fantasy and Fugue in C minor for orch.   (Elgar op. 8

Orchestration of Parry's 'Jerusalem'

'Let us lift up our hearts,' motet by S. S. Wesley, orchestrated.

'O Lord, look down from heaven,' motet by Battishill, orch.

Overture in D minor, Handel, transcribed for orch.

Jehova, quam multi sunt hostes mei, motet by Purcell, orchestrated.

Funeral March by Chopin, arr. for orch.

Transcriptions

IONS

ritten	Published	First Performance
early	? 1907	?
?	1902	?
911	MS.	14th September 1911. Worcester Festival. From the tower of the cathedral before performance
?	?	?
21–2	1921–2	As Op. 86
922	MS.	1922 Leeds Festival
923	MS.	6th September 1923. Worcester Festival
923	MS.	6th September 1923. Worcester Festival
923	1923	2nd September 1923. Worcester Festival
929	MS.	10th September 1929. Worcester Festival
932	1933	25th February 1934. London Philharmonic Society Memorial Concert

APPENDIX B

BIBLIOGRAPHY

Anderson, W. R., 'Introduction to the Music of Elgar.' (London, 1949.)

Barber, Cecil, 'Enigma Variations' (original finale). (*Music & Letters,* Vol. XVI, 1935, p. 137.)

Bennett, Joseph, 'Analytical notes on the cantata King Olaf.' (London, 1896.)

Bonavia, F., 'Elgar' in *Lives of the Great Composers.* (London, 1935).

Buckley, R. J., 'Sir Edward Elgar.' (London, 1905.)

Cardus, Neville, 'Elgar' in *Ten Composers.* (London, 1945.)

Cumberland, Gerald, 'Elgar' in *Set Down in Malice.* (London, 1919.)

Dann, Mary G., 'Elgar's Use of the Sequence.' (*Music & Letters,* Vol. XIX, 1938, p. 255.)

Dunhill, Thomas F., 'Elgar.' (London, 1938.)

Elgar, Edward, 'Falstaff: analytical essay by the composer.' (London, 1913.)

Ffrangcon-Davies, Marjorie, 'David Ffrangcon-Davies.' (London, 1938.) (Contains Elgar letters.)

Fox Strangways, A. H., 'Elgar,' (*Music & Letters,* Vol. XV, 1934, p. 109.)

Gorton, Canon, 'Interpretation of the Librettos of the Oratorios: 1. The Dream of Gerontius. 2. The Apostles. 3. The Kingdom.' (London, n.d.)

Gray, Cecil, 'Edward Elgar' in *A Survey of Contemporary Music.* (Oxford, 1924.)

Howes, Frank, 'Edward Elgar' in *The Heritage of Music,* Vol. III (Oxford, 1951.)

Jackson, Sir Barry, 'Elgar's "Spanish Lady."' (*Music & Letters,* Vol. XXIV, 1943, p. 1.)

Jaeger, A. J., 'Analytical and descriptive notes.' 'The Dream of Gerontius, by Edward Elgar.' (London, 1900.) 'The Apostles, by Edward Elgar.' (London, 1903.) 'The Kingdom, by Edward Elgar.' (London, 1906.)

Jose, Everard and Cranston, Heath, 'The Significance of Elgar.' (London, 1934.)

Appendix B—Bibliography

Lambert, Herbert, 'Modern British Composers,' seventeen Portraits. (London, 1923.)

Langford, Samuel, 'Musical Criticisms,' ed. by Neville Cardus, pp. 13–27. (London, 1929.)

Maine, Basil, 'Elgar: his Life and Work.' 2 vols. (London, 1933.)

Music & Letters, special Elgar number, Vol. XVI, 1935, No. 1. (Articles by Donald Tovey, Hubert Foss, Vaughan Williams, Brent Smith, Frank Howes, and W. H. Reed.)

Musical Times, special Elgar number, No. 1094, April 1934 (also contains a list of articles on Elgar published in this journal during his lifetime).

Newman, Ernest, 'Elgar.' (London, 1922.)

Porte, John F., 'Elgar.' (London, 1921.) (A catalogue of works with brief descriptions.)

Powell, Richard, 'Elgar's "Enigma."' (*Music & Letters,* Vol. XV, 1934, p. 203.)

Powell, Mrs Richard, 'Edward Elgar: Memories of a Variation.' (London, 1937; 2nd ed., 1947.)

Reed, W. H., 'Elgar as I knew him.' (London, 1936)——'Elgar' ('Master Musicians' series). (London, 1939.)

Shaw, G. Bernard, 'Sir Edward Elgar.' (*Music & Letters,* Vol. I, 1920, p. 7.)

Sheldon, A. J., 'Edward Elgar.' (London, 1932.)

Shera, F. H., 'Elgar: Instrumental Works.' ('Musical Pilgrim' series, Oxford, 1931.)

Thompson, Herbert, 'Analytical notes on the Cantata Caractacus.' (London, 1898.)

Turner, E. O., 'Tempo Variations: with Examples from Elgar.' (*Music & Letters,* Vol. XIX, 1938, p. 308.)

APPENDIX C

1900   Hon. Mus.D., Cambridge.

1904   Knighthood.
Hon. Mus.D., Durham.
Hon. LL.D., Leeds.
Member Maatschaapij tot Bevordering der Toonkunst (Holland).
First Richard Peyton Professor, Birmingham University.
Hon. member Royal Academy of Music.
Elected member of the Athenaeum Club.

1905   Hon. Mus.D., Oxford.
Hon. Mus.D., Yale.
Hon. Freeman, City of Worcester.

1906   Hon. LL.D., Aberdeen.
Hon. member Royal Swedish Academy.

1907   Hon. LL.D., Western University of Pennsylvania.
Hon. M.A., Birmingham.

1911   O.M.
Hon. Freeman, Worshipful Company of Musicians.

1912   Associé Académie des Beaux Arts (Belgium).

1914   Hon. Academician Regia Accademia di Santa Cecilia (Rome).

1919   Corresponding member Accademia del Reale Instituto Musicale (Florence).

1920   Member of the Royal College of Music Council.
Corresponding member of the Institut de France.
Commandeur, Ordre de la Couronne (Belgium).

1924   Master of the King's Musick.

248

Appendix C—Honours and Distinctions

1925 Gold Medal of the Royal Philharmonic Society.

1928 K.C.V.O.

1929 Corresponding member of the American Academy of Arts and Letters.

1931 Hon. Mus.D., London University.
Baronetcy (first baronet of Broadheath).

1933 G.C.V.O.

INDEX

INDEX

Where there are many references, those in heavy type give most information.

Index

Index

Index

Index

Index

Index

Index